Perpetual Motion

Electronic Mediations

Series Editors: N. Katherine Hayles, Peter Krapp, Rita Raley, and Samuel Weber

Founding Editor: Mark Poster

(continued on page 229)

Perpetual Motion

Dance, Digital Cultures, and the Common

Harmony Bench

Electronic Mediations 59

UNIVERSITY OF MINNESOTA PRESS

MINNEAPOLIS

LONDON

Published by the University of Minnesota Press
111 Third Avenue South, Suite 290
Minneapolis, MN 55401-2520
http://www.upress.umn.edu

Printed in the United States of America on acid-free paper

The University of Minnesota is an equal-opportunity educator and employer.

Library of Congress Cataloging-in-Publication Data
Names: Bench, Harmony, author.
Title: Perpetual motion : dance, digital cultures, and the common / Harmony Bench.
Description: Minneapolis : University of Minnesota Press, [2020] |
    Series: Electronic mediations ; 59 | Includes bibliographical references and index.
Identifiers: LCCN 2019009190 (print) | ISBN 978-1-5179-0052-6 (hc) |
    ISBN 978-1-5179-0053-3 (pb)
Subjects: LCSH: Dance and the Internet. | Dance and technology. | Dance—Social
    aspects. | Interactive multimedia—Social aspects.
Classification: LCC GV1588.7 .B46 2020 (print) | DDC 792.8—dc23
LC record available at https://lccn.loc.gov/2019009190

UMP BmB 2020

In memory of
Jule and Georgia

Contents

Acknowledgments

This book would have been impossible without the contributions and support of family, friends, and colleagues. I have many people to thank at The Ohio State University, especially Candace Feck, Karen Eliot, Hannah Kosstrin, Susan Petry, Susan Hadley, Nena Couch, Shannon Winnubst, Ana Puga, Shilarna Stokes, Katey Borland, Paloma Martinez-Cruz, David Staley, Isaac Weiner, Leigh Bonds, and Mike Hardesty. My doctoral advisees Mair Culbreth, Alex Harlig, Kelly Klein, Janet Schroeder, Lyndsey Vader, and Benny Simon have been wonderful interlocutors and provocateurs along the way. I thank them for their intelligence and curiosity. Conversations with Victor Quintanilla, David Cook-Martín, and especially Elizabeth Kolkovich made the task of writing much easier. For offering generous feedback at many different stages of writing, I thank Eugene Holland, Clare Croft, Jeannine Murray-Román, Lynn Itagaki, Cindy García, Ryan Skinner, Melissa Blanco Borelli, Kate Elswit, VK Preston, and Anthea Kraut. I remain grateful to Susan Leigh Foster for her consistent advocacy, counsel, and critique. I also thank my anonymous reviewers for their feedback and direction.

Many thanks are due to Norton Owen, Arianna Brawley, and Pamela Tatge at Jacob's Pillow, for supporting me with a research fellowship in 2016 during a final stretch of writing, and to Sherril Dodds, who provided invaluable feedback while I was a Visiting Scholar in Residence at Temple University. A 2017–18 Faculty Professional Leave from The Ohio State University provided the time and space to revise the manuscript. The folks at OSU's STEAM Factory, especially Charlene Brenner, have been welcome companions throughout, and I thank them for providing a space to write. A grant from the Open Access Monograph Initiative helped to realize the digital manifestation of this project, and for assistance with that I am especially thankful to Maureen Walsh, Meris Mandernach, and Sandra Enimil. Many thanks additionally go to the editors of the Electronic Mediations series, N. Katherine Hayles, Peter Krapp, Rita Raley, and Samuel Weber, as well as the University of Minnesota Press, especially Danielle Kasprzak, Jason Weidemann, Mike Stoffel, and the indefatigable Anne Carter. Many thanks also to Holly Monteith for her copy editing. I am deeply appreciative to Jonah Bokaer for allowing me to use the cover image featuring his choreography.

Thanks also go to Simon Ellis, Carolina San Juan, Sara Wolf, and Ali Potvin for their friendship. For sanity-preserving Friday nights on the patio, I wish to recognize the gang on "The Glen": Mike, Rod, George, Georgia, Marcina, Suzanne, and Jeff. My parents, Mike and Sheree, siblings Alisa, Cameron, and Aubrey, their spouses, and many nieces and nephews have been both encouraging and grounding. Finally, thanks are not enough to convey my appreciation to Debra Burrington. Thank you for everything.

Introduction

Dance as Common

I open my iPad, a second-generation model, and find the 2014 application *Passe-Partout* produced by the 2wice Arts Foundation. I tap the app's icon and am greeted with what sounds to my ears like a confused piano. The work's title appears onscreen, after which I am provided with a brief tutorial and then prompted to "tilt or tap dots to start."[1] I tap a gray dot, one of five different colors of dots on the left side of the screen. A duet begins between dancer Daniel Ulbricht and dancer-choreographer Justin Peck, both of the New York City Ballet. Both men wear gray shirts, and a gray bar extends across the screen to indicate the video's progress. Despite *New York Times* dance writer Gia Kourlas assuring me that I'm the choreographer in her article on *Passe-Partout*,[2] my first time through, I am comfortable with my role as spectator and just watch the duet from beginning to end. The sequence is a friendly balletic competition of earthy athleticism that lasts about a minute. At the conclusion, I am invited to play back, share, or save the resulting video, or to start over. I start over. 2wice has produced a handful of iPad apps for dance, and I am curious to see how this one differs.

I tilt the iPad one way, then another, then another. The men's solos and duets fill the screen, overlapping and fading in or out in response to my movements. Colored bars streak across the screen, indicating where each of the five segments comes in and goes out. Producer Patsy Tarr tells Kourlas, "As you work with these layers, you start to see unison and symmetry and repetition," noting that the idea was to convey core principles of choreography.[3] My second time through, however, I don't notice the men's movement so much as my own, since it cues the different musical scores that accompany each scene. Am I doing it right? As the men's dancing images proliferate onscreen, the sounds of piano, clarinet, marimbas, and harpsichord, among other instruments, layer atop each other as well. But because I'm tilting and moving the iPad, it's difficult to track what the dancers are doing onscreen.

On the next round, I intend to sit still and investigate Ulbricht's movement qualities when accompanied by drumming in the pink sequence, but when I start over, the pink and blue dots have been replaced by red and white ones. I decide to use the dots to control the timing of each sequence. The dots double in diameter when I tap them, and the scenes overlap without fading unless I tap the corresponding dots again. The two ways of interacting with *Passe-Partout*—tilting or tapping—have rather different effects on the outcome. Kourlas coaches, "In this choreographic pursuit, there are

Figure 1. Screenshot of choreographer and dancer Justin Peck (in foreground) and dancer Daniel Ulbricht in the iPad app *Passe-Partout* (2014). Concept and design by Abbott Miller, video by Ben Louis Nicholas, music by Aaron Severini. Produced by 2wice Arts Foundation.

no wrong choices. And unlike ballets for the stage, which disappear once the curtain falls, [these] can be saved or shared through social media."⁴ I decide to play back the video of my arrangement. The dots and bars disappear, leaving only a video of the overlaid performances and sound scores. Peck and Ulbricht seem suspended as they dance in their all-white performance space, a prominent aesthetic used in dance-media. I am happy with the result and contemplate whether to post the video online.

Many of the major formal devices this book explores around dance in digital cultures are visible in just the example of *Passe-Partout*: situating dance onscreen, employing repetitive and recombinatory approaches to composition, inviting users to have co-ownership in the creation of a dance experience, and enabling users to share the rendition of a work that results from their participation. These have become familiar, even expected, approaches to reimagining dance for digital screens. Focused on the twenty-year period from 1996 to 2016, *Perpetual Motion: Dance, Digital Cultures, and the Common* proceeds from the position that digital technologies, and especially internet technologies, have thoroughly saturated the practices, creation, distribution, and viewers' experiences of dance. Why should this sea change in dance creation and reception matter? It is not only that digital media have radically reformatted dance for an era of information globalization, accelerating and expanding the ways that bodily motion proliferates as it is uploaded, downloaded, and shared as data—though these are important considerations. It is that, in thus remediating and reformatting dance, digital media throw open, magnify, and broadly disseminate dancing's already powerful physical articulations of how we act in common.

We is of course a fraught term. It is both presumptuously inclusive and manifestly exclusive. It draws a boundary that separates what does from what does not belong. But the "in-common" tempers this *we*. Acting in common requires coordination and thus implies both the nonconformity of multiplicity within a collection and an enabling agreement that gathers, organizes, and directs participants' energies. Acting in common implies proximity and mutual participation as well as beginning from shared ground or moving toward a shared goal. Dancing, whether done alone or as an ensemble, physically enacts and thus makes visible the relationality within a social sphere that enables this in-common to emerge and take shape. Formal changes brought about by digital media alter screen-based

representations of how we act in common. But dancing as a physical practice also registers the constraints and possibilities of these spaces, merging
embodied realities with screen spaces to imagine and enact new ways moving together. Dance-media, in other words, not only make visible the ways
we already move together and act in common in an era of computing and
information globalization but also craft new possibilities through their
specific combinations of bodily expression and digital cultural production.

COMMONS, COMMON

My primary framework for understanding how dance circulates through
digital cultures is the common or commons. The participatory commons
appeals as an alternative to the extractive neoliberal financial logics that govern much of contemporary life in the United States and beyond, and scholars across academic disciplines have turned to the commons to explore
these alternative social and economic arrangements. As a historical and
theoretical model for social organization, the commons primarily relates
to land and water rights and the administration and distribution of natural
resources. Although there are many examples of communities sharing and
sustaining common-pool resources, as economist Elinor Ostrom and others
have amply demonstrated,[5] scholars typically invoke the commons in Europe
that were, for the most part, eradicated during eighteenth-century enclosure movements that forcibly removed peasants from common lands and
privatized natural resources. In such discussions, scholars tend to emphasize enclosure as a social, political, and economic tragedy while leaving to
the side the European feudal system of which these commons were a part,
thus enabling a contemporary discourse in which the commons signal
open access, anticapitalism, and radical democracy. Although this romanticized version of the commons may be useful for imaging contemporary
social projects, historically, the commons were not the progressive social
model they have been made out to be.

Dance scholar Ramsay Burt offers one application of this model of the
commons in his book *Ungoverning Dance: Contemporary European Theatre
Dance and the Commons*. He argues that the dance practices that European
movement artists working within the theatrical tradition produce and
employ are usefully viewed as a commons. Contemporary dance constitutes a field of knowledge in which movement techniques, improvisational

practices, and choreographic processes are shared among practitioners. Burt argues that "many aspects of dance as an art form—such as dance techniques, theatrical devices, generic compositional structures or improvisational processes—are common-pool resources accessible to dance artists."[6] It almost goes without saying that a community is identified by its shared practices,[7] but in calling contemporary dance a commons, Burt points to an economic model underlying theatrical dance that, he says, contradicts the institutionalization of these practices with the contemporary dance market. Burt can make the claim for contemporary dance as a commons because he focuses his investigation on a specific genre of dancemaking within the geocultural boundaries referred to as Europe. In contrast, the digital media at the forefront of my own investigation reach farther and wider than the festivals and metropolitan theaters to which European dance artists might tour their stage-based productions. Furthermore, these media bring all possible dance forms into the flattening space of the computer screen, blurring distinctions among movement practices and communities and disarticulating them from their histories and cultural situations. Whereas Burt posits the commons of contemporary dance, I employ Michael Hardt and Antonio Negri's language of the common to distinguish my usage from a default understanding of the commons as a shared resource.

In their book *Commonwealth*, Hardt and Negri note the inadequacy of the commons as both precedent and metaphor for contemporary reinvestments in a cultural commons. They write instead of the common, of which they posit two main types: the "natural" common of limited resources, such as land, air, and water, and the "artificial" common "that resides in languages, images, knowledges, affects, codes, habits, and practices" as well as gestures.[8] They define the common as "those results of social production that are necessary for social interaction and further production."[9] Ideas, customs, and practices that are collectively generated and make it possible to live together are exemplars of the artificial common. Produced rather than discovered, the common is neither public nor private, and it provides an alternate avenue for theorizing social and cultural production. Hardt and Negri's aim in exploring the common is to uncover market economies' ongoing dependence on—and their corruption of—the common for the purposes of continued financial growth. The common provides the resources and ingenuity upon which neoliberal capital depends. However, in registering that "contemporary forms of capitalist production and accumulation, paradoxically make possible and even require expansions of the common,"[10] Hardt and Negri do not attend to the negative consequences or imbalances of that expansion. They analyze capitalist expropriations of the common but do not fully consider the politics of dispossession by which materials are appropriated *into* the common. In other words, they do not acknowledge the parallel structures of neocolonial and neoliberal logics that unevenly distribute the benefits of access.

If the common expands infinitely within globalization,[11] what gets appropriated into the common that was previously privately held, owned, or shared within an exclusive community? Kimberly Christen summarizes these tensions in her work on the rights of indigenous peoples to curate the flow of cultural heritage information through digital media. In internet culture, she remarks, "the commons signifies openness, the exclusion of intermediaries, and remix culture that is creative, innovative, and politically disobedient."[12] However, she contends, "ongoing legacies of colonialism cannot be jettisoned for the wish of a global commons."[13] Dance scholar and political theorist Randy Martin similarly advises wariness of the common or commons in the current era of financialization: "What it means to own something, just like what it means to be possessed of oneself, undergoes significant modulation under financialization . . . [which] spreads ownership around in vexing ways."[14] He goes on, "Now that ownership is so thoroughly spread around, far more can partake of the entitlements of others."[15] For Martin, parceled out and indiscernible ownership does not portend greater social responsibility or ideals of the common good. On the contrary, under such circumstances, what is common is generated through dispossession, which refuses to share in the wealth generated by and predicated on the very availability of the common.

Partnered with the ideology that "information wants to be free," digital technologies have altered the means, reach, and speed of information dissemination. The emergence of an exuberant ideology promoting freedom, open access, and the digital commons within the space of the internet positioned itself as resistant to corporate greed but did so without distinguishing among knowledge communities and their relative (dis)empowerment. Christen assiduously observes that an uncritical celebration of openness "has resulted in *a limited vocabulary* with which to discuss the ethical and cultural parameters of information circulation and access in the digital realm," limiting conversations to binaries of open or closed, public or private.[16] This limited vocabulary impacts all sides of the debate, not just those who favor unlimited and unregulated access to the world's knowledges and practices.

For example, scholarship in dance studies continues to favor the explanatory framework of cultural appropriation to describe the spread of dances and movements beyond the communities invested in their production. This is due, in part, to the focus of much dance scholarship on the politics of modernist aesthetics in concert dance of the first half of the twentieth century. Scholars have demonstrated that within this field, ideologies of openness and cultural fluidity rooted in the notion that dance is universal have historically favored those with greater social capital. Some artists, generally hailing from outside the community in question, were in a better position to profit individually from something that had been created and maintained collectively. Notably, Brenda Dixon Gottschild has forcefully demonstrated how white ballet and modern dance choreographers were heralded for their innovations when they incorporated uncredited Africanist aesthetics into their work, and Jacqueline Shea Murphy has likewise shown how white American choreographers observed and appropriated imagery from Native American dances.[17] Jane Desmond and Priya Srinivasan have sifted through the creation of early modern dance choreographer Ruth St. Denis's orientalist dances.[18] And Susan Manning has described the process by which white choreographers turned the experiences of African Americans into a "universal" metaphor of struggle.[19] Scholars have repeatedly shown that, in the field of dance, unregulated access to a cultural commons results in the enrichment of the cultural mediators who facilitate dance's reproduction beyond the communities that create and sustain these practices.[20]

Histories of appropriation among ballet and modern dance choreographers are irrefutable. However, present-day participation within global digital cultures involves complex corporeal negotiations that cannot necessarily be reduced to so many examples of cultural theft or capitalistic expropriation in an era of information globalization and participatory media. One aim of this book, then, is to contribute to the vocabulary through which to articulate how dance perpetually moves through digital cultures without favoring openness for its own sake or condemning what performance theorist Diana Taylor calls "acts of transfer."[21] In approaching dance as common, it is necessary to continuously examine how the common repackages ideologies of freedom and universal access in the project of proliferating and circulating movement, while simultaneously acknowledging how dancing can craft a sense of mutual belonging through the sharing of movements and gestures.

For these reasons, my approach to dance as common includes movement as common-pool resource and shared vocabulary as explored by Burt, but it also includes the common as a shared orientation that arises from what theater scholar Elizabeth Dillon calls *commoning practices,* of which dance is a notable example. Dance is not only a resource of gestures and steps that dancers can mine as they generate material; it is also a means of recuperating common spaces and performing a common world. Here I follow Dillon's articulation of the "performative commons" in *New World Drama: The Performative Commons in the Atlantic World, 1649–1849.* Examining a colonial public sphere in the "long 18th century," Dillon explores the social and cultural work of theater in forging—through representation—"the common people as a sovereign political force."[22] Much like social media today, eighteenth-century popular performance functioned as an avenue for political expression and representation in which audiences vigorously participated. Dillon foregrounds corporeal practices and dramatic performances rather than the written word, which, in her study, expands a consideration of the eighteenth-century public sphere in the Atlantic world beyond the lettered peoples of a Habermasian public sphere to include the participation of indigenous, colonized, and enslaved populations whose expressivity was channeled into nonliterary forms. In her view, a performative commons enables an account of commoning practices, or the means available to "articulat[e] relations of mutual belonging in a collective whole."[23] For Dillon, the commons is spatial, interpersonal, and, above all, a relation.

I similarly find that digital media, especially the space of the internet, offer contemporary performative commons in which individuals both perform and contest their belonging through practices such as dance. Notably, I do not argue that dance *is* common, because such an assertion rests on the modernist precept of universality that scholars have worked to debunk. Whether and when dance *is* common is a point of conflict and debate within movement communities, because core ethical, political, and aesthetic values are entangled in the question of what is common. Indeed, with nationalist and populist sentiments on the rise throughout the West, ascertaining what is common and determining what boundaries of community result from that articulation is an urgent social and political issue for the twenty-first century. Employing the lens of the common allows me to approach the ways dancers corporeally and rhetorically configure dance within digital cultural practices. What can dance, movement, and gesture afford—and what conflicts arise—when they are perceived as common or utilized to enact a common? How, why, and for whom are assertions of dance as common meaningful in digital contexts? In *Perpetual Motion*, I consider these questions in the ways interactive media purport to make-common by inviting users into the creative process of dance composition, in dancing's activation of the common dimensions of public spaces, in how artists employ dance to appeal to and perform a common world in a global era, and in the sharing of a corporeal common of movement and gestural resources that circulate across dancers' bodies.

APPROACHES AND CONSTRAINTS

When I began thinking and writing about dance in digital media, I was very confident about the dance forms represented. For the most part, what I saw came from the same lineages of ballet, modern, and postmodern dance in which I had trained for decades as a performer. Digital dance was a niche phenomenon, and participation was a mark of privileged access to the enabling resources and technological infrastructures that enabled high-profile collaborations between choreographers and technologists— seen, for example, in Paul Kaiser and Shelley Eshkar's large-scale collaborations with choreographers Merce Cunningham, Bill T. Jones, and Trisha Brown.[24] This was in the late 1990s and early 2000s. Screendance artists were not yet sharing their films on Vimeo, the general population was not yet recording and uploading videos to YouTube, and there were no gestural interfaces for video games. With few exceptions, there was a wide gulf between "serious" artists developing new technologies to support their aesthetic investigations and amateurs posting animated GIFs of dancing hamsters online.[25]

That gulf has all but disappeared. Now movement artists routinely make work specifically for online consumption. Online archives documenting performing artists' careers make lifetimes of work freely available in digital form. Music video has migrated from television to the web, where fans and satirists post videos of themselves performing versions of popular dance routines in response. Studio dance instructors share videos of their classes and combinations to showcase their talent and improve their employability in the commercial dance industry. Video games and online tutorials offer opportunities for the dance-curious to learn new moves without social pressure. Dance challenges regularly circulate through social media, and pop music and dance artists turn to the internet for inspiration for their latest creations. I have followed dance's travels through digital and online spaces as it looped in all manner of dancing and dance styles. Many of these practices have now grown into significant genres of digital performance worthy of sustained investigation in their own right.

Rather than reinforce divisions among these practices by cataloging markers of generic identity or reasserting a hierarchy between formal and informal performance modalities that dance scholars have long eschewed, I determined early on that all examples of dance in digital cultures were legitimate expressions. However, I struggled with how to include them within the reach of this book without it becoming either an encyclopedia or an unorganized mess. I decided, in the spirit of the ascendance of social media during this time frame, to foreground how amateurs, fans, spectators, and bystanders are invited to participate in and contribute to dance onscreen, how digital cultures reimagine who gets to be a dance performer or choreographer, and how digital technologies mediate bodily proximity among dance practitioners. I placed some additional explicit limits on what I address in this book, largely due to attention such work receives from other scholars. I do not address intermedia works made for the concert stage, nor do I include Hollywood dance films even though they circulate online as part of a vast archive of popular culture.

I am most interested in how digital logics reformat our understanding of how dance artists make and share their work and how dance enthusiasts make and share their responses. *Perpetual Motion* thus cuts a very particular trajectory through multiple and multiplying examples of dance-media, drawing on examples from across digital milieux, although the book tends heavily toward the web as a site that gathers and circulates these creative expressions and YouTube as a privileged (and era-specific) platform for this sharing. I attempt to think these various practices together in the manner that I have experienced them together, as someone who participates in the circulations of dance onscreen and who thus jumps among various media platforms and practices. I have also tried to capture some aspect of the global reach of dance in these digital media. Nevertheless, *Perpetual Motion* is positioned within a Western, specifically white, English-language-dominant, U.S. worldview, which manifests clearly in the examples I have included. My IP addresses, my online search histories, my interpersonal connections, my social positions, and my aesthetic inclinations have all acted as content filters prior to my curating examples for inclusion. Even with its expansive scope, this book thus represents a snapshot rather than a survey, and my examples are indicative rather than exhaustive of how dance appears, circulates, and functions in digital cultures.

I contend that the scale of danced participation in digital cultures demonstrates that, despite being identified as the art of the body par excellence, dance proliferates across bodies in large part because of its perpetual movement through digital media. Far from realizing some techno-utopian dream of disembodiment, each of the examples I consider in this book points to the ways in which digital cultural production implicates corporeality. Dance makes visible how cultural processes recruit participants at the level of their embodiment, offering an opportunity to consider the various political, cultural, and technological projects into which we are enlisted without our full awareness or knowledge. Dance scholars thus have an opportunity—perhaps even a mandate—to contribute their deep investments in bodies as sites of knowledge and practice to such analyses of digital cultures as I pursue in *Perpetual Motion*.

An additional consideration when writing about dance in digital spaces is that the phenomenon of disappearance, that specter that haunts discourses of performance,[26] never ceases to be a problem. The "consecrated theoretical motifs [of] immediacy and disappearance,"[27] in dance and performance studies, alongside more recent articulations of ephemeral media,[28] thus inform my approach to writing this book, namely, in my extensive use of description. Description is critical for analyzing practices that do not enjoy widely shared forms of documentation or techniques of inscription.

I employ movement description here because, even though dances are now widely recorded and shared on video and other digital media, I have been writing about dance in digital environments for long enough to understand that, like performance, these media are unstable. Web pages disappear on a daily basis. A longitudinal study of link rot by the Chesapeake Digital Preservation Group discovered that in the seven years between 2007 and 2014, over 50 percent of the URLs in their sample no longer worked.[29] As digital theorist Wendy Hui Kyong Chun remarks, "the always-thereness of digital media was to make things more stable, more lasting," yet, she argues, "digital media is degenerative, forgetful, eraseable."[30] Although my digital objects of analysis linger for longer than the duration of a single performance event, changes to software and hardware resituate ephemerality at the heart of digital media's documentary capabilities. System and software updates may stall obsolescence somewhat, but in many ways, rapid changes in technology push digital media's recent past to a distance beyond reach, a distance created by the inaccessibility of digital artifacts rather than the passage of time per se.[31]

For example, the iPad app with which I opened this introduction, the 2014 piece *Passe-Partout,* was no longer supported when Apple released iOS 10 in 2016. The production company did not update the application for the new operating system. Ironically, I was still able to access the work in 2018 because my iPad is too old to support a system upgrade. I have no empirical data regarding the failure and disappearance of websites, CD-ROMs, videos, applications, games, and other forms of dance-media, but experientially, I know it to be quite high. The absence of works in this book that other scholars might consider exemplary is thus due not only to my own curatorial choices but also to my timing. I am certain that I am not aware of many examples of dance in digital environments that could have productively contributed to this book because they became obsolete before I could encounter them. Thus this book represents an archive of my own experiences, and I must rely on other scholars to fill out additional dimensions of dance in digital cultures not included in this text.

Readers will also note that I have included web-based works that no longer function. More, surely, will go offline in years to come. I have provided original URLs so that readers may find at least some of these works through the Internet Archive's Wayback Machine at https://archive.org/.

This does not provide a solution for the CD-ROMs, apps, and video games that will soon become obsolete and inaccessible, for which screenshots and additional visual materials will necessarily function as a partial archive. Just as historians pull together fragments of past dances and dance practices from firsthand accounts, drawings or photographs, and the occasional film clip, so too will future scholars rely on a combination of written descriptions and snippets of media to better understand dance's leap into the popular media of the internet era as the devices and platforms for which they were made cease to function. I have tried to facilitate future scholarship with both the descriptions and extensive number of screenshots I provide.

Methodologically, I employ choreographic analysis throughout *Perpetual Motion*. Although choreographic analysis is rooted in dance studies, choreography has for some time exceeded dance as its principal or privileged object and enables a consideration of any structured movement.[32] My intersecting investments in dance studies, media and performance studies, and critical theory and cultural studies shape how I employ choreographic analysis in this book to connect dance-media to larger social and political trends. In my view, choreographic analysis foregrounds the forces through which movement is produced, maintained, constrained, accelerated, directed, and made legible. As a social analytic, choreography is concerned with issues of bodily discipline and regimes of movement. It is worth emphasizing, however, that choreography is necessarily plural. Any complex system simultaneously brings together multiple contradictory forces and pressures, along with multiple structures for organizing movement. These may materialize in the form of dance, or they may materialize in the forms of gestures, postures, mobilities, constraints, pathways, and flows, among other manifestations.

Choreographic analysis offers many ways into movement, dance or otherwise. For example, a choreographic analysis of *Passe-Partout* might consider the steps Peck has composed in each of the scenes, the gendering of the performers and what their movement suggests about masculinity in contemporary ballet, and/or their use of space and their timing in relation to each other and the music. It might also address the dancers' relationship to the camera, the mobility of the camera within the performance space, and the way the camera presents an additional set of spatial logics in its conical view of the space in which the men dance and how it frames them. A choreographic analysis could also include the iPad's affordances and limitations as a technological platform, including the arm, hand, and finger movements required for someone to manipulate and interact with the device. It might further explore the algorithmic elements that incorporate user input into each performance of the work, and how sharing final videos dispatches traces of the work into social media to circulate independently of the iPad application. A choreographic analysis might also evaluate the artists' choice to invite users into the roles of co-composers and distributors in light of similar trends in social, political, and economic domains.

In *Perpetual Motion,* I attend, at various points and to varying degrees, to each of these dimensions: choreographies of dances and specific arguments or claims embedded in them, choreographies of the camera as it frames dance content for viewers, as well as choreographies of the interface and the ways digital platforms enlist and entrain bodily participation. My concern, however, is not with what choreographic analysis can reveal about dance but with what choreographic analysis and dance together can illuminate about articulations of the common in digital cultural production.

STRUCTURE OF THE BOOK

Perpetual Motion consist of four chapters, each of which focuses on a single web-native dance created in the twenty years from 1996 to 2016, bolstered by numerous additional examples drawn across digital media during this same time period. The case studies that anchor each chapter are outliers among dance-media explored in this book in that they are lengthy and episodic or consist of multiple scenes. Their structural complexity allows me to delve more deeply into the compositional and relational trends in dance-media they represent. *Perpetual Motion* opens prior to the advent of social media with a consideration of interactivity at a historical moment when artists turned to the early web and CD-ROM to explore dance and movement composition for the screen. It closes before social media came under scrutiny for promoting inflammatory rhetoric and politically polarizing its users. The time period under consideration thus represents social media on an upswing, and *Perpetual Motion* reflects a kind of playful hopefulness embedded in the works discussed. A project that continued beyond

2016 would need to address the darker sides of social media, which I do not pursue here.

I begin *Perpetual Motion* before Web 2.0 in part for reasons of history: social media offer the current culturally dominant logics of creation and circulation, but how dance operates in social media appears in greater relief when considered in context with dance experimentations on the early web. By and large, dance experiments from the late 1990s and early 2000s have not been written about, and many of them are accessible only in deteriorated form. Nevertheless, they paved the way for later incarnations of dance in digital cultures and established expectations about the ways dance can be presented in nonproscenium digital environments. These expectations include the promise of freedom and democratization through interactivity and the use of repetition in composition.

Chapter 1 thus takes repetition as its central theme in an analysis of intersecting replay loops in hyperdance, with specific attention to the 2003 web-based Macromedia Flash work *Somnambules* by Nicolas Clauss, Jean-Jacques Birgé, and Didier Silhol. I turn to Gilles Deleuze's analysis of repetition and difference in conversation with Friedrich Nietzsche's formulations of the eternal return to argue that, contrary to claims of freedom of interaction and navigation that produce ever-different user experiences, the looped structure and limited possibilities for input prevent users from introducing differences that can make a difference. Hyperdances cannot deliver on their promise of freedom of choice and collaborative authorship because interactive systems are designed to facilitate selection rather than creation. While outwardly, hyperdances seem to foster inclusivity and making-common by bringing interactors into the work, they also constrain users' agency and trap screen dancers within replay loops. This shared lack of agency masquerading as freedom becomes a narrative focus for *Somnambules* and other works that dramatize onscreen performers' digital capture. I argue that it is not until the choreographic structures of interactive media give way to participation that the repetition built into dance-media experiences can transform into something new through what Jean-Luc Nancy calls unworking.

Building on and intensifying the early-web rhetoric of interaction and democratic co-composition, dance in social media developed along many trajectories that favored participation. The participatory media of Web 2.0

were to succeed where interactive media failed by providing platforms to facilitate social interactions rather than dictating which interactions could take place within a system. Where interactivity focused on the human–machine interface, participation focused on computationally mediated human–human connections. The shift in how dance appeared onscreen could not have been more profound. Animated GIFs, the early motor of the web in motion, fell out of favor (only to make a comeback in 2012), and fewer artists created screen-based dance works in specialized software such as Macromedia/Adobe Director or Flash. Instead, YouTube was the preferred platform, followed by other video-sharing sites. Fulfilling YouTube's slogan-as-command to "broadcast yourself," dancers turned their video cameras on themselves. Online dancing videos varied widely in aesthetic, purpose, and production values, but a few trends emerged from the mid-2000s to early 2010s. Professional dancers and fun-loving amateurs recorded themselves dancing in public, whether solo or in large flash mobs; choreographers and filmmakers turned to techniques of crowdsourcing their content to showcase the diversity of humanity; and the mechanized repetition of interactive media became the reperformance of shared choreographies in social and participatory media, with people posting videos of themselves dancing routines from music videos and video games. These trends are explored in chapters 2–4.

Chapter 2 considers the impact of dancing in public, particularly in a post-9/11 American landscape. The chapter focuses on the 2011–12 online serial *Girl Walk//All Day* directed by Jacob Krupnick with lead performances by Anne Marsen. I additionally discuss an array of flash mobs and other dances performed in public spaces, documentation of which circulates on the internet. By introducing the unexpected into public spaces, particularly transit hubs such as airports and train stations, flash mobs, group dances, and even solo performances transform the affective dimension of these sites. Turning to commentary by Judith Butler on assembly, Hannah Arendt on appearance, and Jacques Rancière on the politics of aesthetics, I argue that such public performances have a loosening effect on sites that have tightened under the regulating tendencies of state surveillance and policing. Occurring onsite and circulating online, public performances activate the shared dimension of public sites by enacting the very common to which they lay claim. Such performances can thus recuperate a sense of the common within public spaces.

The performative enactment of a common is further developed in chapter 3, which extends this enacted common from a public space to a world. This chapter focuses on the series of YouTube videos that appeared in 2005, 2006, 2008, and 2012 under the title Where the Hell Is Matt?, in which Matt Harding travels the globe performing a quirky, signature dance. His relationship to the inhabitants of the locales he visits changes over time, moving from postcard images of sites emptied of people except himself to scenes full of participants sharing in his project of bringing the world together through dance. Harding is only one example of utilizing dance to unite a world through movement and gesture and, moreover, of leveraging the creativity of the crowd to do so. Inviting participation from others, artists extend their reach and contribute to a performing world that specifically uses dance to stage being-in-common in an era of globalization. Utilizing different strategies for organizing incommensurable differences within the space of the screen, I argue that the pieces analyzed in this chapter move from what Jean-Luc Nancy describes as the abstract and meaningless globe of *globalization* toward what he calls *mondialisation,* or a worldly world that holds meaning for its inhabitants.

What constitutes a common world and how it is enacted are also central concerns for chapter 4, which builds on the notion of shared gestures and choreographies and considers how they travel between the culture industry and fans. My principal case study in this chapter is Pharrell Williams's 2013 durational music video *24 Hours of Happy* and the ways fans reperform the work and use it to facilitate their own social interactions and even promote themselves. Digital media facilitate the perpetual movement of gestural information that fans embody, thus enabling them to share in a corporeal common that globalization makes available. The ethics of these gestural transfers across cultures and movement communities are ambiguous. Digital cultural production as a global phenomenon thus requires a rethinking of how gestures and dances can circulate through media and across bodies without repeating the colonial violence of dispossession in the name of open access. In this final chapter, I turn to anthropological theories of the gift, including by Marcel Mauss, to analyze dance at the intersection of gift and market economies in music videos, video games, and online spaces. I argue that in digital cultures, dances migrate as a gift of the common. As common, dances circulate freely, but as gifts, they circulate with social obligations attached—including obligations of reciprocity. With this notion, I think through dance's circulation beyond the boundaries of community while preserving an ethics of transmission.

Perpetual Motion takes a snapshot of dance in digital cultures from 1996 to 2016. The account provided here, which contributes to a contemporary history of dance onscreen as well as critical cultural commentary on popular media, is not intended to be exhaustive. But by gathering examples of dance-media across two decades, *Perpetual Motion* asks what is achieved as dance circulates through digital spaces and how digital cultural production and movement practices mutually inform and shape each other in the first decades of the twenty-first century.

CHAPTER ONE

Interactivity and Agency

◆

Making-Common and the
Limits of Difference

The web browser window opens onto a nightmarish vision of death, disembodiment, and decay engulfed in the darkness of a black screen. Twelve thumbnail snapshots lie in a grid, each linking to a corresponding scene.[1] Mousing over the grid of images stirs up sounds of an audience's restless chattering as they wait for a performance to begin. Dancing specters and haunted souls—casualties of digital disembodiment—appear throughout *Somnambules,* a 2003 Macromedia Flash hyperdance with digital visual art by Nicolas Clauss, music and sound by Jean-Jacques Birgé, and dance by Didier Silhol.[2] Each violent, melancholic scene displays a different site—picture frames, mirrors, docks, ballrooms, and many more indeterminate electronic sites in which the dancers execute never-ending cycles of repeating movement, caught in loops of time and unable to escape their nightmare. As a dance made for the computer screen, *Somnambules* emphasizes the computer user's navigation and exploration: "Click, enter, get out, that's all, but everyone in his or her own way," the introductory screen advises.[3] Users do not simply click through *Somnambules* following hyperlinks, however. Their mousing movements cue changes in visual, sonic, and choreographic elements throughout the piece, summoning new sounds, images, and motions. Visually, users explore sensuous fields layered into dense textures of reds, blues, greens; physically, their fingertips glide across the smooth, small geographies of a mouse pad or track pad as the speed and trajectory of their touch shape the piece's landscape as well as soundscape. The sound score adds malevolent violins, scratching record players, drizzling drips, and spooky circus tunes. With its layered sound and imagery, multiple scenes, and exploration of the possibilities of user interaction beyond point-and-click, *Somnambules* represents a level of aesthetic and technological sophistication that few other artists attempted and fewer achieved with dance online in the early 2000s.[4]

This chapter considers several of what I call *hyperdances,* or choreographies created for computational devices, including choreographies for web, CD-ROM, and tablet that support user interaction but do not incorporate user-generated content. Although the term *hyperdance* has an archaic ring, referencing, as it does, hypertext and hypermedia from early web and optical disk technologies, it proves more flexible than terms that specify an exact medium or platform, such as net.dance, while also serving to distinguish this constellation of works from dances that appear in other contexts, such as social media, art galleries, the theatrical stage, or film and video. Because artists constantly blur the boundaries among these approaches, I do not intend to define the contours of hyperdance as a genre that can be easily policed but rather to gather together diverse practices that share key formal attributes. Hyperdances are composed of media elements that appear on a computational device and that invite or require what has been called "nontrivial"[5] interaction from a user. Dancers and viewers are not physically co-present, and the dance occurs in a context of personal computing rather than in the context of spectators gathered together to simultaneously observe or participate in an event. In this chapter, I want to focus on the repetition of looped sequences as a key formal device that most hyperdances use to create a sense of movement, momentum, and rhythm in digital spaces and the use of repetition in tandem with user interaction.

For a book that largely concentrates on dance as a commoning practice in social media spaces, it is not obvious why I should begin with interactive web-based dance experiments of the late 1990s and early 2000s or with repetition as a compositional device in these digital works spanning two decades of creative investigation. Admittedly, hyperdances follow a different logic than the examples of what I call *social dance-media*[6] that make up a majority of this book. However, they are extremely important in the ways they created a space for dance in digital environments in the years prior to social media's cultural dominance and in the ways they migrated from one digital platform to another. Hyperdances laid the conceptual and technological groundwork of user interaction in dance onscreen, setting the stage for later experiments with user participation that feature in the remainder of the book. Furthermore, the centrality of repetition and reperformance to contemporary social dance-media finds a precursor in hyperdance.

Indeed, repetition is key to dance practices, regardless of where they circulate. Repetition makes-common by making an idea, gesture, or style familiar. Built into dance training as a mode of cultivating bodily discipline, and fused with the practice of rehearsal, which works movement into muscle memory, repetition is signally important to dance as a physical practice and performing art and is a recurring theme in choreographic structures, where it can function to establish symmetry, call-and-response relationships, or meditative spaces. It can manifest as citation, mimicry, and parody or as narrative foreshadowing, memory, and déjà vu. Repetition can call out the importance of a movement idea or, conversely, act as the means through which a gesture or sequence of gestures disintegrates into indistinguishable equivalencies. Already familiar as an aesthetic of postmodern dance, repetition, rather than movement invention, has become a dominant compositional logic of dance in early twenty-first-century digital cultures. In the digital environments of the mid-1990s to the mid-2010s— the time period on which this book focuses—repetition offered artists a practical means of enabling continuous motion onscreen, while at the same time maintaining manageable file sizes and processing speeds. Repetition is a vital ingredient in creating new dance experiences across a diverse and changing set of technological platforms, from the zoetropic cinema of animated GIFs in the 1990s and their resurgence in the 2010s to the early twenty-first-century phenomenon of internet memes and their iterative logic, the looped six-second video clips on the popular but short-lived platform Vine (2013–16), or the many apps and online videos that perpetuate themselves through repetition and reiteration, generating an online movement commons through a process of replication that makes-common through circulating and proliferating.

But repetition does not occur in isolation; interactivity is another key element that informs hyperdance, and it is with the question of user interaction that I begin this chapter. Many authors have attempted to define inter-activity as a way to differentiate modes of engaging with digital versus analog media, but rather than defining interaction per se, I find it more useful to think about what interactivity meant in the 1990s and 2000s. I use the first section of this chapter to introduce many hyperdances so as to make visible these early practices that social dance-media have now eclipsed in volume and reach. In the next section, I follow Gilles Deleuze's analysis of neorealist cinema to consider a crisis that dance artists faced when crafting dance for digital environments, initially overcoming the limitations of the early web's static HTML pages, but then falling into the infinite motion introduced by replay loops. As examples, I turn to Carolien Hermans's web-based dance *Trilogy* (2003),[7] scenes from the multisited *Invisible* (2002–5)[8] by Compagnie Magali et Didier Mulleras, the iPad app *5th Wall* (2013)[9] produced by the 2wice Arts Foundation and choreographed and danced by Jonah Bokacr, and the web-based *Somnambules,* described earlier, which is the principal case study I explore in this chapter.

Some hyperdances dramatize the repetition of the replay loop, and I turn, again with Deleuze, to evaluating the role of repetition in *Somnambules* and *windowsninetyeight: lo-fi kitchen sink dancing* (1996–98) on CD-ROM.[10] *Somnambules* is the most ambitious of Clauss's choreographic ventures and explores darker themes than much of his other work, which generally tends toward cinematic storytelling structures and richly painted visual textures. *Windowsninetyeight* was produced and directed by the London-based digital artist Bruno Martelli and choreographer Ruth Gibson, known collectively as Igloo. This piece fashions a soap opera out of the lives of three women, where the tedium of maintaining a household is a promi-nent theme. Part of what interactivity signaled in hyperdance, as in other interactive media, was a democratization of creativity, with interactors positioned as co-creators. But when repetition drives narrative and is not only an engine for the generation of movement, the ability of both screen performers and interactors to intervene and introduce meaningful differ-ences into the unfolding work is suspect. Using Deleuze's explorations of difference and repetition, I posit what I call *indifferent differences* at work in these narrative hyperdances.

Acknowledging the rise of social computing, around 2005, some dances in digital spaces pushed beyond interactivity toward user-generated content in a move that aligned with Web 2.0 aesthetics. Inviting users to upload their own video and other material for inclusion in the work, such pieces broke away from the compositional norms of hyperdance. At the end of this chapter, I discuss one such example, Katrina McPherson and Simon Fildes's *Move-Me* (2006–8),[11] as a way to show how repetition remained an important structuring device for dance in digital spaces even as social media opened new avenues of dance exploration. As we will see in chapters 3 and 4 especially, repetition as reperformance is equally vital to the ways dances circulate through social media environments, particularly in the embodiment of danced gestures by fans. What is key in *Move-Me* is the way participants' contributions repotentialize the choreographic scripts they each follow. Bringing Deleuze's analysis of the Nietzschean concept of the eternal return as a "gift of the new"[12] into conversation with Jean-Luc Nancy's concept of unworking, I suggest that the way these and other artists have opened up their work to crowd-based interventions destabilizes a singular identity of the work, while simultaneously reasserting the work's identity as an assemblage of its iterations. Such dances break out of the restrictive cycles of automated replay loops and employ the creativity of the crowd, whose collective unworking produces a gift of the new. Through such unworking it is possible to produce the uncommon from the common, mundane space of repetition.

WHAT WAS INTERACTIVITY?

In "The Enduring Ephemeral, or the Future Is a Memory," media theorist Wendy Hui Kyong Chun urges scholars to ask not what new media "is" but rather "what was new media?"[13] In a similar vein, in situating *Somnambules* and other hyperdances historically, it no longer feels appropriate to ask what interactivity is but rather to consider what it was. This is a difficult task since, on one hand, the utopian rhetoric that greeted early digital media built up a seductive narrative that paired interactivity with democracy and introduced untenable ontological distinctions among media to reinforce the newness of new media. On the other hand, interactivity is now so normalized in everyday digital media use as to be completely unremarkable. In his now-classic book *The Language of New Media*, cinema and media theorist Lev Manovich contends that "to call computer media 'interactive' is meaningless—it simply means stating the most basic fact about computers."[14] Still, even though yesterday's new media appear quaint by today's ever-evolving standards, it is important to understand what the promise of new media was. That promise hinged in large part on interactivity.

In a 1998 essay tracking the development of interactivity as a concept, communications scholar Jens F. Jensen offers the following summary of a turn-of-the-century perspective: "The concept seems loaded with positive connotations along the lines of high tech, technological advancement, hypermodernity and futurism, along the lines of individual freedom of choice, personal development, self determination—and even along the lines of folksy popularization, grassroots democracy, and political independence."[15] Such inflated hopes for interactivity reflect the priorities of business communities and advertisers as much as cultural commentators. In 1997, Jon Katz declared in the technology and culture magazine *Wired* that "the world's information is being liberated, and so, as a consequence, are we."[16] The scholarly community was not untouched by the hype around interactivity. For example, the early theorist of hypertextual literature George Landow follows Roland Barthes's distinction between classical readerly texts and more contemporary writerly texts to argue for a similar shift from readerly to writerly modes inaugurated by electronic hypertext.[17] For Barthes, a reader absorbs a readerly text but coproduces a writerly text; a writerly text displaces the centrality of authorial intention and requires a reader's active participation. Landow compares this scenario of coproducing meaning in literature to interacting with hypertexts, going so far as to suggest that electronic hypertext fulfills Barthes's vision of the writerly text, which "make[s] the reader no longer a consumer, but a producer of the text."[18]

Where Landow emphasized the nonlinearity of hypertext and the user's active engagement in producing meaning, other authors emphasized that this active engagement was specifically a bodily engagement with the text. Media theorist Margaret Morse, for example, argues that audiences "have always *cognitively* 'interacted' with the text by filling in the gaps," but that interactive media are different in that "the interactive user/viewer *corporeally* influences the body of a digital text itself . . . in real time."[19] For Morse, the difference is that interactors must use their bodies in some way to shape a text at the moment of its unfolding; the text emerges only in relation to that corporeal engagement. "One interacts," Morse contends, "by touching, moving, speaking, gesturing, or another corporeal means of producing a sign that can be read and transformed into input by a computer."[20] Media theorist and philosopher Mark B. N. Hansen likewise contends that digital media put the body to work and that "the self-differing condition of the digital 'medium' . . . requires bodily activity to produce any experience whatsoever."[21] David Saltz, a scholar and practitioner of interactive theater, also attempts a definition of interactive media. His parameters are a bit less fleshy and include a "sensing or input device" that translates input into computer-recognizable data, output that relates to the input, and the translation of output "into real-world phenomena that people can perceive."[22] These definitions of interactivity from the late 1990s and early 2000s show a shared understanding that physical engagement made interactive media different from other forms of media. By interacting with digital texts, users were supposedly emancipated from their previous roles as mere consumers and passive spectators. From this perspective, interactive media opened a door to creative collaboration in which users coproduced what occurred onscreen.

The speed of technological change troubles the rhetoric with which interactive media were heralded, whether as tool of liberation or of artistic co-creation. Still, keeping with what interactivity *was* rather than what it *is*, it is crucial to remember that at the turn of the twenty-first century, web media and especially Flash animations were a novelty,[23] a seemingly radical departure from static web pages, streaming video, and other uses of internet technologies associated with the one-to-many distribution of so-called Web 1.0, but not yet achieving the many-to-many dissemination of Web 2.0's socially integrated models.[24] Whereas platforms such as YouTube, Vimeo, and especially Instagram dominated the way users created and shared dance online by the mid-2010s, a spirit of experimentation permeated early examples of dance on the internet, which made a space for dance in computational environments only equipped for textual communication.

For example, Richard Lord's *Progressive 2* (1996)[25] stands out for its early use of Macromedia Director, which could support video as well as more complex animations, and its gridlike structure anticipated the aesthetics of juxtaposition used by many hyperdances in the early 2000s. His later work *Waterfall* (2002),[26] a multifaceted work on CD-ROM, features Emma

Diamond dancing atop a river, below the ocean's surface, on a cresting wave, in a rainforest, and on a glacier, among other sites through which users navigate. *Invisible* (2002–5) and *96 Détails* (2006–9) by Compagnie Magali et Didier Mulleras recontextualize material from stage-based choreographies and installations as hybrid web-based works that combine video and interactive media. Both *Invisible* and *96 Détails* allow users to set small clips in motion and change their position within a grid to experience the complexities of repetition and juxtaposition core to minimalist choreographic approaches. Screendance artists Katrina McPherson and Simon Fildes have a series of what they call "hyperchoreographies," such as *Big* (2002)[27] and *The Truth: The Truth* (2004).[28] In both of these pieces, dancers cycle through movements in multiple frames, offering users an opportunity to compose the brief video clips into a multipaned choreography. *Triad HyperDance* (1999)[29] repurposes material from a telematic performance by butoh performer Akeno and modern dancer Molissa Fenley, enabling users to move their dancing images within the screen space. And Koert van Mensvoort's *Drift* (2003)[30] features a motion-captured dancer that liquefies and shatters in response to user movement.

Taken together, these hyperdances demonstrate the basic repertoire of interactive possibilities, which remains the same across media platforms. This repertoire includes simple navigation; means of cuing scenes or sequences such as with play and pause controls; and the ability to resize images, change their orientations, or reverse movement sequences. In Igloo's CD-ROM *windowsninetyeight,* for example, users move the dancing images around the screen, alter their size and scale, and trigger the women's performances of caretaking and loneliness. Similarly, in the iPad app *5th Wall,* interactors can select from a few preset arrangements of the four windows in which choreographer and dancer Jonah Bokaer appears dancing his four movement phrases, or they can move and resize each of the viewing panes. Some pieces, such as the web-based *Somnambules,* also layer dancing images with other visual and sonic elements that users can trigger. *Somnambules* limits user interaction to a combination of mousing, hovering, and clicking—no dragging or resizing—but provides a rich landscape of sound and imagery that registers user input. For example, in the scene "Frontal," the user peers down onto dancer Anne-Catherine Nicoladzé, who stands and faces sixteen replicas of a seated Didier Silhol. Hovering over Nicoladzé produces whistling and chirping sounds to accompany her arms sweeping to the side and overhead or gesturing presentationally in front and to the side of her body. Mousing over the images has a comical effect: as though responding to the force of the mouse pushing its way through the seated crowd, each Silhol topples forward and circles back to his default seated posture, righting himself like a child's punching bag toy each time he is struck. Clicking on Nicoladzé, the user is taken to a duet between Nicoladzé and Silhol (only one of each), again seen from above. Without user input, they approach and retreat from each other, swaying back and forth like out-of-sync pendulums in what Alexander Galloway calls an "ambience act" in his analysis of video games,[31] but mousing over the dancers' images causes their arms to extend into the space around them and a complicated conversation of gesture and sound—she chirps and tweets while he screeches and creaks—to unfold between them.

According to Morse and Hansen, interactive digital artworks are built on a premise of bodily participation, not of observation at a remove. In hyperdance, a user's bodily movements explicitly shape the images and sounds, and changes onscreen have the capacity to provoke new bodily responses and movements. For many artists and scholars, interactivity in arts practices hearkens back to the disruptive participatory performances of the 1960s,[32] which employed techniques for interfering with the autonomy of a work and upsetting the sanctity of the art world and its exhibition spaces. Hyperdances similarly explore the aesthetics of interruption and nonlinear progression seemingly to open or repotentialize a screen-based choreography. Artists create possibilities for encounters, determining the nature, number, and types of objects and behaviors in advance, but their authorial intentions otherwise recede into the background, making room for interactors to discover and play with the work on their own, taking as much or as little time as they prefer. Artists provide the interactive framework and the media elements, and then computers and computer users perform the work together. In this way, the ideal spectator is not someone engaged in dispassionate contemplation but one whose experience is predicated on their physical engagement with and immersion in the interactive scenario.

Like a performance score or script, digital artworks realize their dynamic potential with the execution of their code, which disappears as it is executed by a computer, and with the performances of computer users, who "play" the digital work.[33] Writing about hypertext, media theorist Rita Raley even contends that such work "must be conceived in terms of performance."[34] She includes "the processing done by the computer, which itself performs or is even performative, and . . . the performance of the user who operates as a functioning mechanism in the text" in her understanding of performance.[35] Hans Dieter Huber likewise compares the web browser to an orchestra conductor, arguing that "the browser performs the score and displays it on the surface of the monitor."[36] The interactive artwork thus emerges between the computer, where output is informed by such variables as internet bandwidth and processing speeds, and the computer user, whose interactions are informed by visual and sonic feedback. While participatory artists in gallery and community settings cannot always control for the unpredictability of co-present human spectator-performers, artists working with interactive media have a great deal of control over which human behaviors and environmental factors will be accounted for and recognized in the unfolding of an interactive artwork. Most scenes in *Somnambules,* for example, establish a causal logic, and users can detect the correlation between the modes of interaction available to them—mousing and clicking—and specific results. This does not negate surprise, however, and indeed, discovering the correlations between one's actions and on-screen events is part of the pleasure of engaging with interactive media. Nevertheless, even organizationally complex works like *Somnambules* allow users only to cue preprogrammed events.

User input does not, indeed cannot, give rise to choreographic, visual, or sonic events that the artists have not already put in place. Discussing her piece *Trilogy,* Carolien Hermans muses, "The user has considerable freedom to create his own unique art work out of the original composition,"[37] but she offers a caution as well. "The interactivity suggests openness and freedom of interpretation: in reality personal interpretations are restricted and limited."[38] Following Umberto Eco's articulation of the open work,[39] Hermans suggests that rather than describe her work as interactive, perhaps "an artwork in movement" is more apt.[40] Dance-media artist and scholar Susan Kozel likewise contends that "in the end, [interactivity] refers primarily to decision-based mechanisms for screen-based media such as DVDs and Web sites, or automated bank teller and subway ticket dispensers."[41]

Kozel prefers to describe her own media installations and performance work in terms of "responsiveness" rather than interactivity. The difference, she notes, is that "the structure of a responsive work is such that we are made aware *that* we are responding *while* we are responding, that we are playing a role in a greater system of responsivity extending beyond our isolated subjective choices. This takes some of the control away from us: we do not control, we respond."[42] For Kozel, interaction is thus fundamentally a question of selection or causation, not of creative participation.

It would be difficult to assess whether interactors feel they are controlling or responding to hyperdances, which are self-contained works composed of a finite set of images and interactive elements, programmed to recognize predefined user input that triggers predefined output. It would be even more difficult to ascertain the threshold at which apparent control gives way to response and whether these states are fundamentally about the work or the interactor. Morse would counter that such a functionalist understanding of interactivity as Kozel posits relies too heavily on unstable binary distinctions between human and nonhuman interactants or open and closed systems.[43] Yet, overemphasizing the freedom of choice offered to users in interactive artworks seems too simplistic for a generation of users reared under a regime of compulsory participation and data collection. Art critic Hal Foster, for example, cautions against "a shaky analogy between an open work and an inclusive society . . . a democratic community . . . [or] an egalitarian world,"[44] and media theorists Alexander Galloway and Eugene Thacker have lamented, "Today's media physically require the maintained, constant, continuous interaction of users. This is the political tragedy of interactivity."[45] What seemed to be an avenue for encouraging greater user freedom by opening more choices for customizable and unique experiences showed that it could also curtail freedom by compelling ongoing user performance in service to repetitive iterations of the digital work.

Interactivity implicates users and their bodies in the performance of hyperdance, which requires user navigation, as Hansen remarks, "to produce any experience whatsoever."[46] But interaction also loosened a bind that accompanied dance's entrée into online spaces. Whereas dance had easily migrated to film and video, prompting vast experimentation combining bodily movement with the moving image, early web browsers severely curtailed onscreen motion. Working within the constraints of HTML, many of the earliest hyperdances, including Molissa Fenley's *Latitudes* (1996),[47] Troika Ranch's *Yearbody* (1996–97),[48] Marianne Goldberg's *Be to Want I* (1998),[49] and Vivian Selbo and Carl Skelton's web-based documentation of Ralph Lemon's *Tree* (2000),[50] were composed of text, still images, and animated GIFs, which allowed artists to respond to the logics of the internet in a way that streaming video alone did not.[51] As artists continued to experiment with representing dance onscreen while making these dances more responsive to user engagement than a video's simple controls, they turned to replay loops, including looping animated GIFs or very short video clips, to support dance as sustained movement in an environment built for static text. Replay loops thus presented a solution to a crisis of movement that the static HTML pages of the early web represented for hyperdance.

A signature element of digital art "circa 2002," as Raley notes, the replay loop is "incorporated as both design element and thematic content"[52] in hyperdance. A replay loop is a computer programming statement (do while; do loop; repeat until; do until) that repeatedly executes a block of code as long as the conditions for its execution remain true. As soon as they become false, the loop ceases. The condition that ends a loop's repetitions may be internal to the code, for example, if a programmer indicates the number of times an element should execute in advance, or external, for example, when user input fulfills another programmed condition that overrides the replay loop in a hierarchy of behaviors. With few exceptions, the interactive elements that characterize hyperdance take place in the context of and in relation to looped movement sequences. If replay loops solved hyperdance's first crisis of movement, however, they introduced another crisis—one of infinite motion produced by the loop's repetitions.

CRISIS OF MOVEMENT: REPETITION

In a scene of *Somnambules* called "Melting," Silhol and Nicoladzé perform a contact improvisation duet. Contact improvisation emphasizes bodily engagement, exploring movement and touch as both objects and means of interaction. A physical practice of generating movement through the exchange of sensation between (typically) two dancers, contact improvisation offers a particularly poignant take on interactive media with which it shares a democratizing promise. But "Melting" does not portray a radical openness to the other as one might expect. Or rather, the dancers' openness in performance does not extend across time and space to the user, whose mousing gestures have limited effect on the dance. When Silhol and Nicoladzé appear onscreen, they seem to have already been dancing for quite some time. Silhol lays on his back with Nicoladzé at his side. Nicoladzé leans into him as he suspends her feet in the crook of his elbow. They are momentarily fused, paused there, weighing the moment as they wait for gravity or a subtle intention to change their course. Silhol lowers Nicoladzé's feet, propelling her around. She slides between his hips and ribs, perpendicular to him. Nicoladzé finds her feet and plants them, ready to stand. But it seems she changes her mind. She gives in once more to the downward pull, and her elbow leads the rest of her body into the ground. A mouse click causes Silhol and Nicoladzé to increase their pace, while mousing across the frame summons overlays such as a weathered and torn page of text, splotches of red splatter, or a blackness that threatens to engulf the entire image. Silhol and Nicoladzé sit back to back. Silhol reaches

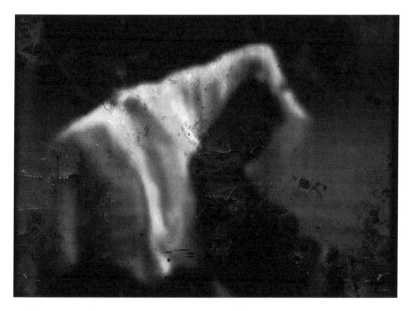

Figure 2. Didier Silhol and Anne-Catherine Nicoladzé perform a contact improvisation duet in the "Melting" scene of *Somnambules* (2003), by Nicolas Clauss, Jean-Jacques Birgé, and Didier Silhol. Courtesy of the Ars Electronica Archive and the creators. Reprinted with permission.

behind, takes Nicoladzé's hand, and guides her into a brief sideways embrace. They unfold and reverse the sequence. Silhol absorbs and redirects Nicoladzé's velocity at each of the clip's end points, and they repeat and reverse again and again, moving forward and backward through time infinitely. As tender as their duet is, neither Silhol nor Nicoladzé has the power to escape it, nor can an interactor transform the scene in any substantive way. Mousing produces changes in foreground and background imagery, but a user can only alter the speed of the duet or leave it behind completely by navigating back to the main menu. Users neither alter the dancers' movement pathways nor bring the dance to a conclusion; they are there as witnesses to a dance that, owing to its looped content, is endless.

Although repetition is built into performing arts training, composition, rehearsal, and performance, replay loops introduce a mechanized form of repetition that is of a different order than these reiterations. The replay loop as a popular strategy of propelling onscreen movement in the late 1990s and early 2000s coincides with a historical moment in which, as dance and performance theorist André Lepecki notes in *Exhausting Dance,* experimental choreographers in Europe and the United States responded to violence and catastrophe on a global scale by practicing stillness onstage instead of dancing, because "political events in the world were such they could not dance."[53] This was an era of war in the Persian Gulf, race-related riots in Los Angeles, and ethnic cleansing in Bosnia and Herzegovina as well as Rwanda. Not long after, fears of a computational apocalypse took hold due to rumors of Y2K programming errors that threatened to wipe out bank accounts. In the first few years of the twenty-first century, especially after the events of September 11, 2001, global terror was advertised as a constant threat. The sentiment of political powerlessness in the face of global violence and existential threats was recurrent and widespread. Stillness, Lepecki observes, was one response to the resulting fatigue. Because of the weight of the political-historical moment, dancers were unable to return to what philosopher Peter Sloterdijk calls the "being-toward-movement" that is the hallmark of the dancer as such.[54] Choreographers thus composed moments of stillness.[55] The crisis of movement that resulted in stillness in stage-based dance performances led to perpetual motion with the use of replay loops in computer-based hyperdances. Though their approaches to motion contradict each other, both are historically and affectively aligned. Replay loops in particular resonate with what Deleuze calls a crisis of the action-image in neorealist cinema, which I explore subsequently through *Trilogy* by Carolien Hermans, *Invisible* by Compagnie Magali et Didier Mulleras, *5th Wall* choreographed and danced by Jonah Bokaer, and *Somnambules*.

In hyperdance, there are loops that only display identical repetitions and others that integrate user feedback. Some displace the play and replay functions onto the user, who is compelled to perform or actualize the repetitions built into the work.[56] Or looped movement can comprise additive modules in a larger combinatory choreography. Coded hierarchically, loops may compete for screen time, especially as user input informs which images display and when. In other words, digital loops are not singular structures but arrays of strategies that may be used to either perpetuate repetition or, through user interaction, interrupt it. Raley identifies two aspects of loops as they appear in electronic literature: "recurrence, whereby the loop cycle does not achieve a perfect re-iteration but is instead altered with each sequence, and feedback, whereby the system and its environment interact and modify each other."[57] Between these two types of loops—the recurring elements and the enfolding of the computer user—the interactive digital work emerges. As loops, recurrence and feedback necessarily produce differences, imperfect reiterations of sequences and deviations in the text. Yet, as a programming command, the replay loop does not admit difference. It is not even a question of the differences among so many copies; the replay loop as a performative command suggests that a computer is merely executing the same block of code, not reproducing or duplicating it. The replay loop is thus predicated upon the assumption that a computer can render the same information exactly—that it can and does achieve perfect reiterations.

For a majority of hyperdances, the replay loop represents a default state. Once launched, a user can navigate and explore a work actively or, having set a few images in motion, can withhold further input. In the latter case, the replay loop reigns. Movement sequences continue to play, gesturing toward their own eternality. With users as audience to their repetitions, dancing images recycling their motions appear contemplative, executing a phrase a second, third, fourth, or nth time, unable to cue a change of scene. Whereas HTML threatened dance with stasis, the use of replay loops renders screen-dancers beholden to a single choreographic idea or movement phrase from which they cannot deviate. This inability to act signals a crisis of movement in hyperdance similar to that explored by Deleuze in his analysis of cinema.

Deleuze opens his second study of cinematic signs, *Cinema 2: The Time-Image,* with a crisis. Whereas realist cinema required action of its characters, Deleuze argues that neorealist films are full of characters who can no longer react to their situations. There is a relaxation of the sensory–motor connection that had driven realist plots: action, reaction. Neorealist cinema, in contrast, is "a cinema of the seer and no longer of the agent."[58] Characters become viewers, witnesses, or bystanders who are helpless to respond. According to Deleuze, the crisis of action reconfigures the function of dance in cinema as well. In the musical comedy genre, which is his principal framework for understanding dance onscreen, dance generally signifies a break with reality, a rupture. As dream, hallucination, or spectacle that disrupts the narrative, dance, according to Deleuze, "has already lost its motor connection."[59] Dance postpones or prevents action. It represents a world of inaction, a "to-and-fro which replaces action."[60] In Deleuze's reading, dance sequences thus provide an ineffectual stand-in for action, a hesitation or unproductive diversion of energy funneled into the realms of wishful thinking and daydreams. Characters play out their fantasies of wealth, beauty, and courage through dance's alternate realties.

For Deleuze, characters in neorealist and new wave cinema are immobilized by sight, by their efforts to comprehend their situation through vision rather than responding with action. Action or agency, as authoring one's own movement in response to a situation, is no longer possible. "Thus movement can tend to zero," Deleuze remarks of cinema, or "be exaggerated, be incessant, become a world movement, a Brownian movement, a trampling, a to-and-fro, a multiplicity of movements on different scales. What is important," he continues, "is that the anomalies of movement become the essential point instead of being accidental or contingent."[61] Such anomalous movements abound in hyperdances. Caught in continuous loops, the dancers are no longer agents of their own motion. They have forfeited their self-propulsion to computational processes and computer users.

For example, "The Elbow Room," one of three scenes in Hermans's interactive dance *Trilogy*, explores the space of the dancer's wardrobe. Onscreen text conveys the dancer's inner monologue, while her movements appear minimal and stilted. "My body is the centre of action: it receives and returns movements," the screen reads.[62] She waits, still, lying down but propped vertically on the screen—apparently naked, except for bright green socks. Mousing over this image causes the screen-dancer to open and close the wardrobe doors, repeatedly concealing and revealing herself. Navigating to the next window, the user encounters the dancer's encircled knees, an animated insect, and another text: "I am moving in the smallest / imaginary space possible. / *walking-running-jumping-rolling* / It has all become impossible. / I have to learn new habits soon / since my body has become / completely dysfunctional in here."[63] Hermans's reflection on her cramped closet and musing on how a body adjusts to that space bring dysfunction to the foreground, perhaps prompting a consideration of a user's own corporeal navigations of cramped spaces, including those of mouse pads and browser windows. Onscreen, Hermans's spatial limitations are also temporal. Her left arm sweeps down, and the momentum lifts her right heel, which crosses her body. Left fingertips find her right elbow, crooked overhead. Her left arm sweeps down, and the momentum lifts her right heel, which crosses her body. Left fingertips find her right elbow, and so on.

Loops at once set dancers in perpetual motion and fetter that motion, containing the dancers' movement and foreclosing the possibility of any future action that deviates from their infinitely recurring gestures. Whatever agency the dancers might have initially exercised in their moment of technological capture is removed from them and displaced onto the user. But users' agency is also circumscribed by the behaviors and possibilities choreographed into the code. Even when producing a maximum of motion, the gestures of both the dancers onscreen and interactors in front of the screen remain limited. "It is as if action floats in the situation, rather than bringing it to a conclusion or strengthening it," Deleuze remarks.[64] And indeed, resolution is perpetually deferred throughout *Trilogy*, which instead sustains an ongoing investigation of small spaces and an infinitely expanding present moment. The different scenes in *Trilogy* promote exploration without predetermined end or sense of conclusion,

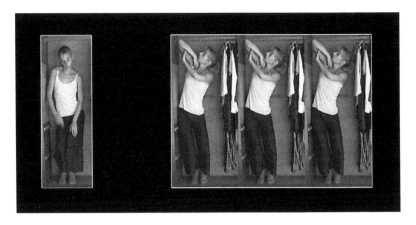

Figure 3. Carolien Hermans dancing in a closet in the "Elbow Room" scene of *Trilogy* (2003) by Carolien Hermans. Screenshot from the Internet Archive.

such that movement, like the sound that accompanies the work, becomes "atmospheric."

Invisible by Compagnie Magali et Didier Mulleras is a work that unfolded across multiple sites, encompassing iterations on stage, as installations, and in site-based performances,[65] as well as an online work that encompasses both videos and interactive segments. Unlike *Trilogy* and *Somnambules,* which sustain a specific media investigation across multiple scenes, *Invisible* is an overarching umbrella that contains various media types. Only the hyperdances in the work rely on the continuity provided by automated replay loops. One of the scenes, "Chambre 317," is composed of a four-by-four grid of which a cinema of rapidly sequenced images takes up the four central squares, leaving an empty perimeter. Mousing over the central image pauses the sequence, while clicking it populates one of the frames on the perimeter with the same image. The entire perimeter can be filled with these smaller images, and mousing over them produces both ambient sound and frustratingly brief video clips. A hallway, a locked door, a man slouched in a chair, a dour woman looking on, a set of stairs. Are they clues? The center images move too rapidly to make sense of what they portray, and the small images on the perimeter offer too little information to determine the relation among the people, the space in which they are gathered, or what they intend to do or have done. "Characters do not move," Deleuze remarks; rather, "the camera causes the movement . . . 'motionlessness at a great pace.'"[66] Nothing in this room moves, but the image itself produces a surplus of movement, leaving faint impressions rather than an understanding of just what is going on. Viewers peer into this world of waiting, a world held in tense suspension but in which nothing seems to happen.

In another scene of *Invisible*, "Velours," a woman enters through each of nine curtained doorways displayed on a three-by-three grid. She emerges tentatively, only to be pulled back every time. With each hopeful, if cautious, attempt, she is jerked backward and hidden from view. Dragged by foot or head, caught by arm, waist, or neck, she will never make it beyond the doorway. Though she never appears desperate, her perseverance seems increasingly ridiculous and tragic in the inevitable failure of her attempts. In "Assis," also on a three-by-three grid, a seated man faces away from the interactor. Mousing over the nine images of the man causes him to topple over, head down, butt in the air, and sometimes the image changes color from bluish white tones to bright red. His hands smack the ground with a distorted electronic thwack, and he rights himself when the user mouses away. Like *Trilogy*, *Invisible* makes use of textual elements that layer onto the visual imagery. In "Assis," the significance of the words and phrases remains mysterious, but they are suggestive: *assis, debout, allongé, il est là, endormi, rêve, nuit* (seated, standing, outspread, he is there, asleep, dream, night). The toppling man does not enact these terms, but, like *Somnambules*, they situate his perpetual falling within a space of dream and slumber.

5th Wall, choreographed and danced by Jonah Bokaer, is accompanied by a slightly melancholic sound score by Eric Beach, Josh Quentin, and Jason Treuting. It is among the first screendances made specifically for the Apple iPad. One might expect that, coming a decade after the peak of hyperdance online, *5th Wall* would share little in common with previous generations of hyperdance. In fact, *5th Wall* uses many of the same conventions, not least of which is the juxtaposition of replay loops. Bokaer dances in a box, but as the box rotates around its x-axis and the camera cartwheels around its z-axis, Bokaer's dancing onscreen appears right side up, upside down, and sideways. Bokaer's physical orientation to a ground is made indeterminate through his own inversions (supporting his weight on his hands) as well as those of the camera. As a result, viewers experience their own disorientations and reorientations in trying to make sense of the different orders of space Bokaer occupies in his box and onscreen. In his box, Bokaer performs four short choreographed phrases, each of which is filmed as a single take and then played on a loop. Each sequence appears onscreen in one of four windows set side by side or stacked one on top of another. The movement phrases are similar enough to each other that discerning the differences between them is a bit of a visual conundrum. The phrases are slightly different lengths, ranging in duration from just over one minute to just under two, and they are repeated indefinitely, with their starting and ending points coming in and out of sync. The similarity of the phrases ensures continuity across the clips, but their varying lengths and the user's ability to move and resize each frame prolong user interest with the possibility of new juxtapositions. Just as is the case with live performance, each encounter with a hyperdance produces

Figure 4. Screenshot of choreographer and dancer Jonah Bokaer in the iPad app 5th Wall (2013). Concept and design by Abbott Miller, video by Ben Louis Nicholas, music by So Percussion. Produced by 2wice Arts Foundation.

a unique event; the encoded relationships between user input and media output remain defined by a choreographic score that enables a nearly infinite range of iterations.

Replay loops provide the electrical charge, the motor force behind the condensed dramas portrayed in hyperdances—even those without overarching narratives. As programming statements, replay loops imply strictly identical reiterations, but because hyperdances frequently combine replay loops of different durations and incorporate user input, loops give rise to both slight and considerable variations that Raley calls recurrence. Hyperdance's repeating movement sequences are entwined in a feedback loop that includes the user, whose input via mouse, keyboard, or touchscreen creates new performances out of indefinitely repeating choreographic elements. Interactors halt or initiate new repetitions and shift the layering of movement and sound in hyperdance's audiovisual composites. Replay loops serve as a foundation to which interactive elements are added, introducing the possibility of difference into the system that would otherwise foreclose alteration. However, the persistence of the loop's iterations renders repetition and difference indistinguishable. Difference effaces itself and takes up the mantle of repetition. The digital replay loop serves both structural and metaphorical functions, and some hyperdances stage dramas out of the repeating elements caught in a loop's perpetual motion. Indeed, Lev Manovich suggests that "the loop [may] be a new narrative form appropriate for the computer age."[67] As I explore in the next section, when such repetition and its attendant crises of movement are not only aestheticized but also narrativized, as in *Somnambules* and *windowsninetyeight,* hyperdances represent a world that has lost its capacity for action. Through repetition, movement becomes indistinguishable from stasis.

INDIFFERENT DIFFERENCES:
ON THE FAILURES OF INTERACTIVITY

Bookended by an overture and a coda that establish and reinforce the tone of the piece, *Somnambules* questions the ability of both onscreen characters and interactors in front of the screen to intervene in this nightmarish space. In the overture, Silhol appears and disappears from view, ducking his head to leave the frame. He looks suddenly to the left and right as menacing footsteps torment him, and he appears surrounded by hands grabbing at him from all sides as he rolls his head, just out of reach of their clawing fingers. In the coda, as though seen through a trick mirror, Silhol jumps from side to side, Nicoladzé cartwheels back and forth, and a caged hand taps out a strange code. The images sway back and forth like a pendulum, hypnotizing interactors. Similarly, in *windowsninetyeight,* built around the experiences of three women in a high-rise, the artists offer interactors many opportunities to prompt behaviors from the system. However, even as new scenes and therefore new opportunities for exploration open up as the women's day goes by, there is not a sense that users can have any transformative effect on the women's reiterative choreographies or relieve the women of their challenges presented as nightmares. Dishes stack up and fill the screen, and table settings frame and serve up dancing images to viewers for consumption. Washing machines hum with activity, rooms require cleaning and redecoration, and the weight of solitude slowly creeps in. In both *Somnambules* and *windowsninetyeight,* the repetitive gestures of the screen-dancers take on sinister overtones as they become core drivers of narrative. Whereas interactivity had promised to open works up to the consequential input of interactors in an overall democratization of art and authorship, these two pieces employ repetition as a form of temporal torture, whether haunted souls trapped in a cyberpurgatory or women overwhelmed by caretaking responsibilities and loneliness. All the screen-dancers are compelled to repeat themselves as they await an ever-deferred conclusion.

In *Difference and Repetition,* Deleuze seeks to correct what he sees as an error in philosophy, which has not approached either repetition or difference as concepts with adequate rigor, resulting in a subordination of difference to repetition. In his study, he identifies two types of repetition that are entwined: one of a static sort he calls "bare repetition" and another of a dynamic sort with difference at its core. Bare repetition is an envelope or shell, an exterior effect that disguises an interior difference: "variation is not added to repetition in order to hide it, but is rather its condition or constitutive element, the interiority of repetition."[68] For Deleuze, difference is neither opposition nor diversity, nor even analogy nor resemblance,[69] but that which gives diversity as a given, "that by which the given is given as diverse."[70] Reading Nietzsche's philosophy of eternal return, to which I will turn shortly, Deleuze posits repetition as a function of difference.

Rather than reduce difference to identity, this maneuver repopulates the category of the same without rendering all elements equal and interchangeable. Deleuze paraphrases Heidegger on this point: "The equal or identical always moves toward the absence of difference, so that everything must be reduced to a common denominator. The same, by contrast, is the belonging together of what differs. . . . The same gathers what is distinct [whereas] the equal, on the contrary, disperses them into the dull unity of mere uniformity."[71] Deleuze broadens the scope of difference within repetition, allowing difference to diversify the same. Difference is an originary multiplicity, while repetition is only "difference without a concept."[72] Deleuze gives difference back to repetition and the same from which, he argues, it had been excluded but always remained in disguise.

In this section, I would like to think further about difference without concept, not to affirm bare repetition or the subordination of difference to repetition within Western philosophical thought but to suggest that in the context of hyperdance, the play of difference that seemed so crucial to digital artists is a surface effect. As we saw earlier, the rhetoric of early interactive media promised that the differences that users introduced into digital artworks were consequential. User interaction activates and amplifies the "self-differing"[73] of digital media through feedback, but while the replay loop's repetitions are internally differentiated, experientially and narratively, it is repetition rather than difference that dominates. In examining hyperdances that narrativize repetition, I argue that the differences they generate are differences that refuse to differentiate, differences that make no difference, or what I am calling indifferent differences.

Loops impede and constrain dancing images such that their continuous motion mimics the effects of stillness as "going nowhere"—a condition that achieves narrative import in windowsninetyeight and Somnambules. It is possible that, being screenic dancing images of the dead and the dreamt, the screen-dancers in Somnambules and windowsninetyeight are simultaneously overburdened by and disconnected from the past. Hence they are doomed to repeat it, unable to act in any other capacity. The past requires a measure of forgetfulness to allow room for life in the present.[74] In Somnambules and windowsninetyeight, however, forgetfulness does not function to enable life or to unburden the present. Rather, stuck in a time outside of time, the performers take their own digital forgetfulness to a radical extreme. Caught in a perverse form of temporal synthesis that offers only a relentless present, they are unable to recognize that they are infinitely reiterating the past. Both *Somnambules* and *windowsninetyeight* explore a loss of agency by dwelling in the space of infinite reiteration, and they challenge this loss of agency and implied inability to act by working through the repercussions of return. However, screening replay loops from which dancers and users cannot escape serves to aestheticize the absence of agency. The computer's memory counters the dancers' forgetfulness and regurgitates their movement through the incessant motion of replay loops that circumvent the possibility of alteration. "It is as if total and anarchic mobilizing of the past now responds to the character's motor powerlessness," Deleuze remarks of neorealist cinema. "Dissolves and superimpositions arrive with a vengeance."[75] The performers are reduced to a pure present beyond which they are unable to move, unable to access either past or future except as an explosion of the now rendered through the multiplication of their superimposed images. Hyperdances do not offer a place from which the screen-dancers can act, nor do they offer an alternative to spinning one's wheels—they expose bare repetition or repetition of the identical as the core of turn-of-the-century interactivity.

The looped sequences in *windowsninetyeight* and *Somnambules* suggest a passive state that allows for differences, but only differences that cannot make a difference: indifferent differences. The dancers onscreen cannot propel themselves into subsequent action, nor transmute their gestures into reiterated movements of a higher order, nor annihilate or dissolve the identity of their repetitions through return. In *Difference and Repetition,* Deleuze briefly mentions indifferent differences as a mark of repetition's blindness to difference: "repetition is attributed to elements which are really distinct but nevertheless share strictly the same concept. Repetition thus appears as a difference, but a difference absolutely without concept; in this sense, an indifferent difference."[76] Dissimilarities, reduced to similarities or repetitions, are indifferent and unrecognizable. In hyperdance, prolific differences can be observed in changing color palettes, soundscapes, spatial configurations, gestural vocabulary, and so on, yet all of these differences have been rendered indifferent, inconsequential. As an aesthetic, difference has been gutted of any transformative capacity.

Windowsninetyeight: lo-fi kitchen sink dancing on CD-Rom offers an example of indifference in narrative hyperdance. It is a meditation on being stuck. Some dancers get stuck in their repetitions of familiar gestures—short or long phrases of movement—while others are fixed in their stasis, awaiting a user's interventions to temporarily give them back their motion by mousing over them. In their own performances of stillness, some images in *windowsninetyeight* cannot move unless the user provides his or her own movement to support or partner the dancers. Interactors thus enable the dance's unfolding, but rather than users exerting control over the interactive scenario, the image borrows movement from them, whose interactions feed and sustain the work in such moments.

Windowsninetyeight opens with still shots of urban environments cast in shades of purple. An apartment high-rise comes into view. Sounds of a clock ticking, birds calling, children playing, and cars driving by weave a sonic landscape as shadows cross the buildings and clouds change shapes. Still photographs bleed into one another: people and cars come into view but soon dissolve into the next image. Three white squares frame windows on the apartment building, indicating to the user that these are each points of entrance into each of the three women's lives. Clicking on any of the three buttons takes the user to the first clip in that particular series. The clips are connected to the time of day depicted onscreen, which in turn represents how much time the user has spent with the piece. *Windowsninetyeight* compresses a day into approximately twenty-four minutes, at which point all clips are available for perusal. At the end of twenty-four minutes, the twenty-four-hour cycle recommences, but user access to the clips is not restricted accordingly. Rather than coming to a close after twenty-four minutes, the piece continues indefinitely. Days go by, but all conditions for access have been met and all iterations may now recur.

Artists Ruth Gibson and Bruno Martelli describe the work as a nightmare of sorts, exposing the deepest fears of three women. They state:

> *Windowsninetyeight* is a provocative portrait of three women living alone in a highrise. One evening, a mysterious event takes each on a cathartic ride through the deepest fears of the other. The saga chronicles a single 24 hour cycle in the lives of these women. The magical world of their

private behaviour, their habits and chores, their dreams and fears, becomes exposed to our scrutiny. As we navigate a passage through their
day, three raw and personal domestic existences open up for our viewing
pleasure.[77]

Domestic disturbances are confined to the infernal realm of housekeep-
ing: decorating rooms, removing spots from carpets, and, of course, doing
the dishes. While the artists describe the piece as nightmarish, there is
little to suggest the horror of these chores, except for their unceasing continuation and the women's inability to escape. Household chores, it would
appear, have a tyrannical hold on these three women who are unable to
opt out of the scenes depicted onscreen. They wait, suspended in time,
anticipating a change, hoping that morning will liberate them from their
domestic labor, but it does not. Catharsis is never achieved, because the
nightmare never concludes. At best, interactors can walk away from the
nightmare by closing the application, but the women's characters will
always be fixed in "the deepest fears of the other."

It is notable that these women's "dreams and fears" pertain to laundry,
dishes, and loneliness. The artists bring humor to their feminist critique,
offering advice on home décor and modern living. Their quasi-camp aesthetic makes it difficult to distinguish, at times, between what is an aspi-
ration and what a horror. Humor and campy nostalgia, however, do not
mitigate the real sense of alienation these women at times convey through
snippets of video, which is exacerbated by the pressure that reiteration
exerts on the depictions of cleaning and waiting.

One woman waits at the window, blinds closed. With a mouse click,
the blinds open, revealing the seated woman who turns to stand and look
out, sits opposite from where she had just been, and then retraces her
revolution to return to her original position. Is she waiting for a friend?
A lover? Someone to rescue her from boredom and isolation? Seated
again, the blinds close in front of the watching woman who continues to
wait, unseen. Later, she dances confined to a snow globe where flecks of
digital plastic snow swirl around the dome. Imagining herself unable to
escape from the prison of a bookshelf tchotchke, the woman performs a
meta-commentary on her entrapment and the aestheticization of that
condition.

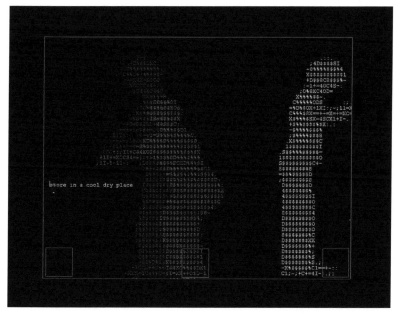

Figure 5. Screenshots of scenes from the CD-ROM *windowsninetyeight: lo-fi kitchen sink dancing* (1996–98) by Ruth Gibson and Bruno Martelli.

Elsewhere a green ASCII silhouette dances against a black screen. Her body-as-code gathers the empty space around her, pouring dollar signs into her body, which has multiplied into a trio of dancers. She is as liquid as her assets. She financially manages her household, keeping track of expenditures and other transactions as commercial interests invade the screen: "But luxurious doesn't mean expensive," "do not apply to broken or irritated skin," "money back guarantee."[78] Representing the individual as the sum total of one's data, this figure is rendered in terms of marketing strategies and purchasing power. The person animating the data has disappeared; only information remains as Derridean "supplement"—though propped up by the dancer, the data have already taken her place. She is tethered to her information, but it circulates freely in excess of her, entering into systems of exchange without her awareness or agency.

In another scene, the third woman arches backward over her couch to reach the carpet below, but the stains she hopes to remove do not respond to her innovative cleaning technique. A doorbell rings and she runs down the stairs, up the stairs, or down a hallway to answer, but she never arrives, and no guest enters. Past dinner parties remain as residues—martini glasses, table settings, dirty dishes, laundry, and carpet stains—but the outside world cannot trespass into these women's socially sealed-off spaces, nor can these women leave their apartments. They are cut off and tucked away.

Because the movement sequences are looped, users cannot hope to see any dance through to its completion. The dancing, which can always be mined for choreographic possibilities and juxtapositions, will always continue beyond the user's ability to see it. As a result, the dances are always cut short. The reiterative bodies gesture toward an idealized whole through continuous motion, though the work never reaches a final conclusion or resolution. There is no abrupt waking from the women's bad dreams. Repetition has become nothing more than a mechanical operation, and it has rendered these women passive. They have relinquished their agency to nightmares, computation, and user manipulation. Any difference introduced into the work by an interactor is not enough to provoke a transmutation that would electrify and give purpose to their reiterations. *Windowsninetyeight* offers viewers a vision of the diversity of the same, combining the return of the identical in replay loops with differences introduced through user input and feedback loops, but diversifying the same is inadequate for the task of introducing efficacious differences—differences that can make a difference within the overall work. *Somnambules* similarly stages repetition without agency and difference without concept. Where *windowsninetyeight* portrays a feminist nightmare—women confined to their homes with only chores to keep them company—*Somnambules* takes a gothic approach to nightmare, combining rich coloration with the frailty of the images—ghosts and shadows surrounded by blood spatter onscreen. *Somnambules* plays with light and pixilation, shadow and saturation, in its vision of death, disembodiment, and decay. These not-quite-bodily images acquire a digital texture, a depth and materiality based on information divorced from the bodies of their donors. Yet, the bloody visual references to violence and trauma bring this play of colors and pixels back to bodies as memories of corporeality prior to their seduction by a video camera, before the traces of their movement were ingested by a lens and rendered onscreen. Gasping breath, grabbing hands, menacing mechanical dolls, clockwork, creaking doors, and shadowy reflections feature throughout the work.

The fantasy and fear of disembodiment is a recurrent theme in Western metaphysics and artistic practices. Media historian Jeffrey Sconce traces the parallels between the history of communications technologies and the dead, the alien, and the disembodied. He notes that electronic media have seen their fair share of hauntings and that they repeat a utopian rhetoric of technologically facilitated liberation from the human body and physical labor.[79] *Somnambules* also participates in this fantasy, creating monstrous bodies that can occupy cyberspace, disembodied bodies extolled by prophets of the internet as a fleshless domain, bodies of information reduced to genetic or binary code. The idea that information exists without material instantiation or that information is more essential than matter is undermined in a piece like *Somnambules*. Rather than presenting ideal consciousnesses or information free of bodies, *Somnambules* constantly brings users' attention back to the confinement that attends the immateriality of its dancing bodies as the program compels the dancers to repeat their movements indefinitely. These fleshless, lifeless, reiterative bodies are not the incorporeal ideal that so many cyberenthusiasts hoped for. They are instead dilapidated technologic ghosts, the bodiless spirits of trapped and tormented souls controlled by the program's constraints and a user's whims.

"Docks," the seventh of *Somnambules*'s twelve acts, includes approximately ten sound tracks distributed over the frame's four quadrants and the browser window, which change in relation to each of six randomly ordered visual landscapes. The number and ordering of these visual terrains and the many different sounds make it difficult to discern whether an image is exactly as it appeared before—whether an image is identical or if, instead, it is the same. Mousing inward, sounds increase in complexity— from gasps and footsteps to drizzling drips and cavernous echoes to carnivalesque music. But they do not remain consistent across all the images. Each mouse click produces an alternate scene. Vivid, light-filled blues and greens surround an eerily empty space. Vertical lines, glitches in the visual field, travel horizontally across the screen. Sepia tones alternate with violent red spatter. The dancers, all images of choreographer and contact improvisation dancer Didier Silhol, are placed within each of these scenes, sometimes alone and sometimes in tandem. One Silhol is seated, rocking from side to side while he crosses and uncrosses his legs. Another hops in a circle, arms extended and left leg reaching behind, pushing at the capacity of his white suit. A third Silhol stands, swings his arm like a weighted pendulum, and steps out. His arm catches at waist height, and he reverses the gesture. There are only these three distinct movement phrases in "Docks," but Silhol's placement onscreen, his reflections and shadows, and the visibility of his dancing images constantly shift in relation to the other onscreen events. Furthermore, in *Somnambules,* Clauss has looped both forward and reverse motion. Thus dancers do not continually move forward through the choreography and time, only to be stopped in their tracks at the end of the movement phrase, as occurs in *windowsninetyeight*. Rather, the dance unfurls and retracts in equal measure.

Though their movement multiplies infinitely, the dancers in *windowsninetyeight, Somnambules,* and the other hyperdances discussed in this chapter are fundamentally immobilized. Advancing and retreating, the dancers neither gain nor lose ground. They achieve an equilibrium that equates movement with stasis and evacuates difference, rendering it indifferent. Unable to produce "real" or significant differences, the dancers' screened gestures are devoid of efficacy—their insignificance is a mark of their difference neutralized and subordinated to an oppressive repetition. That users are unable to intervene except superficially by rearranging parts of the whole only adds to the disempowerment of this difference: the danc-ers cannot break out of their temporal cages, and users cannot free them. Indifferent differences show the faulty logic of the liberatory rhetoric that greeted interactive media early on. Enthusiasts promised user determina-tion in partnership with artists, but the interactive scenario is ultimately not one of collaboration or coauthorship. Pursued insistently and drama-tized in these pieces, repetition comes to represent a politically disabling surrender to the present, an inability to transform the rote, mechanical movements portrayed onscreen into action.

Confined by their movement, the dancers remain overdetermined by the repetition to which they are consigned. The disempowerment portrayed in *Somnambules* and *windowsninetyeight* is not intrinsic to repetition or re-iteration, however. The screen-dancers in *Somnambules* and *windowsninety-eight* are committed to their gestures—executed to the *n*th degree—but the dancing images cannot transmute their movement into a higher form or make room for what Deleuze calls a "creative instant of time" through which repetition "consists in beginning everything again, in ascending the path which is imprisoned by the cycle."[80] In his reading of Nietzsche's concept of the eternal return, Deleuze suggests that repetition, with dif-ference at its core, is transformative. Repetition can give rise to something new. To examine this type of repetition, I turn from the preprogrammed behaviors of hyperdance toward social dance-media, which invite greater participation from users than does interaction alone.

THE CREATIVE INSTANT AND
CHOREOGRAPHIC UNWORKING

Nietzsche suggests what the eternal return might be across passages in multiple texts, but he nowhere fully develops it as a concept. As a con-glomeration of enfolded and sometimes contradictory ideas, the eternal return is further complicated in that it appears variously as a cosmologi-cal principle, as an ethical stance, and as a philosophical postulate of being as becoming or, as Deleuze suggests, as the "being *of* becoming."[81] Often, Nietzsche indicates some combination of these ideas. For example, in the parable *Thus Spoke Zarathustra*, Nietzsche intertwines three types of unspecified repetitions throughout the narrative: the return of the iden-tical through cyclical time, the return of difference through the complex combination of all possibility, and the eternal return as the synthesis of past and future in the present moment. Each type of return introduced in the text is distinct in its conceptual and ethical implications, but Nietzsche seems to keep all three versions in continuous play, while at the same time positing the eternal return as difference's only exception: *"excluding the return,* there is nothing identical."[82] Yet it is difference, and not the identity of repetition, that Deleuze foregrounds in his analysis. In this final section, I would like to shift my focus to how repetition, with difference at its core, might give rise to a Deleuzian creative instant by which to escape entropy and produce something new. The primary example I turn to is *Move-Me,* an installation and online work by Katrina McPherson and Simon Fildes. *Move-Me* straddles the interactive aesthetics of hyperdance and the partici-patory aesthetics of social media. In particular, I contend that *Move-Me* activates the creative instant through reperformance and not through the mechanical repetitions we see in hyperdance. Such reperformance opens a space of choreographic "unworking" in Jean-Luc Nancy's terminology. I thus bring both Deleuze and Nancy to bear on the iterative performances found in *Move-Me* and their repotentialization of repetition.

In his first study of cinematic signs, *Cinema 1: The Movement-Image,* Deleuze briefly elaborates on repetition in the cinema of surrealist Luis Buñuel and the literature of Raymond Roussel. As he contemplates the psychology of characters driven to repeat their actions, whether to recover what has been lost (Lucius Egroizard's daughter in Roussel's 1914 *Locus solus*) or to rediscover a moment of salvation (the Angel's guests in Buñuel's 1962 *The Exterminating Angel*), Deleuze configures their repetitions in terms of the eternal return, through which he seeks a repetition that saves, that changes life.[83] Within repetition lies the possibility of differentiation, the possibility of escape, even the possibility of resurrection: a "creative instant"[84] that will bring an end to the cycle. Deleuze thus distinguishes a reproductive from a creative version of eternal return: "It is repetition which ruins and degrades us, but it is also repetition which can save us and allow us to escape from the other repetition. . . . To the eternal return as reproduction of something always already-accomplished, is opposed the eternal return as resurrection, a new gift of the new of the possible."[85] Deleuze seeks a "decisive instant" that will overcome the failure of indefi-nite repetition as a closed repetition and bring about a radical difference through an open repetition that "recreates the model or the originary."[86] Hyperdances, however, espouse indifferent differences, which mark the greatest gap between the loop's reiterations and the ethical imperative of repetition underlying the eternal return and its capacity for transmutation. In hyperdance, digital loops fall into exactly the impulses of undifferentiation that Deleuze, following Nietzsche, critiques: identity, equality, equilibrium.[87] An agential return is thus impossible in hyperdance, where dancers have lost their ability to act, but we can find it in other examples of dance circulating online and, in particular, in the phenomenon of reperformance that is prevalent in social dance-media. Although reperformance is not unique to digital cultures,[88] it is of signal importance in considering transmissions of dance vocabularies and choreographies via the web. As I will discuss in depth in chapter 4, reperformance engages choreography as a gift that travels through the bodies of internet users and video game players, dispersing cultural capital and masking indebtedness as it circulates. Amateur dancers and dance fans participate in dance as shared cultural object, part of a gestural or corporeal common rather than personal property, and thus often do so without regard for the communities of practice that have developed the dances to which digital technologies open access.

Similar to contemporary dance artists' restagings of work drawn from the archives of dance's pasts,[89] reperformance restages and reinterprets choreography of the present. Writing on the phenomenon of reenactment, Lepecki notes that "one re-enacts not to fix a work in its singular (originating) possibilization but to unlock, release, and actualize a work's many (virtual) com- and incompossibilities, which the originating instantiation of the work kept in reserve, virtually."[90] "Fixing" a work is more the approach taken by artists who wish to achieve some sense of historical accuracy or authenticity by reconstructing dances, whereas reenactment, according to Lepecki, unlocks them. As dance theorist Mark Franko observes in his introduction to *The Oxford Handbook of Dance and Reenactment,* "the concern was no longer to demonstrate how the dance could be redone by simulating the original dance and the dancer's appearance; the emphasis was rather on what it was like to *do* it again."[91] For both Franko and Lepecki, reenactment destabilizes the identity of a work, reanimating a dance by doing-again rather than simulating a prior manifestation. Thus we see two types of repetition play out in the field of dance's engagement with embodied choreographic histories: a repetition that attempts to recover a lost past, to hold on to that past as static and unchanging and thereby to reaffirm the identity of a work, and a repetition with difference at its core that reimagines a work such that it becomes an assemblage of iterations. An assemblage, Manuel DeLanda observes in his Deleuzian social theory, "can have components working to stabilize its identity as well as components forcing it to change."[92] The primary process through which an assemblage achieves stability is repetition,[93] yet it is also repetition, in the form of reenactment or reperformance, that, in Nancy's language, unworks or infinishes a work. Thus, as we will see in *Move-Me,* participants' reperformances of choreographic scores serve both to consolidate and to repotentialize the choreography in a manner very similar to the reenactments Lepecki and Franko describe. Reperformance activates what Deleuze calls a "creative instant" to actualize what Lepecki describes as a dimension of the work held in reserve. Reperformance offers the return of the new.

Migrating the phenomenon of reperformance from the stage to the web, McPherson and Fildes's piece *Move-Me* foreshadows the online explosion of restaged flash mobs and music video choreographies from 2009 on. *Move-Me* offers a site of repetition in which differences *can* make a difference. Repetition and reperformance work together toward an unworking of the eight choreographies that feature in the work, disrupting their wholeness or totality through participant engagement such that, through repetition, the scores manifest latent vectors of difference embedded in them. Crowd-based participation and collaboration, which I discuss in more depth in chapter 3, enable the artists to explore what Nancy calls in *The Inoperative Community* "unworking"[94] and in *The Muses* "infinishing."[95] For Nancy, it is not enough for art to gather fragments into a whole, which finishes them. Infinishing or "infinite finishing" suggests at once the finitude of the infinite and the opening up of the finite toward the infinite. Unworking refers to the interruption through which cohesion as completion is disrupted. If a work, for example, a work of art, can be said to be finished, then unworking engages in the activity of infinishing. A work concludes, whereas unworking perpetually defers closure, proliferating versions or remaining forever a work in progress.

An unworked work is infinished, but it is not the same as an open work, which Umberto Eco describes as a work that offers performers a variety of interpretive avenues within "a range of rigidly preestablished" possibilities.[96] Examples of open works include both the hyperdances we have discussed in this chapter and the crowdsourced, participatory choreographies we will consider in chapter 3. An open work establishes capacious parameters for containing what unfolds under the auspices of the work; unworking opens and repotentializes what had previously been closed or complete. Hyperdances offer interactors nonlinear navigation, which gives rise to multiple experiences with different entry points and perhaps different outcomes, but nonlinearity still leaves the work intact. As interactive works, hyperdances are coded to select from and activate available assets that have been correlated to specific user input. Unworking, by contrast, is allied with Deleuze's characterization of the eternal return as a nonreproductive gift of the new. *Move-Me* leverages broad participation, and the work is fragmented and multiplied through the many participants who contribute to it. In this way, participation from the crowd links *Move-Me* to social media and to choreographic unworking through reperformance. However, accessing these videos through a specially designed user interface that encloses all of the contributions in a single work also connects *Move-Me* to hyperdance. What is unworked in *Move-Me* is not *Move-Me* itself, which is an example of an open work expanding to accommodate the contributions of participants. Rather, with each contribution, participants unwork the choreographies that guide their performances. They offer a remarkable array of unpredictable interpretations held together only by the scores themselves and not by any overarching aesthetic, movement vocabulary, or style.

Combining contemporary choreography with participatory installation art and web media, Katrina McPherson and Simon Fildes gathered movement scores from eight well-known choreographers, established a means of collecting movement from participants on location, provided an online structure to house movement contributions, and offered others access to this content for further use or elaboration. The modified photo booth in which contributors performed traveled throughout the United Kingdom, Australia, and New Zealand, collecting videos from both amateur and practiced dancers. Participants entered the booth solo, in pairs, or in

Figure 6. A young man follows choreographer Raphael Bonachela's instructions in this screenshot from *Move-Me* (2004) by Simon Fildes and Katrina McPherson.

groups. Inside, they chose one of the eight choreographers whose choreographic score they wished to perform, and a camera recorded their actions and responses to the choreographers' movement prompts. The recordings are made available in an online database, where viewable performances include interpretations of scores by American postmodern choreographer Deborah Hay, who coaches her *Move-Me* participants to sing a song in an imagined language; British hip-hop choreographer Jonzi D, who names specific body parts to move in time with the beat of the music; and the London-based Spanish crossover choreographer Raphael Bonachela, who tells the dancers in the booth that a wasp has flown out of their eye, which they must catch and, finally, eat.

"The core of this project," Fildes explained in an interview, "was the relationship between the choreographer's instructions and what you choose to do as your interpretation of the dance."[97] Some participants do their best to fulfill the choreographers' requests, and others abandon the choreography altogether. With each performance of the choreography, the dancers introduce differences, but in contrast to the hyperdances discussed in this chapter, these differences diversify the same, repopulating the category of the same with the difference that, for Deleuze, is its proper concept. There is no romanticized conflation of dancer and dance in *Move-Me*; choreography is understood as external to the performers and available to all for reembodiment, reinterpretation, and reenactment, an idea central to chapter 4. Choreography acts as a score to be interpreted and interrupted as it is reperformed, generatively replaying through the bodies of participants and linking them together without reducing them to the identical or to a difference without concept. *Move-Me* bridges interactive and social media, taking hyperdance's core feature of repetition and setting it in a social situation before video sharing platforms made such an activity commonplace. *Move-Me* points to ways repetition as unworking gives rise to the new, which we will see again and again throughout the remainder of the book.

Hyperdances short-circuit user input, promising creative difference through interaction but achieving only indifferent differences. In contrast, social dance-media activate the transformative potential of repetition. When dancers perform or parody music video choreography for wedding celebrations or political protests, or when they participate in building an affective archive in response to popular media, they engage a form of repetition through participation that interaction alone forecloses. They do not produce mere differences without concept as we see in hyperdance. Rather, they occasion repetitions that reveal the diversity of the same. Uploading their danced offerings to YouTube and the like, amateur dancers and dance fans generate an archive of the present, participating in dances—even set choreographies—as shared cultural objects rather than individual intellectual property, perpetuating their circulation across bodies and sites. Collectively, their dancing makes-common. The politics of this common are ambivalent; dancers exhibit obliviousness to cultural differences in some circumstances and reassert the sociality of embodied objects such as movement and gesture in others.

In the next chapter, we will see how dance is deployed in public settings to loosen restrictions on freedom of movement in a time when threats of domestic and international terrorism are cited as reasons to control and limit where, when, and how people move through open spaces and transit sites. Videos of events such as dancing flash mobs circulate online, where they sustain and promote a greater openness to public space. I contend that dance in public is engaged in a long-term project of recuperating public spaces as common spaces, reorienting negative affects in the wake of mass shootings and bombings and facilitating the use of these spaces for political demonstration and protest. However, while dance in public endeavors to disrupt excessive policing in a manner that facilitates other uses of common spaces, the effects of loosening public space through dance cannot be determined in advance.

CHAPTER TWO

Dance in Public

◆◆

Of Common Spaces

A girl stands on the corner of Broadway and Wall Street, across from Trinity Church. In the never-ending construction zone that is New York City, orange cones alert drivers to roadwork, and barricades prevent pedestrians from spilling into the street. Nestled against this construction site, the Girl performs a forlorn confusion that any ballet lover would recognize—one hand outstretched into the unknown, the other curved over her heart, she silently pleads for those around her to acknowledge her presence as Peter Gabriel croons, "I want to touch the light, the heat, I see in your eyes."[1] Actively ignored (one man even runs past so as to remain unmolested), she switches tactics and sound tracks. Her body sinks with the newfound downbeat, and her hands fling upward from extended arms, "gangsta" style, a gesture that plays ironically on her white body, but this does not last long. Quickly, she shifts again—kick, cartwheel, booty shake, twirl. Lean back. Lean back.

Directed by Jacob Krupnick, the 2011–12 web video sensation *Girl Walk//All Day* is set to the seventy-one-minute album *All Day* by mash-up artist and fair-use advocate Gregg Gillis (aka Girl Talk).[2] Gillis released the album, which is constructed of samples from more than 350 songs,[3] in November 2010 as a free download. It provides the architecture as well as atmosphere for the entire film, which begins with the Girl clearly out of place in a ballet class. Frustration with the dance combinations and the ballet mistress results in a convulsive breakdown. The electric guitar of Black Sabbath's "War Pigs" tears through the ballet class's piano accompaniment, and the Girl sloughs off the prescribed movement vocabulary with spasms and shudders, gnashing her teeth and flailing her limbs to Ludacris's "Move Bitch (Get Out the Way)." Once out of the dance studio, the Girl, played by Anne Marsen, pursues a single mission: to get the city dancing. Sometimes she seems oblivious to those around her, sometimes she incorporates their gestures or features into her own movement, and sometimes she actively enlists others to join in. Co-stars Daisuke Omiya as the Gentleman and John Doyle as the Creep offer a love interest and a nemesis, respectively, to propel what is otherwise a very loose narrative. Referencing a long history of Hollywood films, musicals, and music videos featuring dancing in the street[4] as well as the comparatively recent phenomenon of flash mobs, they dance throughout New York City, transforming every available surface into a site for their physical expression. From the Staten Island Ferry to the High Line to Times Square to Zuccotti Park filled with Occupy Wall Street (OWS) protesters, the entire city becomes their stage.

Dance in public catches people by surprise. As Melanie Kloetzel and Carolyn Pavlik explain in their introduction to *Site Dance: Choreographers and the Lure of Alternative Spaces,* "unusual movement in a public place will capture your eye, call your attention to the present, and expand your awareness of your surroundings."[5] Passersby linger in parks or on street

Figure 7. Screenshot of Anne Marsen as the Girl dancing on the Staten Island Ferry in *Girl Walk// All Day* (2011–12), directed by Jacob Krupnick with music by Girl Talk.

Figure 8. Screenshot of Anne Marsen as the Girl dancing throughout New York City in *Girl Walk// All Day* (2011–12), directed by Jacob Krupnick with music by Girl Talk.

corners to watch as artists transform their experiences of everyday environments. But this type of public display is not always welcome. As site-based choreographer Stephen Koplowitz observes, "after 9/11, no one wanted to hire artists to do things in public."[6] Reflecting on the uses of public spaces particularly in social movements, Judith Butler notes that we must think through how acts of coming together "reconfigure the materiality of public space, and produce, or reproduce, the public character of that material environment."[7] She continues, "We miss something of the point of public demonstrations, if we fail to see that the very public character of the space is being disputed and even fought over when these crowds gather."[8] One cannot presume that public space is already given as a common or shared space that is automatically receptive to whatever acts of speech or movement members of a population might choose to perform therein. Dance in public, which asserts the public character of public spaces, exists in a historico-political moment informed by the pervasive threat of, and government responses to, global and domestic terrorism.

This chapter focuses on both solo and group dances in public from approximately 2008 to 2013 to consider how they lay claim to public spaces and rematerialize them as common spaces open to individual and collective expression. Indulging in the unexpected, dance in public provokes and measures collective tolerance for deviance from post-9/11 kinesthetic and social norms, at the same time that it helps to normalize such encounters. This same stretch of time is also marked by the increasing importance of social media in daily life. Providing an avenue of broad circulation, social media proliferate and reinvigorate spaces reimagined through dance, proving indispensible to the aesthetic and political work of dance in public. Thus the examples I consider in this chapter stage dance in public and circulate online. In addition to analyzing Krupnick's episodic film *Girl Walk//All Day* throughout the chapter, I examine the spatial and affective claims of dances in public, such as Angela Trimbur's Dance Like Nobody's Watching series (2011–13), the Round Dance flash mobs of Idle No More's Indigenous rights activists (2012–14), and the Spanish anticapitalist organization Flo6x8's flamenco flash mobs (2010–16). Whereas other chapters focus more explicitly on specific dance works, this chapter grapples with dance in public as a larger phenomenon borne out across innumerable examples circulating through social media as a cumulative and shared project of performing a common in public spaces. Public space becomes especially fraught in circumstances where land, for example, is continuously removed from the public realm and expropriated into the sphere of private property, and where perceived threats or acts of violence invite a further policing of urban environments in particular such that how populations move through public space can produce anxiety and suspicion. Under such circumstances, the very presence of dancers in public sites acts as a means of collectively creating or activating the common character of those public spaces, of reclaiming the common space of the city.

Sometimes this recuperation takes place without interference, but not always. For example, in 2008, Mary Brooke Oberwetter organized a group of Libertarian friends to dance with her at the Jefferson Memorial in Washington, D.C., in celebration of Thomas Jefferson's 265th birthday. Soon after they had begun rocking out to their private tunes, the celebrants were forced by police officers to leave. Oberwetter refused and was arrested. She was charged with "interfering with an agency function" and "demonstrating without a permit."[9] A judge later determined that the Memorial was a "nonpublic" forum and thus the park police acted reasonably in arresting Oberwetter: "That the Memorial is open to the public does not alter its status as a nonpublic forum. Visitors are not invited for expressive purposes, but are free to enter only if they abide by the rules that preserve the Memorial's solemn atmosphere."[10] Oberwetter and her friends' dancing illustrates the political risks and resonances of moving as a collective body in public and the potential danger of claiming the publicness or commonness of private, nonpublic, or indeterminate spaces. As another example, the Oakland, California, group Turf Feinz has produced a number of RIP videos to commemorate the lives of young black men who have been killed.[11] The dancers employ urban and street dance forms in their responses to a violence that never ceases, a violence like that which feminist anthropologist Elizabeth Povinelli describes as "ordinary, chronic, and cruddy rather than catastrophic, crisis-laden and sublime."[12] These videos also circulate online, reminding viewers that there is a racialized politics to being in public spaces and therefore to dancing in public. Memorably, in "RIP RichD" (2009), dancers on the corner of 90th Street and MacArthur Boulevard are harassed by police officers on patrol, making visible, according to dance scholar Naomi Bragin, the "existential criminality of blackness" that "frames the demand for black performance."[13] The politics of identity are clearly at play in any use of public space, and depending on one's racial or ethnic background, gender or sexual identity, or even political leanings, one may find oneself exposed to different degrees of risk when dancing in public. Both of these are important examples of how interventions in public spaces flirt with the boundary of the law and show how "just" dancing in public can be a deeply political act.

Dance in public coincides with social movements and political demonstrations that vocally proclaim an overt political agenda, such as OWS, which began in July 2011 (inspired by the so-called Arab Spring and fomented by a domestic economic downturn) and gathered thousands of participants as the months wore on. Unlike the durational protest/performance that was OWS, however, dance in public seems to have embraced the guerilla tactic of ephemerality, leveraging what has been described as an ontological condition of performance in general and dance in particular into a sociopolitically disruptive position. OWS was notable for how long protesters held on to their occupied territories and how many were drawn into its embrace of the 99 percent, but dance in public is notable for its here-and-gone spatiotemporal ruptures that access longevity through their mediated circulation on the internet, at a remove from the people and places implicated in performance. Still, the ephemeral spectacle of dance in public rechoreographs the affective landscape of public spaces in a way that complements the carnivalesque spatial reimagining seen in OWS encampments.

It is of distinct importance that shopping centers, train stations, airports, and public squares have proved to be locations of choice for dance in public. Reflecting the amplified anxieties of the United States post-9/11, these sites are under additional pressures of both threat and surveillance and are spaces in which dance does not "belong." Dance in public revitalizes public spaces as sites of mobility and mobilization alongside the public acts and occupations undertaken by protesters. More to the point, as Randy Martin has argued, dance is a "kinesthetic practice that puts on display the very conditions through which the body itself is mobilized."[14] As a genre of public performance, dance in public displays these conditions, sometimes concealing the spatial occupations and reclamations it enacts behind a mask of playfulness and joy.[15] "Why are you dancing?" the Hasidic man asks the Girl in *Girl Walk//All Day*. "Because I'm happy," she replies.[16]

Dance in public also challenges notions of private property, intellectual property (in its gestural and musical quotations), and freedoms of speech and assembly. It actively disrupts distinctions between private and public, performer and audience, art and commerce. Dance's inherent ambiguity results in an overabundance of signification, which makes it both powerful and easily usurped by the forces of capital and the state.[17] But this same ambiguity allows dance to reinvigorate public space as common space through its bodily mobilizations and affective modulations. In particular, I argue, dance in public transforms what anthropologist Marc Augé calls the "non-places" of postmodernity,[18] which are also spaces of surveillance in an era of crisis generation and management, into what political philosopher Hannah Arendt calls "spaces of appearance,"[19] which she identifies as the precondition for politics. This transformation comes about through dance in public's ability to, in philosopher Jacques Rancière's terms, "redistribute the sensible."[20] The implication of this redistribution is to recuperate a spatial common via performance, a recuperation carried out through danced gestures and dancers' physical occupation of public spaces. The affective intensity and emotion behind these public performances vary, from grief to rage to pride to joy, but the effect is the same: triggering appearance through the spectacle of dancing in public.

It is not, I contend, simply a matter of dance changing a social relationship to public space once and for all but of continuously deterritorializing and reorganizing the affects that inhere in public spaces. As the post-9/11 United States shifted from reactive defense toward preemptive securitization,[21] it gave way to a global war on terror that, as Michael Hardt and Antonio Negri claim, "has to be won again every day"[22] both domestically and abroad.[23] Security, they contend, proactively shapes the environment[24] and thus must be countered in the space of the metropolis with "joyful encounters."[25] Dance in public's project of redistributing the sensible is not a singular event but is necessarily a repeatable process that ruptures the shape of security in the face of attempts to consolidate, secure, and exclude in the name of antiterrorism. Dancing in public disrupts security, even as the political and ideological forces that promote insecurity to justify securitization remain in place. It reclaims public spaces not only from those who are intent on inflicting harm but from the political and security forces that turn common spaces into non-places of surveillance.

Dance in public lays claim to public space as a common space by physically occupying that space. Furthermore, it performatively declares a right to have certain rights within that space: a right to appear, to peaceably assemble, to experience freedom of movement, to inhabit a body, and use it as a means of expression. In Rancière's concise formulation, "the 'rights of man and of the citizen' are the rights of those who make them a reality."[26] The violence that accompanies such contemporary movements as OWS and Black Lives Matter continues to show that when demonstrators gather and refuse to move, they expose themselves to violence, making their bodies available to the state as so many surfaces upon which to display its force. Such demonstrations, Butler remarks, "[pose their] challenge in corporeal terms, which means that when the body 'speaks' politically, it is not only in vocal or written language. . . . Both action and gesture signify and speak, as action and claim."[27] Dance in public makes visible how such claims are also made within the cultural field. As an alternative to the chants and slogans we have come to expect of political demonstrations, dance in public offers an especially powerful indicator of what a body can do, and what bodies can do when acting in concert.

DANCING ONSITE, DANCING ONLINE

Circulating as video on the web is key for dance in public. However, online access is not what makes dance "public" for the purposes of this argument. With the term *public,* I am speaking more specifically of public spaces, which is to say, built environments and physical locations, even though my analysis focuses on the circulation of videos featuring these spaces through media channels. As a viewer, I have largely encountered these public performances in private or quasi-private settings, sitting alone with my computer or smartphone. Even while I use the term *public* to refer primarily to the location of performance, dance in public intertwines multiple aspects of public and private realms, as articulated in different analytical disciplines: viewed from the position of governance, for example, the public sphere is the place of political discourse and debate, while the private sphere presents an ever-negotiated limit of the state's reach. From the position of economics, public goods and resources are managed by the state, while private goods are treated as individual property with market value. From a social perspective, the public refers to sites in which heterogeneous individuals gather and coexist while remaining strangers and private spaces are those in which individuals inhabit by themselves or with family and other close ties, and over which they have some measure of control. Scholars have long insisted that public and private cannot be so neatly distinguished, and network and media scholars in particular have demonstrated their overlap. For example, internet discussion boards, social media sites, and peer file-sharing offer examples of "networked publics,"[28] while cell phone users notoriously bring their private telephone conversations into public spaces even as others leverage the private spaces of their mobile screens to withdraw from the public realm.[29]

Dance in public does not follow the distinctions between public and private based on property ownership: for my purposes, dance in public excludes the private sphere as domestic site (even though dancers routinely record their private dances for public circulation online), but it does not exclude private property, nor private or semiprivate experiences of public places. Dancing in public is as much about exposure to onsite spectators (who may not actually be the target audience) as it is about dancing in venues that are available and accessible to the general public. Dance in public includes venues such as parks and beaches, whether publicly or privately owned; malls, shops, and parking lots; and sites of transit, such as airports, railway stations, and modes of public transportation, such as planes, trains, and busses. Dance in public also includes busking—the practice of giving unsanctioned performances with the hope of collecting gratuities from onlookers. It does not include home dances,[30] dance in social clubs, dance studios, theaters, competition venues, or any form of outdoor performance taking place on a temporary stage set up for the occasion, regardless of whether videos of these circulate on the web.

In brief, dance in public describes dances that take place outside of areas that have been specially designated or set aside for dancing. They may occur with or without permission. They may lend themselves to any social, commercial, or political agenda or may exist primarily as entertainment. Dance in public does not *require* social media, but, like planking, horsemanning, Tebowing, Hadoukening,[31] and other viral photography memes, as a genre of public performance, dance in public is greatly facilitated by the channels of distribution that social media offer, and its meaning is accentuated by other similar circulations. The online life of dance in public is thus a central consideration, and it is therefore difficult if not impossible to separate dance in public from social media in an era when the latter are determining forces of contemporary social life and engagement. Dance in public avails itself of the digital commons, which both circulates and provides audiences for these videos. As a result, many of the public performances seem to target an audience of internet users more so than co-present spectators.

Take, for example, the Dance Like Nobody's Watching videos, which began circulating on YouTube circa 2012. Actress Angela Trimbur briefly became something of an internet sensation by dancing alone at various Los Angeles venues: an Echo Park Laundromat, an LAX airport baggage claim, and a shopping mall.[32] Other users followed suit, posting videos of themselves dancing in malls, grocery stores, cafés, and plazas across the United States and Europe.[33] The solo genre of dance in public in which Trimbur and her followers participated does not benefit from the strength in numbers that dancing flash mobs provide, as we will later see. These solo performers expose themselves to public scrutiny and possible censure, suspending rules of decorum that govern such environments for the belated approval of an online audience. In these videos, dancers wear headphones or earbuds such that co-present spectators cannot hear the music to which the dancers are responding, though a music track is laid down for the benefit of internet viewers. Other editing is minimal: some Dance Like Nobody's Watching videos are compilations of various dancers and venues, but Trimbur's videos and those modeled on them are single takes; viewers see Trimbur just after she begins recording and just before she stops—her fuzzy face and upper body filling the frame as the camera tries to focus on her too-close body. Because these public performers have charged themselves with dancing like no one is watching (from the familiar poem), they interact little or not at all with the people around them—as though they are invisible. Trimbur interacts with others a little more than her freestyling followers, but even she is not performing "for" a co-present audience. All of the dancers in these videos face the camera, performing for an audience of asynchronous internet spectators. Here documentation does not serve the function of historical preservation, that is, recording a fleeting performance in a more durable medium. Rather, documentation of dance in public sits somewhere between what Roland Barthes calls the "that-has-been" *(ça a été)* of the photographed subject[34] ("pics or it didn't happen," as the familiar catch-phrase goes) and what Philip Auslander describes as "performed photography," or photographs that do not merely document a performance event but are the medium of its enactment.[35]

Girl Walk//All Day similarly exemplifies the importance of social media for dance in public. Filmed throughout 2011, the video was crowdfunded through Kickstarter. Calls for participation went out to give local communities an opportunity to appear in the film, which premiered online one section at a time on the New York news website The Gothamist from November 2011 to January 2012 and remain available for online viewing at no cost at http://www.girlwalkallday.com/. Audience access is at the core of *Girl Walk,* even in the ways the film frames and presents dancing. In a *New York Times* Artsbeat interview, Krupnick notes that in directing the work, he wanted Marsen's dancing to be relatable to audiences who "just love to really shake it when they feel it."[36] Dancing to Gillis's epic mashup *All Day,* Marsen borrows freely from a vast range movement repertories without lingering long enough in any form for it to actualize as such. Marsen's body gives corporeal form to the indifferent differences discussed in chapter 1: her movement is a melting pot, a gestural collage of the global contemporary. Structured atop a music mash-up, crowdfunded, performed in familiar sites throughout New York City, drawing from a global database of movement references, and performed with acute amateurism, *Girl Walk//All Day* epitomizes social media aesthetics and modes of production. Couched in a narrative of which passersby on the street are unaware, the affective impact of Marsen's dancing is far more profound for asynchronous viewers than for those who briefly encountered her antics in person. Onsite, both Trimbur and Marsen maximize their potential for spatial disruption, but online, that disruption transforms their respective cityscapes into what Krupnick calls a "positive spectacle."[37]

Circulating on the web, videos of dances in public have the effect of altering viewers' relationships to public spaces.[38] As dance scholar Mark Franko notes, "The way in which dance alters public space by occupying it is full of political innuendos, as is any unprecedented use of public space for the circulation of bodies."[39] How, then does dance occupy public space, and what does its occupation or temporary hijacking of public space bring about in the cultural field? Dance in public disturbs the peace, providing microbursts of utopianism in public space, dissipating the negative affects that have inhered in public space throughout the first decade of the twenty-first century. Even melancholic dances in public shift perceptions of what

Figure 9. Screenshot of Angela Trimbur dancing at a baggage claim in LAX in her YouTube video *Dance Like Nobody's Watching: Airport* (2012).

public space is and what kinds of activities may take place there. In this way, dance in public recalls what theater scholar Jan Cohen-Cruz has noted of radical street performance: it "creates visions of what society might be, and arguments against what it is."[40] It is because dance, particularly the joyful and playful types of dance employed by flash mobs and amateur dancers, is generally seen as trivial, apolitical, and even antipolitical, that it serves as a foil to various attempts to lock down and excessively police public uses of space. In addition, whether audience delight or empathy serves as a primary aim, dance in public facilitates the renewal of social bonds[41]—made tenuous due to xenophobic suspicion, mass shootings, police violence, electoral politics, and economic warfare—thus helping to recuperate public space as a shared or common site of sociality.

Dance in public meets social movements on the same ground, with recourse to similar tactics of occupation that forcefully assert the public dimension of both publicly and privately owned spaces, folding them back into the common. This spatial operation unfolds choreographically in relation to a separate claim that dance is itself a common resource, an argument that I will explore more fully in chapter 4. Dance in public, and the amateur aesthetics that frequently accompany it, offers dance as a shared principle or practice that fosters social cohesiveness and even, as I will argue in chapter 3, creates new worlds. It is an integral part of multifaceted movements to recuperate the political public sphere via common spaces—which cannot be presupposed but must be produced and reproduced through the performance of that very commonness. The performative production of common space takes the form of mobilization, which is necessarily plural: "No one mobilizes a claim to move and assemble freely without moving and assembling together with others," Butler argues.[42] Mobilized, dancing bodies reclaim and rechoreograph terrains that ought to exclude them. They reappropriate spaces for public action and reorient expectations for public behavior. More than this, the ambiguous and sometimes silly act of dancing in public asks its audience to consider how one moves "freely" in a state of exception—in the wake of violent events that transform a population's relationship to public spaces and policing, and in the wake of financial collapse that transforms a population's relationship to public institutions. In an era when public space is itself fraught and contested, dance in public proves to be a crucial mechanism for critiquing, reclaiming, and transforming public space into a space of the common.

This is precisely the scenario encapsulated in the 2011 *Adbusters*[43] image associated with the initial call for a mass occupation of Lower Manhattan, which featured a ballerina perched atop the iconic Wall Street Charging Bull. What could be more indicative of OWS's challenge than juxtaposing the female dancer and the male bull, the aesthetic practice of dancing against the economic function of markets, the disciplined against the out of control? At the same time, the dancer and the bull share a fundamental evanescence: the immateriality of money wending its way through financial systems with abandon, and dance as immaterial labor that ostensibly leaves no trace—the dancer and the bull mutually signify production without product. Her affect is cool, calm, and relaxed (though poised) compared to the bull's hot, aggressive tension. This anonymous dancer is undoubtedly classically trained, but even if her pose *en attitude arrière* formally references balletic movement vocabulary, her loose, short-cropped hair, thigh-length pants, and bare feet suggest that as a dancer, she may very well be part of the flexible dance labor force—a dancer who can adapt to the changing needs of contemporary choreographers and choreography—whether those are tied to technical vocabulary, movement style, or affective capacity. Indeed, the dancer on the bull symbolically represents both the status quo of financial capital and resistance to it—her one-legged balance is both threatened by and demonstrates mastery over the precarity of her position. Situating dance where it does not belong, here, atop an aggressive symbol of wealth, gives viewers pause. But this pause, as is true of any sustained balance, is not a static pose but a dynamic inhabitation of multiple contradictory forces, a falling upward that offers an anticipatory breath and provides momentum for what follows. As an image calling for the mobilization of the 99 percent, the dancer balancing on the bull provokes a question that dance scholars and political theorists know all too well: "What can movements achieve?"

When the Gentleman tap dances on Charging Bull in *Girl Walk//All Day,* the reference to the *Adbusters* image is immediately clear, but his dancing achieves something else entirely. Instead of sustaining himself through a masterful stillness, Omiya is constantly in motion. Arms swinging, he stomps and shuffles across the bull's broad back, traveling from top to tail. Omiya's economically precarious position as a tap and contemporary dancer is probably little different from that of the dancer in the image calling for the occupation of Wall Street. However, his dancing on the bull

Figure 10. July 2011 poster in *Adbusters* that initiated the Occupy Wall Street movement. Reprinted with permission.

Figure 11. Screenshot of Daisuke Omiya as the Gentleman dancing on the Wall Street Bull in *Girl Walk//All Day* (2011–12), directed by Jacob Krupnick with music by Girl Talk.

is not a Photoshop trick. His care-free dancing belies the slick bronze surface beneath him, making no distinction between the bull and the other sites and surfaces he occupies with his movement: telephone booths, stanchions, sidewalks, plazas, passageways—all are common spaces of mobility and mobilization.

MOBILIZING MOBILITY: DANCING NEW COMMON(S)

When dance in public is considered as a means of mobilization that takes the form of gestural and rhythmic difference from the corporeal status quo, it becomes easy to see how eruptions of difference in public spaces modify perceptual configurations of such spaces, transforming them into sites that can support spectacular motion. Mobilization of an expressly political variety can hardly occur without a capacity for movement, and it is this capacitation of movement via performatively transformed spaces that is the purview of dance in public. In his 1998 analysis of dance and the political, Randy Martin concedes that "because dance is but a minority of the movement most people engage in, the claims that can be made for its formal political impact or direct social significance are limited."[44] Yet, writing before the advent of social media, Martin underestimates the circulation of dance, which, in his analysis, occurs primarily in dance studios,

theaters, social clubs, or onscreen in commercially produced films and
videos. However, the internet has surpassed these venues and is now arguably the single most important means of accessing dance. As a result,
though it may be true that acts of dancing remain minimal as far as everyday experiences go, more people have an exponentially greater exposure
to dance than when Martin was writing in the late 1990s. And one need
not identify as a dancer to appreciate or benefit from dance's circulation
online. By the same token, one need not individually contribute to the
opening up of public spaces through public displays such as dancing or
demonstrating to benefit from that openness, or participate in acts of violence to feel them closing back down in their wake.

For months, and in some cases years, after 9/11, spaces of transportation were heavily surveilled in the United States by soldiers and national
guardsmen, but because these flat, wide spaces are designed to accommodate many people, they, along with shopping malls and parks, ironically
proved the most hospitable settings for dancing in public. Even airport
terminals, where passengers are constantly advised to report any activity
out of the ordinary, have played host to dancing flash mobs. In his introduction to *Insurgent Public Space,* Jeffrey Hou notes, "In the post 9/11 world
of hyper-security and surveillance, new forms of control in public space
have curtailed freedom of movement and expression and greatly limited the
activities and meanings of contemporary public space."[45] Dancing in public
poses a focused challenge to such limitations of motion and expression, in
the same spaces in which such activities are heavily policed. Dancing acts as
a form of nonviolent resistance to attempts to curtail freedom of movement
in public spaces and takes place alongside political demonstrations, marches,
and protests that share a similar goal. For example, in early 2003, protesters
marched worldwide to voice opposition to the U.S. invasion of Iraq. Not
all city governments allowed protesters to gather, however. In New York
City, where I happened to be protesting, barricades, mounted police, and
officers in riot gear prevented and disrupted the protesters' coalescence as
a group. I do not find it at all coincidental that later that same year, urban
pranksters began staging spatial disruptions and acts of defiance with flash
mobs and that dancers adopted the format for their own public spectacles.

Flash mobs, which are large gatherings of individuals at a specific time
and place in response to a call sent out via email or text, arose with the

expansion of social computing. They have sometimes been feared by law enforcement because of the size of crowds that gather and sometimes dismissed because they seem to have little purpose other than to disrupt public space. Judith Nicholson suggests that while flash mobs "shone briefly and brilliantly," the trend was "officially declared passé" in September 2003.[46] Jeffrey Schnapp and Matthew Tiews describe them as a brief fad that brought together "crowds of the underemployed and overconnected . . . [who] assemble for the simultaneous performance of quirky gestures."[47] If flash mobs seemed faddish and passé in 2003, however, that didn't stop them from morphing into a fully developed genre of public performance by the decade's end.

Dancing flash mobs boomed in 2009 as professional and amateur artists appropriated the flash mob formula and began staging public spectacles for enjoyment, community building, commercial advertising, and eventually consciousness raising around social issues. Whereas organized protests demonstrate strength in numbers and durational commitment to a site, flash mobs find tactical advantage in the combination of camouflage and the suddenness of their spectacles. Unlike protests, flash mobs at their outset made no overt claims except for the right of their participants to appear—a claim that itself seemed risky enough that disappearance was built into their format. At the conclusion of every flash mob, performers merge with the surrounding crowd as a protective measure against reprisal.

Easily the most famous dancing flash mob, an advertisement called *The T-Mobile Dance*[48] that took place in a Liverpool metro station surprised passersby with its size and scale—the enormity of the group, its spectacle of energy and delight, the accessible but precise dancing. But as soon as the last notes rang over the speakers, the performance dissolved. The dancers' everyday clothing made them indistinguishable from nondancers, and they evaporated into the crowd. Dispersing in all directions, they left no trace of their performance or their identities. Far from the quirky incomprehensibility of early flash mobs, dance mobs[49] have adapted the flash mob format to become highly organized public relations events. They share with flash mobs a characteristic disruption of public space and a recognizable structure—converge, perform, disperse—but they are more likely than flash mobs to involve the spectacle of unison dancing and are more likely to become viral videos.[50]

Figure 12. Screenshot of *The T-Mobile Dance* (2009), an advertisement and YouTube video of a dance mob in Liverpool Street Station as part of the cellular phone company T-Mobile's Life's for Sharing marketing campaign.

One of a handful of scholars to consider the phenomenon of dancing flash mobs, anthropologist Georgiana Gore traces the typical development of flash mobs through the call for participants and uploading of tutorial videos to performance onsite and later dissemination online. Of these steps, it is what occurs onsite that interests Gore most. She describes dance mobs as "a spectacular intrusion into public spaces designated for other uses."[51] Dance mobs interrupt the visual field with spectacular choreographies, distinguishing themselves from the more simplified gestures and actions typical of flash mobs. "Designed to create a visual stir," Gore says, "flash mobbing is like soft terrorism, using guerilla tactics."[52] Gore's comparison of flash mobs and dance mobs to terrorism is no trite metaphor. Like acts of terror, at their inception, flash mobs and dance mobs provoked cognitive and corporeal shifts in co-present viewers. Indeed, dancing flash mobs could be likened to a form of homeopathy: combating surprise as terror with surprise as delight[53] or administering temporary

mass occupation as an antidote to state control and corporate expropriation of public space.

For example, during the 2013 *Harlem Shake* dance meme/viral video
craze, the Colorado College Ultimate Frisbee team persuaded a Frontier
Airlines crew and passengers to let them dance on an airplane while in
flight.[54] That dancing was a possibility in such a highly controlled environment where even restroom visits are strictly monitored attests to what
dance theorist Susan Leigh Foster describes as "the flexibility of the social
body to accommodate deviance," which, she argues, "endures in spite of
the tightened restrictions on one's movements resulting from the post-
9/11 orientation toward terror."[55] The social body, however, may be much
more tolerant of such deviations than the state: the online circulation of
the video prompted the Federal Aviation Authority to investigate the dancers and flight crew for possible violations. Dancing in public skirts but does
not escape the law as it lays claim to certain spaces: the law continuously
brings itself to bear on these public displays of organized unauthorized
movement. Perhaps for this reason, the performance of confused surprise
is integral to the choreographic arc of dancing flash mobs. In addition to
blending in with the crowd at the conclusion of such a public performance,
by performing their own confusion at the outset of an event, participants
can plausibly maintain their innocence if law enforcement intervenes. In
videos circulating online, one finds myriad examples of confused spectators revealing themselves to be dancers in the know. It is not unusual, in
fact, to find examples where, in the end, those dancing vastly outnumber
those watching. Befuddled amusement is part of the dancers' performance
and not just the audience's experience.

Without romanticizing dance in public, I want to emphasize the socially
productive potentials in examining what dance in public hopes to achieve
and to argue that dance in public engages in political work, even as, and in
many cases precisely because, organizers refuse political intent. It is, after
all, the persistent idea that dance offers aesthetic form without intellection
or substance that lends the form to advertising. From the phone company
T-Mobile[56] to FOX television's *Glee*[57] to pop star Beyoncé Knowles[58] to Dell's
Streak hand-held tablet,[59] and even Suave hair products,[60] dancing flash
mobs have been called upon to stage attention-grabbing advertisements
for an amazing variety of products and services. Indeed, it is significant to

note that after 9/11, brick-and-mortar businesses suffered from perceptions of public spaces as threatening, prompting Western leaders to encourage their citizens to respond to the terrorist attacks of 2001 by going about business as usual, by which they meant exercising their consumer power.[61] Americans dutifully fulfilled the command to shop, but did so without venturing into public: although it is now a behemoth, the online retailer Amazon.com did not turn a profit until the fourth quarter of 2001, which is to say, in the months immediately following 9/11.[62] Because public spaces were perceived as dangerous, the technology was continuously improving, and the content was continuously expanding, Americans increasingly turned to the "safe" space of the internet as an alternative to public spaces. For this reason, in the years after 9/11, even the most commercially oriented dance mob worked on transforming public space from what I call a nonplace of surveillance into an Arendtian "space of appearance." Above all a relation among people, the space of appearance is transposable, available for instantiation in any number of locations. Dance having been performed in public, and the documentation that circulates online reperforming its choreographic intervention, leaves lasting residues—not just in the specific site of performance but in other similar locations. How, then, might dancing—such a seemingly trivial enactment of bodily mobilization—assist in the project of transforming the street and other similar venues into common spaces and spaces of appearance that enable mobilization toward political action? What does it take to appear?

Marsen poses just this question throughout *Girl Walk//All Day*. In the scene "Dance with Me," the Girl prepares a placard—the type you might expect a doomsayer to wear declaring the end of days—writing the phrase "dance with me" in several languages. The Girl offers a plea to those who pass by her: wherever you are headed, however late you are, take a moment to find a connection through motion. She starts out with some levity, sandwiched in her sign and sporting an old school boom box. Dressed in a purple leotard, pink tights, frilly skirt, shawl, and sneakers, she is quite a sight hanging from streetlight posts and leaping through Grand Central Station. But as her calls for participation go unmet, her intensity increases. Her gestures become sharper, her attitude confrontational. Passersby back away, actively ignore the Girl, or occasionally show hesitant smiles that reveal the ambivalence of their worried amusement. Reflecting on audience responses at screenings of the film, Krupnick notes, "A lot of people react to the film with a bouncy exuberance and insist that, if they'd been there, they would've joined in [the dancing], or they would've smiled, and they can't believe how stone-faced all these zombie-ish New Yorkers are. I like to point out that . . . most of us would look at this crazy dancer . . . and say, *Who cares?*"[63] The nonchalance with which New Yorkers receive the Girl is attributable in part to their high tolerance for the abnormal, since large cities facilitate encounters with the extraordinary on a daily basis. And the Girl does not appear violent so much as volatile, unstable. She is, as Krupnick describes her, a "crazy dancer."[64] She invades people's space, grabbing at some trying to bring them into her world, following them closely with mocking gestures, or otherwise belligerently disrupting their movements. The Girl works herself into a whirling, pleading frenzy until she finally collapses, exhausted by the labor of performing at maximum effort without acknowledgment or reciprocation from those around her. With so many demands on our collective attention, and with lifetimes of practice at turning away, producing appearance is no easy feat.

FROM NON-PLACES OF SURVEILLANCE TO SPACES OF APPEARANCE

Arendt's space of appearance is an idealized space of political action modeled on the ancient Greek polis. The space of appearance is not a site per se but a relation among equals mediated through speech and action, or "the living deed and the spoken word."[65] Notably, equality can be maintained within the polis only due to its prior exclusion of noncitizens from its midst. Arendt notes that the polis was the only place where equality was guaranteed. Outside the polis, it was understood that "men were by nature . . . not equal, and needed an artificial institution . . . [to] make them equal. Equality existed only in this specifically political realm, where men met one another as citizens and not as private persons."[66] Political life excluded the private realm, to which both labor and work, the maintenance of life and the creation of the material world, were relegated. Although the Greek polis serves as Arendt's model, her concept of the space of appearance was centuries removed from the polis's strict divisions between public and private, distinctions that have become even more blurred since her writing. What exists in place of a polis is a proliferation of what anthropologist Marc Augé calls non-places.

Augé tracks the emergence of non-places in relation to an anthropological sense of place: "If a place can be defined as relational, historical and concerned with identity, then a space which cannot be defined as relational, or historical, or concerned with identity will be a non-place."[67] Though non-places are an abstract ideal, never appearing "in their pure form,"[68] according to Augé, they are "the real measure of our time."[69] The time spent in transit or stuck in traffic, the time spent in waiting rooms or standing in line to complete necessary transactions—such suspensions between here and there, beginning and end, are characteristic of non-places. Thus, for Augé, non-places are sites of transit, commerce, and leisure in which people primarily interact with texts—labels, directions, and other instructions for use—or sites that have only textual incarnations, imagined places that "exist only through the words that evoke them."[70] Augé emphasizes spaces that are utilized rather than experienced—motorways and railways, supermarkets and shopping malls, airplanes and airports, and other sites only temporarily occupied.[71] Constant motion and loss of subjectivity mark these indeterminate spaces. In Augé's non-places, one does not enter into a social arrangement but remains remarkably solitary, assuming the temporary identity of a silent addressee for equally silent border controllers, clerks, tollbooth operators, bank tellers, and the like: "a person entering non-place is relieved of his usual determinants. He becomes no more than what he experiences in the role of passenger, customer or driver."[72] A person in a non-place navigates the space by referring to signs—exit here, pick up luggage there, restrooms are this way. People play their parts in the contractual theater of in-between places, retrieving their identities "only at Customs, at the tollbooth, at the check-out counter."[73] Otherwise, anonymity reigns: each individual "obeys the same codes as others, receives the same messages, responds to the same entreaties."[74]

Dance in public refuses to honor the terms of this contract, exploiting the personal anonymity offered by non-places as well as the limits of interdiction. Non-places may be governed by rules regarding loitering, speed, noise, or entry and exit, but few spaces specifically prohibit dancing.[75] Furthermore, given that dances in public frequently rely on dispersal as a technique of evasion and anonymity, they are difficult targets for law enforcement. It is significant, therefore, that Trimbur danced in an airport, that Oberwetter danced in a national monument, that T-Mobile placed its spectacle of motion in the Liverpool Street Station, and that the Colorado College team danced on an airplane. All of these liminal sites are non-places as Augé describes them, and further, all are under near-constant surveillance.

In practice, as Augé notes, a non-place is never perfectly realized, and neither is the universal anonymous subject it presupposes. In airports, one finds oneself sorted according to a global hierarchy of passports and, furthermore, according to an itinerary of suspicion. Religious or cultural dress codes, complete or insufficient documentation, and departures and destinations create divergent pathways through these transit sites, where some individuals are siphoned off into private examination rooms, some circle back because travel documents have been refused, some are taken to police headquarters or immigration services, and so on. Similarly, in a shopping mall, people sort themselves (and are sorted) according to stylistic preferences as well as economic status. Salespeople are formally and informally trained to keep close watch over some individuals for fear of shoplifting, to dutifully attend to others who fit the profile of someone whose browsing might convert into a sales commission, and to ignore the remaining customers. Though the temporary occupants of a non-place may read the same signs, the messages they contain are likely to be substantively different for each individual, who, by virtue of being in a non-place, has also become a sign—of capital or wealth, of danger or criminality, and so on. The individual as such may not matter in Augé's non-places, but the socio-cultural categories according to which people are read and categorized matter a great deal for the regimes of surveillance constructed in and through non-place. How many surveillance cameras dot the ceilings of grocery stores, shopping malls, busses, and trains or line the perimeters of plazas, alleys, and roads, not to mention the virtual surveillance of government agencies, corporations, and hackers alike—each tracking movements, purchases, and sentiments/preferences expressed through internet activity and location-aware computing?

If one is thus visible in a non-place of surveillance, what is the need for a space of appearance? Why is visibility insufficient? First, surveillance (or the fear of surveillance) produces conformity such that only those who seem to be noncompliant or nonnormative are made visible as such, and theirs is a compulsory or even violent visibility. Although American individualism encourages people to stand out from the crowd, in fact, visibility resulting from physical comportment, deportment, style, or general deviation from the norm invites reprimand. Thus panoptic surveillance produces, as Michel Foucault argues, "a state of conscious and permanent visibility that assures the automatic functioning of power."[76] Visibility is therefore not synonymous with appearance as Arendt conceptualizes it. Foucault continues, "He who is subjected to a field of visibility, and who knows it, assumes responsibility for the constraints of power; he makes them play spontaneously upon himself; he inscribes himself in the power relation in which he simultaneously plays both roles; he becomes the principle of his own subjection."[77] Visibility interpellates individuals into a hierarchical social matrix wherein some actors mobilize power as a repressive force over others, with the ultimate goal that self-policing will replace policing by the state or other apparatus. "Visibility is a trap."[78] Appearance, in contrast, is predicated on the co-presence of and recognition by equals who empower themselves by working together in a public realm. Indeed, for Arendt, power exists precisely in this plurality, in "this potentiality in being together,"[79] and is distinct from both strength and force. Crucially, for Arendt, power is a positive energy deployed by the people collectively, whereas for Foucault, power is a system of regulation and regularization that is neither wholly positive nor negative. These divergent conceptions of power undergird their theorizations of visibility as appearance or surveillance. We might say that appearance differentiates among equals without undermining their equality (it is a premise, not a promise, as Rancière argues),[80] whereas surveillance renders equality an undifferentiated mass from which difference can be isolated, extracted, and either fostered or flat-lined.

When New York lifestyle reporter Ben Aaron discovered "Joe," an African American man from Brooklyn dancing down Manhattan's 5th Avenue in 2012, it was clear that Joe's chosen mode of locomotion did not match those around him. Nor was he like the buskers that populate New York City's streets and subways: Joe was not attached to a fixed area within which he danced, and he did not ask viewers to compensate him for his physical effort. He was dancing, but walking. Initially taken by surprise, Aaron momentarily joined him before Joe continued on his way.[81] By dancing, or dance-walking, in public, Joe invited those around him to see him, and for those whose gaze offered recognition or who were contagiously set in motion alongside him, Joe appeared. Unlike other examples of dance in public discussed in this chapter, Joe's dance-walking was captured on video by happenstance. Joe was not performing for the camera; he was dancing for his own pleasure. Disregarding both the scrutiny of tourists and the indifference of New York residents used to unpredictable encounters in the metropolis, Joe's enjoyment was also his courage. Putting his body in motion in this way, and doing so alone, opens a door to harassment. Will dancing render him merely visible and out of place, or will he achieve the recognition upon which appearance depends? Appearance, predicated on equality, is not given; it must be activated, insisted upon, asserted, performed. It must erupt and break through the crystalizing scan of surveillance.

To make public spaces hospitable as spaces of appearance, the whole character of public spaces must be worked upon. In the wake of 9/11, state and media apparatuses latch on to bombings, mass shootings, and similar events, churning out crises to fuel and justify a state of exception as the new status quo. As a result, public spaces and the people in them have been transformed into targets for generating and policing terror. There is no possible return to some nostalgic idea of what the public used to be, but by working in and with public space constantly, dance in public activates the common in these spaces, populating them with unsanctioned activities that nevertheless cannot be labeled "terrorist."

Dance in public modulates space, making room for other actions to occur—without dictating what those might be. The objective is not to change public spaces by managing their transition into some preplanned alternate shape but to open them back up to their potential, to reenliven or recapacitate them by positing that these spaces, as common spaces, can be sites for dance. The consequences of opening up public spaces in this manner cannot be foreseen. This is because, as critics never cease to point out, dance (supposedly) produces nothing.[82] And yet, Arendt notes that the Greeks considered politics a *technē,* like performance: "as in the performance of the dancer or play-actor, the 'product' [of political action] is identical with the performing act itself."[83] Occurring on the street or in public spaces, dance parallels political action, which Arendt describes as unpredictable, irreversible, and anonymous,[84] by setting things in motion.[85] This is precisely what the Girl achieves in *Girl Walk//All Day*, dancing throughout the city and throughout the film without precisely knowing what the effects of her gestures will be. In addition to serving a narrative function in the film, Marsen's dancing ripples beyond the film as well, through the unforeseeable effects on viewers and their future interactions with public spaces.

Marsen's dancing, which confronts viewers with its apparently undisciplined audacity, is a more demanding form of dance in public than Joe's dance-walking. With her wild gesticulations, she certainly ruptures public spaces, but despite drawing from a variety of dance and movement sources to cobble together her unique flavor of freestyle, Marsen's dancing is often illegible and unassimilable for viewers onsite. The Girl's zaniness creates an affective block,[86] which compromises her ability to appear to those around her. *Girl Walk*'s narrative maximizes rupture but subverts appearance. As a character, the Girl is not able to fabricate her own appearance; her demand has to become sensible to others who both can and will offer recognition. One cannot appear alone. Appearance is a relation, and recognition can be withheld, as we see repeatedly throughout the film.

A scene toward the end of the film is a case in point. In "Dance with Me," The Girl is leaping, twirling, and jiving in New York's Grand Central Station. At one point, a man staring at his smartphone enters the frame. She pesters him, jumping up and down, flailing her arms about, and even waving her hands in the space between his face and the screen to disrupt and redirect the attention he has devoted solely to his hand-held device. Without looking up, his facial expressions and body language clearly reveal his simultaneous awareness of her presence and his refusal to engage. That which appears, we will recall from Arendt, is real, while that which does not yet appear maneuvers and exists in a state of unreality vis-à-vis the dominant culture. For the duration of this encounter, the Girl has been assigned to a space of unreality. With so much going on around them all the time, New Yorkers have a well-developed capacity for blocking out unwanted stimuli, including and especially from other people. This dynamic is set up early in the film—in "All Aboard," when many of the Staten Island Ferry passengers refuse to look up from their books and laptops, while others glance at the Girl long enough to register their lack of interest. It is not as if they do not realize she is there; they simply withhold acknowledgment by looking away or returning her gaze with a blank stare. For many, the Girl's existence is irrelevant, and her extreme state of agitated excitement testifies to her fight for appearance. Dancing by herself, without the support of a cohort of dancers, it takes an enormous expenditure of energy for Marsen to be noticed.

The Girl is not deprived of recognition for the whole film. Some people gawk or look on with amusement while keeping their distance, but when Marsen drops character, for example, when she collects a group to perform a modified "Single Ladies" choreography, she is granted the recognition that her character desires. Interactions with other film characters also offer moments of mutuality, for example, in her romantic duet with the Gentleman on the High Line or her temporary absorption into a breaking crew on the Williamsburg Bridge. But appearance is not distributed uniformly; it is contingent; it is not a permanent condition. Thus appearance in one context does not translate to other places and spaces. A space of appearance can only be realized when a demand to appear, a performative enactment of the right to appear, is received and granted. This process is depicted in *Girl Walk*'s concluding chapters: "Chain Reaction" and "For the People." After expending so much effort trying to set the city alight with dance, the Girl defeatedly makes her way through the city, unaware that her unbounded movement and uninhibited presence have finally made an impact on the people of New York. As she walks, the city begins to simmer with choreographic energy, and dancing begins to erupt all around her. Krupnick has edited together found dances, such as those occurring in subway cars, with dancing and movement staged specifically for the film. The mixture of ballet girls and b-boys, social and street dancers, festivals and rainbow parades, has the interesting effect of subsuming the diversity of New Yorkers' physical expressions under the Girl's sphere of influence. In *Girl Walk*'s narrative, the Girl's reappropriations of privatized spaces recuperate the city as a common space for individual and collective expression. The city gathers its churning energies and regurgitates its dancers onto Central Park, where they swarm around an exhausted Girl and buoy her up. The film ends with a resplendent nighttime festival set to John

Lennon's "Imagine." As Lennon sings his final plea, "and the world will live as one,"[87] the film's dancing crowd bursts into cheers, attempting to enact the hoped-for global community toward which Lennon's lyrics gesture.

Girl Walk stages the Girl's quest to get the city dancing as a journey from expulsion and invisibility to inclusion and appearance. The fabrication of a space of appearance at the film's conclusion offers narrative closure but, we should note, is supplied by the filmmaker, not by New York's residents. Although action is unpredictable, according to Arendt—it does not follow a specific trajectory or narrative arc from rupture to resolution—the film resolves the Girl's conflict. It validates her difference, renders that difference readable over the course of the film, and finally gives it a place in the end.

Situating *Girl Walk* within a genealogy of performance practices that disrupt the everyday, film critic Tom McCormack suggests that "the mere disruption of the normal arrangement of public space is a meaningful and potentially radical act."[88] But with recurring terrorist threats to New York City's public places and transit systems,[89] McCormack notes that "the massive popularity of *Girl Walk* comes at a time when such gestures carry an extra crazy little electrical charge."[90] That extra little charge is what makes dance in public a political intervention. Indeed, Krupnick and his crew had reason to feel some hesitation about their disruptions of New York's iconic sites when they were filming the Girl's outburst on the Staten Island Ferry. Krupnick recalls, "It happened to be the morning after Osama Bin Laden had been killed, [and] the ferry terminal was swarmed with dogs and police."[91] As a form of dance in public, *Girl Walk* asks viewers to repeatedly consider where dance belongs. The answer the film gives is "everywhere." All sites are, or ought to be, equally receptive to dancing bodies. But because there is no prior social agreement that dance belongs everywhere, and because people have become accustomed to and subdued by heavy police presence and surveillance in public spaces, Marsen's dancing, like dance mobs and other examples of dance in public, produces ruptures in the social sensorium. Dancing in sites not specially designated for such behavior forces a perceptual realignment for viewers to make sense of what should not be there in the first place.

In *The Emancipated Spectator,* Jacques Rancière brings together a contemporary artwork located in a French suburb after the wide-reaching 2005 riots and a Mallarmé poem, which, like *Girl Walk,* is seemingly apolitical yet set against the backdrop of a "social crisis."[92] Rancière turns to Deleuze and Guattari, who articulate the function of art in their coauthored volume *What Is Philosophy?,* to bring these examples of "critical" and "autonomous" art into conversation. Echoing Deleuze and Guattari, Rancière argues that artists transform sensation: "What the artist does is to weave together a new sensory fabric by wresting percepts and affects from the perceptions and affections that make up the fabric of ordinary experience. Weaving this new fabric means creating a form of common expression or a form of expression of the community."[93] Artists create new experiences in the sensory domain, whether by transforming familiar sensations into unfamiliar ones or by creating new sensory relations among disparate ideas and objects. These new sensations then weave themselves into the sensory fabric that a community shares, becoming an expression of that community or a common tapestry of a shared capacity for feeling.

To be sure, *Girl Walk* transforms ordinary, familiar places into extraordinary sites through dance, in particular, through a mix of socially sanctioned and unsanctioned behaviors. The Girl's ability to transform public spaces is not tied to a propagandistic message embedded in *Girl Walk* per se; it is related more to the ways in which the Girl as a character and *Girl Walk* as a film promote a vision of how we are together and the social fabric that makes our being-together possible—a theme I continue to explore in chapter 3. Aesthetic experiences, Rancière suggests, offer "a multiplication of connections and disconnections that reframe the relation between bodies, the world they live in and the way in which they are 'equipped' to adapt to it."[94] These multiple connections and disconnections create new communities from their alternate sensory distributions. But, like Arendt's political action, the results of this sensuous reconfiguration and bodily capacitation cannot be foreseen. There is no causal relationship that links aesthetic experiences to specific, predictable effects in governance or social relations.

For Rancière, artistic productions that seek social and political transformation as their own proper end point misunderstand the nature of both politics and art and can only be a disappointment insofar as they will never be able to deliver on their promises. Political art may aspire to raise consciousness about this or that social ill, but there is no guarantee that

viewers will be prompted to change their behavior or revolt as a result
of an elevated or renewed critical consciousness. Instead, what Rancière
suggests links the domains of aesthetics and politics lays in "a shift from a
given sensible world to another sensible world that defines different capacities and incapacities, different forms of tolerance and intolerance. What
occurs are processes of dissociation: a break in a relationship between sense
and sense—between what is seen and what is thought, what is thought
and what is felt. Such breaks can happen anywhere and at any time. But
they cannot be calculated."[95] Whatever invites a confrontation between
conflicting sensory regimes—staging dissensus, or the mismatch between
sense and sense—opens up the space of aesthetics in the sphere of politics
and the space of politics in the sphere of aesthetics.

REDISTRIBUTING THE PUBLIC

Up to this point, I have focused primarily on dances in public that do
not seem to have a political agenda attached to their claims to public space
to show that the absence of an overt agenda does not diminish the ability
of these performances to articulate a common space in public space, a space
of appearance in a non-place of surveillance. Indeed, I contend that it is
precisely these types of interventions that provide a format for more politicized actions. In this final section, I would like to shift my attention to two
examples of dance in public sponsored by activist organizations that directly
engage with political claims in the ways they move through and take up
space: the Round Dances of the Indigenous rights movement Idle No More
and the flamenco flash mobs of the Spanish anticapitalist group Flo6x8. As
we have seen, in the years after the first flash mobs began appearing in 2003,
but especially from 2008 onward, dance in public has contributed to reimagining public spaces in ways that complement twenty-first-century political movements. Dance mobs make a collective demand to appear on behalf
of an anonymous crowd, a crowd acting together to rupture the corporeal
and spatial status quo. As performance theorist José Muñoz describes of a
"punk rock commons," dance mobs are engaged in a larger project that
"defies social conventions and conformism and is innately heretical yet still
desirous for the world, actively attempting to enact a commons that is
not a pulverizing hierarchical one bequeathed through logics and practices
of exploitation."[96] Dance mobs by Idle No More and Flo6x8 in particular

challenge established hierarchies and histories of exploitation. They require a shift in collective perceptions of public spaces and public behavior, provoking dissensual conflict in the realms of both aesthetics and politics to transform public spaces into the common spaces they enact.

Before continuing on with the Round Dances and flamenco flash mobs as politicized examples of dance in public, let me pause to further explicate Rancière's use of the terms *politics* and *aesthetics,* particularly how they relate to the partitioning or distribution of the sensible. For Rancière, politics is always concerned with the question of equality, occurring whenever equality is affirmed in the form of a dispute or conflict. Politics as such must give rise to a confrontation between what Rancière calls police logic, or consensus, which orders and legitimates a certain partitioning of social roles or distributions of the sensible, and egalitarian logic, or dissensus, which breaks with that configuration in the name of equality.[97] Politics occurs in the dispute, where a claim to equality confronts its own absence within consensus. In making that claim nonetheless, that is, without prior authorization, the claim to equality undoes the distributions of perceptibility of the police order, which regulates appearance. "Politics breaks with the sensory self-evidence of the 'natural' order that destines specific individuals and groups to occupy . . . specific ways of being, seeing and saying."[98] Insofar as politics is a conflict over appearance—what is visible, audible, legible, and so on—it also has an aesthetic dimension. Insofar as the aesthetic stages a confrontation of heterogeneous elements in the name of equality, it, in turn, has a political dimension. For Rancière, aesthetics and politics each creates dissensual reconfigurations of the sensible and the common associated with it: "If there is such thing as an 'aesthetics of politics,' it lies in a re-configuration of the distribution of the common through political processes of subjectivation. Correspondingly, if there is a politics of aesthetics, it lies in the practices and modes of visibility of art that re-configure the fabric of sensory experience."[99]

In general, when Rancière uses the term *aesthetic,* he is referring to one of two things: (1) a regime of Art,[100] in which works of art claim autonomy from other crafts, trades, practices, or ordinary experience, even as, according to Rancière, the aesthetic regime is marked by the blurring of the very boundaries between art and life or art and nonart that had allowed Art to be demarcated as its own, independent terrain of expression, or

(2) a configuration of what is available to sense perception or what is intelligible within a specific distribution of the sensible, that is, what can be seen, heard, said, or felt. Rancière attaches aesthetics to politics, as the aspect of politics that makes visible what had previously been unseen through the rupturing effects of dissensus. Aesthetics and politics both frame conflicts between sense and sense, struggling for new relationships that include that which is excluded from the realm of the sensible. Rancière continues on the theme of aesthetic experience: "It is a multiplicity of folds and gaps in the fabric of the common experience that change the cartography of the perceptible, the thinkable and the feasible. As such, it allows for new modes of political construction of common objects and new possibilities for collective enunciation."[101] Rancière establishes art's political intervention in its elaboration of new forms of collective enunciation and new images of common experience, images that contradict what was thought to be self-evident. The measurement of art's political efficacy thus becomes disentangled from changes in policy, an arena in which Rancière contends art can only fail to achieve its aims, and aligned instead with its ability to create or establish connections that did not previously exist. In so doing, artistic practices rearrange what is perceptible, or available to audiences for sensory assimilation, enlarging the common sensorium to include the previously excluded. This common becomes a new consensus.

Throughout this chapter, the claims of dance in public to the domains of both art and politics have been ambiguous. Why, then, is it useful to turn to Rancière if dance in public's relationship to both artistic practice and political action is uncertain? As Jill Bennett argues, "the aesthetic is not art's exclusive province but a method of engagement in which art specializes."[102] Classification as art is unnecessary to participate in the aesthetic realm. Indeed, such identification is beside the point, as dance in public is deeply embedded in the logic of the aesthetic regime as Rancière describes it. Dance in public performs exactly the boundary-blurring equivocation that he attributes to the aesthetic regime of art—blurring art, commerce, social work, protest, and everyday life into a choreographic mélange that registers on each of these levels. Dance in public focuses its energies on the dissensual confrontation between public space as a non-place of surveillance and as a common space of appearance in which to manifest a full range of freedoms of movement and expression. It performs an alternate order of space within a society of surveillance and control, discovering "new bodily capacities"[103] and reinventing others, dislodging viewers from their assigned locations within social arrangements through affective disorientation and spatial deterritorialization.

Initiated in December 2012, the Indigenous rights movement Idle No More has sought to raise awareness of atrocities committed against the earth and Native ways of life. The movement arose in response to Canadian legislation that deregulated waterways in First Nations land to facilitate the building of oil pipelines. In addition to Attawapiskat chief Theresa Spence's widely publicized hunger strike and numerous protests and teach-ins around environmental sustainability, First Nation sovereignty, and treaty violations, Idle No More staged Round Dance flash mobs in locations throughout Canada and the United States.[104] In December 2012 alone, Round Dances took place in every Canadian province and territory as well as in cities throughout the United States, including Minneapolis, San Francisco, Los Angeles, Spokane, Portland, Sioux City, Seattle, and New York City. As the Idle No More movement grew, Round Dances continued to be performed throughout 2013 and 2014 in plazas, city centers, and especially shopping malls.

Figure 13. Screenshot of the Indigenous rights organization Idle No More with participants in Saskatchewan in *ONE MORE TIME!! Idle No More 2nd song—Saskatoon, SK Flash Mob Round Dance Video 2 of 2* (2012).

Figure 14. Screenshot of the Indigenous rights organization Idle No More with participants in
Saskatchewan in *ONE MORE TIME!! Idle No More 2nd song—Saskatoon, SK Flash Mob Round Dance
Video 2 of 2* (2012).

Originating among Plains Indians, the Round Dance began as a dance
of healing that transformed into a social dance, a friendship and courtship
form suitable for intertribal gatherings as well as for non-Indigenous participation. Unlike most Native American and First Nation dances, which
are sex segregated and performed with gender-specific movements, the
Round Dance allows people of all genders to dance alongside one another.
Dancers join hands and travel clockwise in a circle (or concentric circles,
if the group is particularly large), around the drummers. Idle No More
gatherings have used the Round Dance format to reach out and foster
relationships with members of settler and non-Native populations, and the
simplicity of the movement ensures an inclusive environment. In a post
for the artist-activist website Beautiful Trouble, Paul Kuttner suggests that
the Round Dance flash mobs "symbolized [Idle No More's] core tenets
of peace and unity, while sending the simple message: 'We are here, our
culture is strong and we will not be silent in the face of destruction.'"[105]
Noting the activist principles at work in the Round Dances, Kuttner further suggests that the dances held an element of ritual and "made it easy
for people from many backgrounds to 'fall into the rhythm' of the action;
they offered participants a direct experience of unity and solidarity."[106]

Some of the Round Dance flash mobs also incorporate call-and-response elements, and as participants join in and respond with their own "hey ya," they bind themselves to this temporary community of dancers sustained for the duration of their mutual recognition and adherence to a rhythm. Together, Native and non-Native participants perform a version of the political recognition that Indigenous peoples seek on a broader scale through such movements as Idle No More.

Marking the one-year anniversary of Idle No More, organizers planned a Round Dance flash mob in Mall of America, a shopping center in Bloomington, Minnesota, where a Round Dance involving nearly one thousand people had been held on December 30, 2012. Organizers were put on notice by the mall's management, however, who noted in a letter that political protests are not allowed on mall property and threatened legal action if another Round Dance ensued. Organizer Reyna Crow responded that characterizing a Round Dance as a protest was both inaccurate and insulting: "If the Idle No More flash mob Round Dance that was held there last year is a 'protest,' so are the Christmas carols and other flash mob events that have been held there."[107] Crow and fellow organizer Patricia Shephard were indeed arrested when they appeared at the mall on December 31, 2013, and mall security set up checkpoints, examining bags and refusing entry to anyone with a drum or other paraphernalia. Even before entering the mall, Round Dance participants were already marked as outside the midwestern mainstream, and those carrying hand drums or wearing additional signifiers of indigeneity could not blend in with the crowd—thus deactivating the signal protective feature of the flash mob format. Although hundreds of Round Dances have taken place across Canada and the United States, this particular one was stopped before it started.[108]

Without an obvious connection to popular culture or commerce like flash mobs of Christmas carolers or dancers accompanied by pop tunes, the Round Dances can only read as protest to mall managers. Idle No More's participants demand to appear in social and political environments that have disenfranchised and rendered Indigenous populations invisible and pre-scripted their visibility within non-places of surveillance. Yet, with their hand drums, chants, and large crowds, Idle No More's Round Dances assert the participants' appearance in a common space. Here dancing in public reenacts daily negotiations between visibility and political appearance, on one hand, and invisibility and state abandonment, on the other. Simply validating Native cultures and practices in a public forum, let alone raising issues of Native sovereignty or land and water rights, is already a political gesture. Such legitimation of a marginalized population's cultural practices is thus only perceivable through the lens of agitation and propaganda unless appearance can break through surveillance. Affirming one's cultural difference, claiming an equal standing for that difference, and doing so without first being given permission to do so are intensely political acts of defiance. As Muñoz suggests, "life in the commons is and should be turbulent, not only because of the various enclosures that attempt to overwhelm a commons, but because disagreement . . . is of vital importance to the augmentation of the insurrectionist promise of the commons."[109] Where legal claims based on treaties and rights discourses appeal to the juridical arrangements that enforce the status quo, interventions such as the Round Dance flash mobs employ a cultural practice as a dissensual, insurrectionist wedge that asserts appearance while simultaneously appealing to social bonds across difference. These are not the indifferent differences of chapter 1—rote repetitions that eliminate the difference within repetition—these are differences that make a difference. They make a difference to participants, to audiences, to property owners, and to lawmakers. Decades of multiculturalism have encouraged people to celebrate their difference, but Idle No More illuminates the edges of tolerance for such differences. As indicated earlier with "Harlem Shake on a Plane," the ability of a social body to accommodate deviation does not translate easily into support from those who own or administer institutions and commercial enterprises.

Dance in public takes place in spaces where it does not belong, highlighting its unspoken exclusion. By thus appearing in such spaces without permission, that is, without acceding to the demands of those spaces through self-exclusion and instead performing equality with other accepted public behaviors, dance in public cuts a dissensual figure out of an existing community of sense, disincorporating what had seemed unified. Dance in public challenges the self-evidence of public spaces and their surveillance. Like politics and art in Rancière's formulation, dances in public "widen gaps, open up space for deviations, modify the speeds, the trajectories, and the ways in which groups of people adhere to a condition, react to situations, recognize their images. They reconfigure the map of the sensible by interfering with the functionality of gestures and rhythms adapted to the natural cycles of production, reproduction, and submission."[110] Blurring the boundaries between dance and protest, indeed, making the distinction between dance and protest irrelevant by foregrounding a population whose aesthetico-political practices have been rendered illegible through this very distinction,[111] Idle No More generates new forms of relationships and new forms of collective life by tying the heterogeneous elements of dance and protest together, both counting on and provocatively challenging the illegibility that such blurring brings about.

In *The Emancipated Spectator,* Rancière describes new forms of collective life as distinctly dissensual: "the intertwining of contradictory relations are intended to produce a new sense of community . . . a new political people. And it is the anticipated reality of that people."[112] Aesthetic practices can therefore prefigure a community to come, perhaps even create a new world, by imagining and staging a possible reality that is not yet but may be. Participating in this reimagining, Rancière notes that "many contemporary artists no longer set out to create works of art. [They want to] induce alterations in the space of everyday life, generating new forms of relations."[113] In his essay "Contemporary Art and the Politics of Aesthetics," Rancière aligns this social turn, the desire to contribute to repairing the social world or a broken public sphere, with a shift in politics that disarms dissensus in the face of terror and exception[114] and subsequently substitutes artistic practices for politics "in the construction of dissensual stages."[115] Art, however, has responded by substituting ethics for politics as artists seek to offer "a testimony of co-presence" or "[witness] to a common world."[116] Both political and aesthetic spheres, Rancière seems to suggest, have largely abandoned dissensus. To remain in the realm of critical art, Rancière argues that art must negotiate two tensions, "[keeping] something of the tension that pushes aesthetic experience toward the reconfiguration of collective life and something of the tension that withdraws the power of aesthetic sensoriality from the other spheres of experience. From the zones of indistinction between art and life it must borrow the connections that provoke political intelligibility."[117] These, in essence, are the tensions that both Idle No More and Flo6x8 maintain in their dance mobs. They stage continuities between art and life with their performed

assertions of a collectivity that does not yet exist and from which they
are excluded, while distancing themselves from everyday life in their use
of music, song, and dance as a multidimensional performance through
which to convey or portray a vision of a collectivity in which they, too, find
a place. Neither Idle No More's Round Dances nor Flo6x8's flamenco
dance mobs promote social healing at the expense of the communities'
own erasure; rather, it is only through mutual recognition that healing is
possible, and mutual recognition requires appearance.

  After the ignominious 2008 collapse of the financial services firm Lehman
Brothers and the subsequent chain reaction in the form of a global economic downturn, the anticapitalist group Flo6x8 began staging flamenco
flash mobs in Spanish banks and financial institutions (where threat of
arrest is ever present) to protest the banking system and austerity measures as the economic situation worsened in Spain and around the globe.
An "activist-artistic-situationist-performative-folkloric collective"[118] named
for the popular flamenco rhythm, Flo6x8 is a "group of average folks"
brought together by their love of flamenco and criticism of the financial
system: "Among the concerns that motivate us, what stands out is the excess not only of the earth's pillaging by the banks, but also the general
silence which meets this destruction, its naturalization and the impunity
with which it is perpetrated."[119] Refusing to be silent themselves, they engage in civil disobedience and direct action in the form of flamenco dance
and song, critiquing the financial system that governs so many aspects of
contemporary life. Singing their laments to ATMs and dancing their out-
rage to bank tellers, Flo6x8 interrupts business as usual, filling bank lobbies
with the droning sounds of complaint, furious heel strikes, and stinging
gestures. As momentum builds and dancers take over additional space,
other participants' *palmas*—hand claps that mark the complex rhythm—
offer support and extend the dancers' energetic reach. *Palmas* are a way of
bringing dancers and musicians into sync but also of bringing a community of performers and audience members into being, focusing energy and
attention, amplifying presence, and bringing one's own body to bear on a
situation.

  Flo6x8 maintains the strict structure that dance mobs have familiarized,
with a singer calling out a few bars before being joined by a dancer, and
then a few more dancers, until an organized group emerges from what had

appeared to be bank patrons awaiting service. Whereas a sizable majority
of dance mobs are accompanied by recorded pop songs (Idle No More's
Round Dances are a notable exception), Flo6x8 creates original lyrical
and musical compositions for their events. These songs protest the bank
bail-outs and policies that further burden the Spanish people with bank
debt even as their own debts are not forgiven. They poignantly reflect on
the experiences of austerity, joblessness, and even homelessness: "The
attitude and the will / my friend, has changed. . . . You have lowered my
salary / and put up the price of everything / To hold my own / I've
even had to pawn the parrot / and I've even had to sell my house."[120] The
"artivists" have no delusions about their ability to influence economic
policy. They consider the entire banking apparatus to be a giant iceberg,
of which ATMs and local branches are the mere tip, and they are like "Lil-
liputians scratching at its frigidly inhuman fissures with ice axes made out
of cardboard rock."[121] Like a submerged iceberg hidden from sight, the enormous hidden infrastructure of financial capitalism and workings of the
invisible hand of the market cannot be countered. Flo6x8 understands that
facing off with the banking system cannot be the objective of their collective activism. Global capital neither resists nor acquiesces—it flows, picking up and incorporating any positive or negative forces into its current.

Figure 15. Screenshot of the activist performance collective Flo6x8 in a flamenco dance mob at a
branch of the Spanish bank Bankia in *flo6x8: Bankia, pulmones y branquias (bulerías)* (2012).

At best, some of its flow can be redirected, siphoned off to support and possibly grow alternatives to global capital. But this is not to say that Flo6x8's efforts are futile. As they say, "pero por algún sitio hay que empezar"—you have to start somewhere.[122]

Commenting on Flo6x8's political orientation, Pepe el Moody's, a pseudonym playing on the credit rating agency, argues that protest is deeply embedded in the history of flamenco but that artists have forgotten. "They have forgotten that flamenco is the music of exploited people, of an exploited country."[123] Flo6x8 brings back indignation and confrontation as core elements of flamenco, recalling the Romani people's misery and full-bodied protest against suffering. It is not only the music that expresses this disgruntlement, el Moody's clarifies: "it's not just words—the body of a flamenco dancer is rebellion in itself."[124] Bringing material realities back to the fore to counter the immateriality of financial capitalism, Flo6x8 has literalized OWS's ballerina on the bull. Knowing that they cannot confront the financial system itself, they dance on its surrogates. The flamenco body, a body, el Moody's says, that is itself a rebellion, dances defiantly. It makes a space for itself in which it can appear while at the same time being out of place or where it does not belong, and thereby it risks not being seen for what it is. Flo6x8 blurs the artificial boundaries between art and protest, reclaiming flamenco as a physical and musical practice of dissent.

Dancing in public calls upon viewers (onsite, but especially online) to make sense of these aesthetic scenes. This sense making is not only a reordering or reconfiguring of the perceptual field; it is a creative act: viewers must *make* sense of what appears before them in order for it to appear as such. The sense that dance mobs perform is a sense of the common, but because our own time is dominated by the spatial and financial logics of free-market capitalism, the sense of the common is most certainly not the prevailing common sense. Being-in-common, which is to say, actively producing the common (as common spaces and as common world) and not simply drawing resources from it, defies the current consensus. When public spaces erupt with unexpected encounters, such as the dance mobs or solo dances discussed throughout this chapter, they break with ways of seeing or sensing that are common to a community within which social legibility takes place. However, the very assimilation of such ruptures into popular consciousness, the very act of making sense of these scenes, gradually pulls them in the direction of intelligibility. As more people stage dance mobs and post them online, they make more sense to viewers. Common sense is built through just such reperformance, which builds sense through a citational process. Even so, the fact that dance mobs make sense to viewers does not mean that they are therefore permissible from the perspective of property owners and business operators, as responses to Idle No More's Round Dances and Flo6x8's flamenco flash mobs demonstrate.

Dancing in public exchanges the common sense that regulates normative behavior in public spaces for a sense of the common, thereby performatively reworking non-places of surveillance into common spaces of appearance. Despite the absence of a right to do so, dance and dancers appear in public and, through their unauthorized gestural assertions, stake a claim to public spaces and refuse to be dispossessed of the common or of their ability to move in-common. Dance in public alters our collective relationship to public spaces in the United States and potentially around the globe by staging dissensus in a joyful, if sometimes zany, manner. Whether performed individually or as a coordinated group, whether choreographed or improvised, dancing in public is a practice of freedom,[125] a playfully serious revolt that recuperates public spaces as common spaces. Recorded, edited, and posted online, each circulating dance in public "[changes] existing modes of sensory presentations and forms of enunciation . . . building new relationships between reality and appearance, the individual and the collective."[126] Dance in public redistributes public spaces along new axes of visibility and affect, offering a dissensual encounter through the simple pleasure of dancing in public. In its rupture of the sensorial field, it presences both common spaces and a corporeal common reflected in its radical embrace of that which cannot be owned: the gestures and movements of dancing, which I explore further in chapter 4.

But not everyone can make this claim to the common-place of dance and public space. In the United States, street performers have come under fire as policies regarding public behavior have begun to shift. New York City now requires the purchase of permits to perform in or near parks and restricts busking locations to a mere one hundred spots,[127] and plainclothes police officers have begun targeting dancers on the subway,[128] resulting in arrests and fines of up to $1,000 for noncompliance.[129] Notably, performing on ferries, such as the Staten Island Ferry at the heart of *Girl Walk//All Day,* is explicitly prohibited.[130] Indeed, cities across the United States, including Las Vegas, Seattle, Venice Beach, Boston, and Kansas City, have similarly sought to ban or restrict street performance, and many performance groups claiming First Amendment protection have brought their cases to the courts, with uneven success. One wonders, then, if *Girl Walk* is "pro-public intervention" as Krupnick describes, who assesses the desirability of such interventions, and with what authority? From the film's beginning moments when Marsen sprawls herself along an escalator handrail, the Girl demands accommodation from those around her, and by and large, they acquiesce. The film's viewers vicariously experience the exhilaration of taking up space in this way, feeling what it might be like to dance whenever and wherever they wanted, taking up however much space they wanted. But in proposing that all public spaces are common spaces, or spaces in which to elaborate a sense of the common, *Girl Walk//All Day* also demands that we consider where reclaiming or materializing the common by taking back public spaces might displace others, exacerbating rather than ameliorating unequal access to the performatively enacted common.

In the next chapter, these questions take on even greater import as the common moves from local sites and public spaces toward a global expansiveness. For such work, the crowd becomes a key creative agent and resource as artists invite contributions and mine collective archives to craft a common world through a praxis of being-with. Just as dancers must continuously assert the public character of public space, however, the common world produced through crowd contributions is never final or total but is rather a partial, contingent, and temporary affective disposition.

CHAPTER THREE

A World from a Crowd

◆◆◆

Composing the Common

At first, there are a couple of voices. "Okay, so just hold it. Just hold it—
don't do anything, just hold it." A man emerges onscreen and centers himself in the frame between stalls at a market. A caption tells viewers that
this scene is in Beijing, and as the city is revealed, the man begins to dance.
Sort of. He shuffles his feet forward and back, and his arms hang loosely,
moving in response to the displacements of his feet. He appears next in
Hanoi, and then in Delhi, doing this same movement. In Bangkok, he
seems a bit hesitant, even rigid. But in Moscow, he thrashes about freely.
"Keep going," prompts an offscreen voice in Los Angeles, and he does—
from city to city, circling the globe with his "dorky dance,"[1] rocking his
upper body side to side, popping his feet up underneath him like he's run-
ning in place, and swinging and poking his elbows while his hands and
arms flail about.

A one-time video game designer,[2] Matt Harding emerged as an internet celebrity in the mid-2000s thanks to the video-sharing powers of social
media. At the urging of a friend, Harding began recording his quirky signature dance in the sites he visited, which he edited together into several
videos, including two sponsored by Stride, the makers of a chewing gum
who liked the idea of Harding's "ridiculously long dance round the world."[3]
As one might imagine, although the videos retain core elements that
maintain consistency across the various iterations, Harding's dance style,
and what it achieves in relation to global populations, shifts over time. In
the 2005 and 2006 videos, Harding dances more or less alone against a

backdrop of each exotic locale. In 2008, Harding extends an invitation for others to join him in his unique style of dance. And in the 2012 video, Harding relinquishes the safety of the dance that made him famous and learns dance styles and movements from those with whom he shares a space and a screen. In this chapter, I use Harding's videos, which are all listed under the title Where the Hell Is Matt? on YouTube,[4] as a way to think through questions of how artists and social media contributors imagine the world, not only as a theatrical representation, but also as a performative achievement.[5] In particular, I ask how they employ the contributions of the crowd in imagining a global community, and how dance participates in this articulation of a worldwide together.

In his introduction to Art and Multitude, Antonio Negri suggests that art manifests a capacity for "reinventing the world."[6] However, he qualifies art's ability to achieve beauty, the traditional domain of aesthetic practices, requiring that expressive acts "transform themselves into a community . . . embraced and contained within a common project." He continues, "The beautiful is an invention of singularity which circulates and reveals itself as common in the multiplicity of subjects who participate in the construction of the world."[7] It is not my objective in this chapter or in this book to pose the question of the beautiful. Yet Negri's understanding of art's deployment of the immaterial and affective labor of the multitude, and the collaboration of art and multitude in exposing a common through projects of world-making, captures the central ideas I explore in this chapter: that many contemporary performance practices attempt to create the world anew, and that they turn to the crowd or multitude to assist in this project of creating a global community that shares in an affective orientation to the world.

I pursue the notion of a globally scaled common through several screen-based dance projects created between 2005 and 2014. In addition to Harding's Where the Hell Is Matt? series of videos (2005–12), which I consider throughout the chapter, I analyze the dance film Globe Trot (2014), choreographed by Bebe Miller and directed and edited by Mitchell Rose;[8] the single-channel video installation Mass Ornament (2009) by Natalie Bookchin;[9] One Day on Earth the Music Video (2012), directed by Kyle Ruddick and edited by Cari Ann Shim Sham* to music by DJ Cut Chemist;[10] and the band OK Go's interactive music video All Is Not Lost (2011).[11]

To analyze the ways these pieces go about creating common worlds through dance and in the space of the screen, I turn to philosopher Jean-Luc Nancy, whose thought is central to this chapter. For Nancy, the world no longer makes sense because globalization has replaced the world with a mere globe. Globalization, according to Nancy, is nothing other than the world destroying itself. In the absence of an orienting world, there can be no sense or meaning to grasp on to, and this feeling of being estranged from the world, which is an estrangement from meaning, is, as Paolo Virno remarks, "an inescapable and shared condition."[12] Parsing the loss of sense as the new common sense of the contemporary world, Nancy posits the French term *mondialisation,* or "world-forming," against the English term *globalization,* which refers to economic globalization and to the world as an abstraction or frictionless world of commerce.

Attempts to make sense of the world, for example, through artistic practice, are not only attempts to come to terms with catastrophe, violence, austerity, alienation, displacement, or ecological crisis, though such themes are certainly present, as will be seen later in this chapter. Nancy asks, "How are we to conceive of, precisely, a world where we find only a globe?"[13] In making sense of the world, I argue that the artists and works I explore in this chapter are also attempting to make-world from the space of globalization. To be sure, a single world is insufficient for Nancy as well as for artistic practice. There are worlds upon worlds in the world. "A world is a multiplicity of worlds, the world is a multiplicity of worlds, and its unity is the sharing out [*partage*] and the mutual exposure in this world of all its worlds."[14] In the same way that *Girl Walk//All Day* (2011–12), discussed in chapter 2, and *24 Hours of Happy* (2013), discussed in chapter 4, are love letters to specific cities (New York and Los Angeles, respectively), *Where the Hell Is Matt?* and the other works analyzed in this chapter are love letters to the world—to the planet and to humanity. Through various techniques of composition and editing, each of these digital and video pieces focuses on humanity explicitly around the world—not just global North and South or East and West but from as many regions as respond to their calls for participation. Each piece generates a sense of the world; thus I turn to questions of sensation and affect in sharing in a world and the importance of fragmentation, or what Nancy calls *fractality,* in presenting this world as a being-together that is singular plural. A sense of the world, while being a shared sense, must remain multiple.

Globalization has both enabled and complicated the project of representing the world such that artists can no longer reasonably justify pursuing such a representation alone. As a result, the projects I discuss in this chapter employ crowdsourcing as a technique of composition. Delegating content generation to the crowd enables a planetary scope impossible except for very rare and highly mobile individuals like Harding. I argue that all of these pieces invest in the globe, in Nancy's usage, as a site from which to create a world. They engage in a process of suturing a world together through shared choreographies or shared gestures that form the linkages necessary for being-with or being-in-common. Turning toward a global human community, each employs processes of delegation or crowdsourcing to gather material from which to create this world. Before turning to the question of how dances might engage in the work of creating a world from the space of globalization, I first consider the broader phenomenon of contemporary artists relying on the creativity of the crowd in participatory art practices.

CREATIVE CROWDS

Like interactive media, discussed in chapter 1, crowdsourced content is now so ubiquitous as to require little explanation. Crowdsourcing is a process of harnessing the knowledge and creative input of a large population, but that large population might be fifty people, or it might be 5 million. Those who utilize techniques of crowdsourcing espouse a belief in what James Surowiecki calls the "wisdom of crowds"—left to their own devices, the collective intelligence of a crowd is comparable to or may even surpass that of a few well-trained experts.[15] Crowd-generated content functions particularly well where users are engaged in the collective production of knowledge and debate (Wikipedia, blogs), products (beta-testers and focus groups), maps (Google Maps), assessments (rating and review sites such as Yelp or Amazon), and the sharing and development of open source software (GitHub). In such instances, the collective labor of many participants will, in theory, produce more accurate results delivered more quickly to better serve a business or community than could be provided by a few knowledgeable people. This model tends to overlook that crowds contain experts (as well as bad actors) and that dedicated amateurs develop expertise over time. Nevertheless, crowdsourcing lowers barriers for participation, especially for the purposes of digital cultural production.

A similar approach to crowdsourcing has been applied as a technique of artistic composition in what has been called participatory, relational, and socially engaged artistic practices. Art critic and curator Nicolas Bourriaud has been a vocal advocate of relational art, which often takes the form of immersive, participatory, transient experiences. In addition to being disciplinarily ambiguous, Bourriaud remarks that the relational art of the 1990s onward manifests a desire to produce greater conviviality and create social bonds, and to do so through art as an encounter or curated experience rather than through representation alone. In this way, art promotes "learning how to inhabit the world in a better way."[16] Bourriaud argues that the place of art is no longer to imagine and represent alternate realities and utopian elsewheres but to directly impact the lives of those who participate by offering "ways of living and models of action."[17] In other words, art should not be contemplated at a distance but engaged and experienced immersively. Theater scholar Shannon Jackson likewise argues that the experimental performance pieces she describes as "social works" offer an opportunity to examine "what it means to sustain human collaboration [and] contribute to inter-dependent social imagining."[18] These contemporary experimental arts practices critically reflect on the enabling conditions of both art and sociality, mobilizing themes of lending and withdrawing support to transform art-making into a form of world-making.

Not all art or cultural critics admire relational works or structures of audience participation or collaborative authorship, however. Claire Bishop, for example, forcefully argues that artworks that take shape through the participation of audience members risk duplicating the structures of neoliberal capitalism, requiring affective investments and uncompensated labor as part of a larger "experience economy."[19] Theater scholar Jen Harvie also remains skeptical of some of the claims that have accrued around participatory arts practices, noting that relationships tend to be short-lived and superficial, though she finds social and political value in what such work attempts. Where Jackson emphasizes mutual support in the performing arts' social turn, Harvie offers a stronger critique with her use of the term *delegated art* to describe the situation in which "people who are

not, nominally, 'the artist,' make or contribute to making, the art or performance."[20] Again, there is a range of participation that falls under this
general category of art-making. Artists may invite spectators to participate in artworks fully conceived and executed with little difference in concept or substance despite audience engagement, or they may turn over
key aspects of the artistic experience to collaborators, workers for hire, or
audience members. While, according to Harvie, delegated art can show
how artistic practices are inevitably "socially embedded and socially dependent,"[21] they can also "conscript audiences and others to produce work for
which they are not properly attributed authorship" and implicate them in
social or ideological projects with which they might not otherwise affili-
ate.[22] More than participatory or relational art, the concept of delegated
art reflects the political and economic ambivalence of artists collecting
contributions from the crowd to compose a digital or video work such
as those explored in this chapter. Although I argue that these works are
engaged in the larger project of creating a world from crowd, it is impossible to ignore the fundamental paradox of crowdsourcing content, which
promotes extracting contributions or requiring voluntary labor in the name
of inclusivity and equality.[23]

  Delegated or crowdsourced art is fueled, ideally, by an ethic of volun-
teerism on the part of participants and informed by participatory and
open arts practices on the part of project directors. Such methods of artistic composition exemplify the ways in which what Virno describes as the
generic capacities of the multitude are put to work[24] and are increasingly
commonplace as a technique of composition. The extent to which artists
rely on the crowd varies across projects, as does the size of the crowd to
which they turn. For example, after his 2005 and 2006 videos gave him
quasi-celebrity status, Matt Harding tapped into his global fan community to create evocative and playful scenes for his 2008 and 2012 Where the
Hell Is Matt? videos. The contents for *Globe Trot* were crowdsourced from
a small community of choreographers and filmmakers, while the content
for *One Day on Earth the Music Video* came from a very large community of
documentary filmmakers. Some artists seem to wish to remove themselves
from the process of content creation, receding into the background but
providing conceptual architectures to organize contributions, while others
exert a stronger influence on what content is generated, for example, in

what Mitchell Rose calls "instructional collaboration."[25] In either case, crowd-generated movement functions as raw material that is combined into a larger whole.

Just as the level of audience or fan involvement in delegated work can vary, some web-based pieces can continue to incorporate crowd submissions over a long period of time. OK Go's *All Is Not Lost* interactive music video has an unlimited number of possible participants drawn from among internet users. Described as a "video dance messenger," it invites user participation in the form of messages to the victims of the 2011 Japanese earthquake and the Fukushima nuclear disaster. In this way, *All Is Not Lost* differs from the hyperdances discussed in chapter 1. Viewers are invited to contribute a message that becomes part of the work, displayed at the end of the song in a global get-well card to the Japanese people in the wake of disaster.

As Harvie notes, attribution of authorship is vague in situations of delegated creativity, exacerbated by the fact that these pieces reflect a networked or internet logic in which the assumption is that contributors are part of an anonymous crowd—just like those who leave product reviews on Amazon. For example, Harding does not give credit to the many participants in his videos, despite their centrality to the overall effect of his *Where the Hell Is Matt?* series. Mitchell Rose credits the contributing filmmakers but not dancers in *Globe Trot*. In analyzing dances that utilize such methods of delegated or crowdsourced composition, I do not presume that these works achieve their aim of cultivating fellow feeling, or that, if they do, this translates into any lasting repairs to the social fabric that would result in, for example, policy changes that extend support on a large scale. Even so, I argue, following Nancy, that each of these pieces begins from a place of globalization and, to a greater or lesser degree, works to create a common world. Crowdsourcing their content from participants around the globe, these pieces imagine the social sphere not as national or regional but as global. They leverage the networks that economic and informational globalization have made available to assert a world in the place of an abstract globe, to create a world from a crowd.

In chapter 2, we saw how professional and amateur artists turned to an aesthetic politics of the street and the public in recuperating an Arendtian space of appearance, or what Nancy might call a staging of coappearance, by gathering en masse in public spectacles of extraordinary and coordinated gestures of *communitas*. These public spectacles exemplify Nancy's claim that "to-be-with is to make sense mutually, and only mutually."[26] Yet, their self-imposed scale of performance is the city or the locale. The videos circulate across space and time and continue to create ruptures in the representational field and thereby continue to impact the material world (from which representation is not separate), but their global reach is an effect of their circulation, not their composition or production. The fabrication of their being-together is localized. In contrast, the pieces in this chapter imagine a much larger common—a global or planetary common from which to make sense of the world. Over the course of the next sections, I follow the evolution in Harding's Where the Hell Is Matt? videos to consider how artists move from an abstract globe to a worldly world, beginning with the world as picture. From there, I move on to examine Nancy's formulation of the world as ethos, praxis, and habitus, which I argue configures the world as performative—something that is brought into being through its enactment as well as its representation.

PICTURING THE WORLD

Harding takes up space. He appropriates space to himself regardless of other occupants. Locating himself in the center of the frame, Harding dances around the world. In his 2005 video, a collage of destinations across Asia and Eastern Europe, Africa, and North America, he dances in urban venues surrounded by people as well as in remote settings where he dances alone. Both of his 2005 and 2006 videos are set to the Deep Forest song "Sweet Lullaby," but in the Stride-sponsored 2006 video, an astonishing number of his sites are unpeopled. The 2006 video begins in Bolivia at Salar de Uyuni, a salt flat where the bright blue sky and cumulus clouds reflect in the shallow water below, merging heaven and earth. Harding walks into the frame. His feet skim the water and leave a small trail behind him. As he arrives center screen, he turns to face the camera and begins to dance. In contrast to the 2005 video, which captures a few impromptu interactions with locals and other tourists, in the 2006 video, if there happen to be others within the frame, Harding pays them no attention. With a few exceptions, for example, among Buddhist monks in Laos and children in Rwanda, they also ignore him. Harding dances on a bridge in Venice as pedestrians pass behind and a gondola emerges from underneath. He dances in a crosswalk in the rain in Tokyo, while a crowd of people maneuvers umbrellas around him and each other without stopping. He dances with giant tortoises in the Galápagos Islands, kangaroos in Australia, walruses in the South Shetland Islands, elephants in Botswana, and jellyfish in Palau. It is as if sponsorship has led Harding to reimagine the world as his stage, but his stage contains only scenery and no players.

Approaching the world as an exotic backdrop for a tourist's pictures, Harding's 2005 and 2006 videos are striking for the ease of his travels as well as their reach. Both videos could be tributes to the magnificence of the planet Earth and the architectural wonders of the world, except for the odd man dancing, who interrupts the serenity of jungles, glaciers, and deserts, challenging the silent authority of Easter Island's Moai statues and Egypt's sandstone pharaohs with his stomping feet and swinging arms. The sites themselves offer up no resistance to his appearance or his centrality in the scene. And he doesn't seem to care much about them either: Harding states, "I'll admit that as the dancing video goes, standing in front of the ancient stuff is largely obligatory. . . . But the Taj Mahal? Pyramids? Parthenon? To me, it's just a pile of rocks that doesn't say anything worth saying."[27] With rare exceptions, the evidence of which is banished to the outtakes, Harding seems able to move into these sites comfortably, without hindrance and without any recognition of the appropriateness or inappropriateness of his dancing in the sites he has chosen.[28] When stopped by security for dancing at the Parthenon and briefly jailed for what amounts to belligerence, Harding made clear that, while he wanted access to world heritage sites, he did not bother with the rules governing such access. He recollects his encounter with security on his blog:

"What you are doing is disrespectful."
"I don't think it's disrespectful."
. . .
"It is against the rules."
"What rules? Show me the sign that says No Dancing."
. . .
"Listen to me. The Parthenon may mean nothing to you, but to us it is a
    HOLY RELIGIOUS SITE!"
Oh really? And when's the last time you made sacrifice to Athena?[29]

Harding's voluntary continuous displacement, not to mention his release by Greek authorities despite his refusal to delete the Parthenon footage, stands out as uniquely privileged. He giddily prances from one place to the next, flattening the world with his gregariously stomping feet and claiming connections that involve no labor to produce except his own circulation, a global access and freedom of movement facilitated by the color of his passport and the currency of corporate sponsorship.

In Harding's 2005 and 2006 videos, the globe seems to exist for his own personal enjoyment. He stands outside the world, stomping across the face of the planet-as-playground. Harding features in these films as a godlike proxy, organizing the world around him; there is no coexistence in these videos. What is presented onscreen is, in a rather literal way, Harding's worldview. As Nancy remarks, "a world 'viewed,' a represented world, is dependent on the gaze of a subject of the world [who] cannot itself be in the world."[30] Here Harding is the subject of the world, but even as he offers viewers his own worldview, by placing himself at the center of

Figure 16. Screenshot of Matt Harding dancing at Angkor Wat in the YouTube video series Where the Hell Is Matt? (2005).

the screen, and by extension at the center of the world, the world is not directly the object of his gaze. It is, rather, the gaze of the camera that functions to transform the world into a picture: Harding faces the camera while the camera faces the world.

In addition to framing the world as picture for online viewers, the videos facilitate Harding's transition among places by erasing the act of "getting there" in what digital performance theorist Gabriella Giannachi describes as "hypertextual travel."[31] Giannachi is referring in part to the virtualized travel seemingly made available by internet technologies, which render events and people present-at-a-distance.[32] Hypertextual travel involves "no *real* movement."[33] "Everything happens," Giannachi remarks, "without us needing to go anywhere."[34] Through video editing, Harding creates just such an experience of hypertextual travel for online viewers. The labor of his travel is compressed into an instantaneous scene change in a flat world without obstacles. Imagining the world as picture, Harding appears in each image but is not really a part of any scene. It is as though he has pasted

Figure 17. Screenshot of Matt Harding dancing in Namibia in the YouTube video series Where the Hell Is Matt? (2006).

himself, free of context, onto each background, and differences among sites have been eradicated in preparation for his entrance. Geographic sites have been rendered flat, interchangeable postcard backgrounds for Harding's image. They are a collection of souvenirs, which, representing a tourist's travels, are more important in the diversity of their collection than their intimacy with each locale. Harding generates a flat hierarchy that equalizes but also radically de-differentiates these locations, reducing them to color or flavor. A shot of one could easily be replaced with another without fundamentally changing the work.[35] As highly interchangeable backdrops, any site can suffice to suggest the one-dimensional idea that it's a small world after all.[36]

With the 2005 and 2006 Where the Hell Is Matt? videos, what appear onscreen are postcard pictures of the world as globe—familiar sites and scenes that collect and represent rather than present the world. Their representations of the world are deeply located within globalization, the economic situation in which images and currencies travel the world more freely than human beings. As Nancy remarks, "it is as if there was an intimate connection between capitalistic development and the capitalization of views or pictures of the world."[37] This is an exacerbation of what Heidegger, on whose work Nancy builds, described as the "world picture": "Understood in an essential way, 'world picture' does not mean 'picture of the world' but, rather, the world grasped as picture. . . . The being of beings is sought and found in the representedness of beings. Where, however, beings are *not* interpreted in this way, the world, too, cannot come into the picture—there can be no world picture."[38] It would seem that a capacity to imagine a world depends on an ability to picture it, to represent it as an image. Without this image of the world, the world itself cannot be imagined. This is the problem to which Where the Hell Is Matt? addresses itself: how do we imagine the world? The picture brings a world into formation, but within Nancy's framework, this world as picture is an impoverished world. It is the world as globe—not an expansive worldly world but an abstract totality. How else might a world come into the picture without removing its inhabitants to make room for a single "bumptious foreigner"?[39]

WE ARE THE WORLD

When watching the 2008 Where the Hell Is Matt?, one is immediately struck by its difference from the 2005 and 2006 renditions. Whereas the earlier videos feature Harding, center screen, with other people appearing in the frame only as background or part of the local color, in the 2008 video, residents of the places he visits join him in an enthusiastic display of collective joy at dancing badly. The idea for including others in the videos came from a scene shot in Rwanda for the 2006 video. Harding recalls, "I went out to this village and started dancing, without any explanation of what I was doing. As soon as I started dancing, kids started joining in, and within a couple minutes, all the kids in the village had circled around and we were all dancing together."[40] Also toward the end of the 2006 video, Harding is joined by a small group of goofy dancers in San Francisco, all imitating his punching, swinging, stomping dance, and in Seattle, a couple of children join him in front of the Fremont Troll. These exceptions became the rule for 2008. The change seems to have struck a chord with viewers, since the 2008 video has logged about two and a half times as many views as the 2006 version.[41] "Sometimes Mr. Harding dances alone," notes Charles McGrath in the New York Times, "but more often—and this accounts for much of the video's appeal—he's in the company of others . . . all copying, or trying to, his flailing chicken step."[42]

The first ten scenes connect the 2008 video to its predecessors: situated among prayer flags in Bhutan, in a field of vibrant red tulips in the Netherlands, on a Christmas Island shore full of crabs, at the foot of the Teotihuacán Pyramid of the Sun in Mexico, Harding dances alone. But just shy of a minute into the video, a rapid sequence of shots overwhelms viewers with waves of people rushing from either side to fill the screen. Harding, who remains roughly center screen, is suddenly immersed in crowds of people to the point where he momentarily disappears in the throngs of others who have come to dance their own rendition of his little jig. McGrath continues, "There is something sweetly touching and uplifting about the spectacle of all these different nationalities, people of almost every age and color, dancing along with an uninhibited doofus."[43] Harding invited dancers who had participated in the 2008 video to leave their impressions and connect with each other on his website. Celene exclaims, "Oh, Matt, I have goosebumps, you've done it again! Thank you so much for bringing us the world, one bad dance at a time!"[44] Roemarie writes, "It brought me to happy tears because it is pure joy, no politics, no attachments, no stress, no problems, just people having fun together doing the same thing (dancing badly) at the same time, all over our big beautiful world."[45] Devin Weiss comments, "Your video is truly a beautiful thing expressing how we all are together in this world . . . and all love to Dance!"[46] Comments such as these reflect a desire among participants and viewers to feel globally connected and to imagine themselves within a human community that exceeds national borders. Though Harding remains at the center of the video as the reason for the crowds that gather around him, as McGrath points out, the video's focus on people besides Harding offers a different sense of the world. Instead of dancing alone in front of aesthetically pleasing backdrops, as a tourist might, Harding invites local residents to share the screen with him, and it is their participation that makes the video meaningful to viewers.

Globe Trot, a collaboration between filmmaker Mitchell Rose and choreographer Bebe Miller, with crowdsourced contributions from dancers, filmmakers, and everyday people around the world, opens in a manner similar to how Harding has structured his videos. It begins with environmental sound. A woman walks directly toward the camera on a Stockholm street, but she is a red herring. A man takes his place just off center as the first chord sounds. A second chord deposits viewers in Yokohama, Japan, and a third in Papua New Guinea. A drumbeat adds another layer to the sound track, and the locations come more swiftly, highlighting the differences

Figure 18. Screenshot of Matt Harding dancing with a crowd of participants in Spain in the YouTube video series *Where the Hell Is Matt?* (2008).

among people and peoples, locales and locations. For the first several shots, participants just stand, looking at the camera, letting their presence register with viewers. As with Harding's videos, architecture plays a crucial role in placing the performers, but even more so, because Rose has not labeled the locations, making viewers even more reliant on distinctive landmarks to identify them.[47] Some locations, however, are less recognizable or more abstract. The Eiffel Tower, a pagoda, a village, a farm—*Globe Trot* travels across all sites equally and easily, regardless of their fame or relative anonymity.

Before they could craft *Globe Trot,* Rose and Miller had to recruit participants, inviting others to share in the vision of the film. They first circulated a video describing a very strict protocol to potential contributors and further gave detailed instructions on Rose's website,[48] including images, sample videos, and a downloadable manual describing the requirements in detail. Whereas Harding provided volunteer dancers with his iconic step to organize their participation, Rose and Miller provided volunteer dancers with brief sections of choreographed material. Each participant was assigned to shoot two seconds (four counts) of Miller's choreography on the assumption that, while performing an entire choreographed dance would be difficult for most people, almost anybody could perform two seconds of movement.[49] In his detailed documentation, Rose indicated where the filmmakers should place their cameras in relation to the dancers and where each dancer would need to begin and end the assigned microphrase of movement so that, when Rose edited all of the clips together, not only would the choreography continue seamlessly despite changes in filming locations and performers but each dancer would pick up the phrase in the precise spot onscreen that the previous dancer had just occupied.[50]

Globe Trot focuses less on the geographic locales as such and more on their presumed inhabitants. Although there are some group shots, most of the film focuses on one performer at a time, which has the effect of individuating the participants, who might otherwise be reduced to tokenized presences. An ode to the world and our common humanity in an era of globalization, there are no specific efforts in *Globe Trot* to assure viewers that the performers and places are what they purport to represent. Indeed, some of the participants are international students studying at U.S. universities, and others are tourists traveling abroad. Rather than criticize the film for a lack of "authenticity," a critique predicated on essentialized notions of identity, I find it more useful to consider the film as a reflection of the negotiation between human mobility and representations of cultural belonging. By not disclosing the filming locations in the film itself, as Harding does, Rose allows viewers to make their own judgments about what ethnocultural identities and geopolitical locations the bodies on-screen represent. He does not falsify the filming locations to preserve a direct correlation between person and place, but neither does he call attention to the discontinuities that globe trotting produces. Rose edits together disparate contributions from all over the planet, including Antarctica, to form a cohesive world picture. The final result is a choreography that unfurls across continents, tying scores of people together in their mutual participation in this crowdsourced dance film.

When watching a rough cut of *Globe Trot,* Rose recalls Miller exclaiming "I love people!" which is exactly the response he had hoped for.[51] Similarly, in responses to the 2008 Where the Hell Is Matt? video, participants and viewers comment on Harding's presentation of the world through its people. As seen with participatory and delegated art aesthetics, it should not come as a surprise that people—we ourselves—should be a focus of

Figure 19. Screenshot from *Globe Trot* (2014), directed and edited by Mitchell Rose, choreographed by Bebe Miller. This shot from Papua New Guinea was contributed by Mark Eby and Steven Vele.

Figure 20. Screenshot from *Globe Trot* (2014), directed and edited by Mitchell Rose, choreographed by Bebe Miller. This shot from London, England, was contributed by Nicky Chatfield and Jonathon Vines.

contemporary art. According to Nancy, previous eras in the European intellectual tradition made sense of the world by positioning a god outside of it. But now, the fields of art and philosophy mutually participate in resolving a distinctly postmodern crisis in meaning by making the world itself meaningful. The meaning of the world is, precisely, us, Nancy contends. We are the meaning of the world.

Like Harding and Rose and Miller, media artist Natalie Bookchin turns her attention to the crowd and exhibits their contributions in the single-channel video installation *Mass Ornament* (2009). Whereas Rose's approach enabled him to create a continuous work in which Miller's choreography organized the gestures of contributors in advance of their participation, Bookchin culled videos from YouTube. Using these videos as raw material, she both composed the dancers' bodily movements in relation to each other and choreographed the ways these YouTube clips appeared and moved as multiple small frames on the larger screen. Instead of providing a specific avenue through which movement donors could choose to participate in the project, Bookchin gathered what had been made publicly available online and devised a new composition from the activities in which the performers engage.

Organizing the video clips into similar color palettes and movement themes, Bookchin creates a spectacle for the information age. *Mass Ornament* refers to the essay by Siegfried Kracauer in which he situates the precision dances of the Tiller Girls in a postwar capitalist frenzy of production. If, for Kracauer, "the hands of the factory correspond to the legs of the Tiller Girls,"[52] Bookchin's kick line of YouTube videos comments on the circulation of movement and the repetitiveness of seeming individuality in our own time, as well as the introduction of surveillance technologies into domestic settings. Many fixed cameras peer into many homes as different women in various stages of undress walk into separate frames. A surfeit of women look in mirrors, lean into video and web cameras, pose in front of furniture, face their cameras, and begin to dance. They salsa and belly dance and pop and twerk, offering greater diversity in their movements than either the 2008 Where the Hell Is Matt? or *Globe Trot*. They kick and spin, backbend and handstand. Throughout, Bookchin combines like videos with like—a row of six variations on the yoga pose Natarajasana (dancer's pose) or nine "Single Ladies." Linking these videos side by side seems to be Bookchin's preference, as one might imagine a kick line of dancers linked arm in arm, but the videos also accumulate, and their spatial relationships change the shape of the whole. Sometimes videos even seem to snake across the screen. Bookchin gives shape to what has already been shared, transforming the sharing of others into an image of shared culture and identity.

Bookchin's invocation of Kracauer and sonic references to the Busby Berkeley film *Gold Diggers of 1935* and Leni Riefenstahl's film *The Triumph of the Will*, widely viewed as Nazi propaganda, suggest that her portrait of "us" has different political stakes than the other pieces discussed thus far in this chapter.[53] Bookchin is more ambivalent about the in-common that she screens. In making "us" the subject of *Mass Ornament*, Bookchin raises a host of provocations and questions, not least of which is the extent to which global informational capitalism promotes the domestication of surveillance technologies. If we are the world, Bookchin troubles the economics and politics of such self-regard. Dance scholar Ramsay Burt, for example, observes that *Mass Ornament* is among contemporary dance works that "have a radical edge that prevents them from being absorbed into an abstracted, apoliticized worldview that tends to divert any critical potential

Figure 21. A collage of video clips gathered from YouTube in the single-channel video installation *Mass Ornament* (2009) by Natalie Bookchin. This screenshot is from documentation of the installation on the artist's website, https://bookchin.net/projects/mass-ornament/.

into a too-often platitudinous, universal narrative about emotional experience and the individual's freedom to express this."[54] Burt's critique of shallow contemporary arts discourse could easily apply to *Where the Hell Is Matt?* and *Globe Trot,* which summon emotional responses from viewers in their portrayals of being-together, and which use dance for the purpose of choreographing postpolitical planetary harmony. Still, like *Where the Hell Is Matt?* and *Globe Trot, Mass Ornament* orients viewers toward a larger sociality by making "us" ourselves, as documented and shared via social media, the meaning of the work. This orientation, Burt notes, "can allow beholders to imagine possibilities for renewing the common space for social and political relations."[55]

In his reexamination of the meaning of the world separate from a god as both the condition for and the meaning of human existence, Nancy builds on Heidegger's consideration of *Mitsein,* or the dimension of Being *(Dasein)* that is being-with. Nancy contends that there is no Being as such or for itself. There is only being-with. For Nancy, Being is irreducibly this being-with. There is no existence except with this "with," no self without exposition toward others and especially no self prior to others. Being-with is not an addition to Being, then. Instead, the self, if there is one, *"is nothing but the exposition. . . . It is being-unto-others."*[56] Everything that exists is plural, everything that exists coexists, and because all existence is irreducibly coexistence, Being is sharing in a common world: "the world is the coexistence that puts these existences together."[57] In addition to being-with, Nancy names this irreducible condition of existence being-together, being-in-common, and being singular plural. Each of these terms reflects what Nancy considers irrefutable: that there is only a "we," and that this "we" is not a question of "cohabitation or contamination,"[58] and especially not of communion but of ontology. This being-with is not manifested in adjacency, proximity, or shared space but is a relation without relation, an in-common that is not a common being, as though community were identical to consensus. The in-common is a shared sense that links or "enchains" as world.[59] Hence, for Nancy, the *with* in *being-with* "must be both an *ethos* and a *praxis*."[60] As praxis, this "with" is constantly put into play between us. Although the "with" is the being of existence, it is not presumed as a given but must instead be enacted to create a world, which Nancy describes, among other things, as "an ethos, a *habitus* and an inhabiting: it is what holds to itself and in itself."[61] If being-with and world function as ethos, praxis, and habitus, then world is performative. A world is not made; it is enacted. It is practiced in relation, in the linkages that knot a world together. It is a praxis of non-self-sufficiency that "effects the agent."[62] Just as theorizations of performativity have demonstrated the emergence of meaning from repeated performances and the materially transformative effects of these performances, for example, as regards gender, so too is the world located in the repeated performances of being-with.

THE PERFORMATIVITY OF BEING-WITH

Nancy understands world as ethos, praxis, and habitus. Interpreting this configuration as performative risks expanding the concept of performativity to the point where it is no longer useful. Performativity as an idea has already migrated and evolved substantially since J. L. Austin first theorized a certain class of spoken statements, which he called *performative utterances,* which did not merely describe or report on phenomena but actually introduced a change of state. He remarks, "To name the ship *is* to say (in the appropriate circumstances) the words 'I name &c.' When I say, before the registrar or altar, &c., 'I do,' I am not reporting on a marriage:

I am indulging in it."[63] Provided that a speaker utters a performative under felicitous conditions,[64] speech can transform people and objects. Speech is not merely a container for information to be transmitted between individuals. Speech can be a form of action.

Judith Butler in particular demonstrates the transformative power of language in her example of a doctor declaring "It's a girl!" thus interpellating the child into a matrix of societal norms that give both the declaration and the so-declared body meaning and intelligibility.[65] Gender identity is thus embedded in language, and though statements about gender differences seem only to describe such differences, they actually constitute those differences and further articulate them in gestures and behaviors. "Such acts, gestures, enactments generally construed, are *performative* in the sense that the essence or identity that they otherwise purport to express are *fabrications* manufactured and sustained through corporeal signs and other discursive means."[66] Carrie Noland, among other dance, theater, and performance theorists, takes issue with Butler's conflation of corporeal and discursive domains, arguing that, while bodies may signify, "the gesture and the word inhabit different registers of experience as well as signification."[67] The expressivity of being-together is not limited to discursive signification; other logics also participate in constituting a world or in creating a sense of the world.

Nancy, like Noland, does not overemphasize language and naming as what makes sense, meaning, and world. Instead, he points to *ethos, praxis,* and *habitus.*[68] World is not, however, *poiesis*—a mode of fabrication attributed to the artist who stands outside of a world of her own making. Stated differently, world manifests in moral character, practical action, and bodily disposition, through which world is enacted—not made. Though Nancy speaks of creating the world, he does not speak of world-making, as making suggests finality and completion. Instead, the world is incomplete, inoperative *(désœuvré)*. Enactments of world through *ethos, praxis,* and *habitus* cite previous scripts to remain meaningful, but they continuously bring a world into being through new, incomplete, ongoing action. Again, according to Nancy, the world no longer derives its meaning from a god-creator who made it. Instead, the meaning of the world arises from its inhabitants. We ourselves imagine, create, and sustain the world. A world, that is to say, being-with or being-in-common, is a physical practice and disposition, a performative enactment that presences the world with each enactment of it. We might suggest, employing Virno's language, that the world is virtuosic. It produces nothing other than itself, for no other purpose than itself.[69] The world is a creation "with neither principle nor end nor material other than itself," says Nancy.[70] Performing-world produces world as being-together, as coexistence. Through this performance of the with or together, the world creates a sense of itself as that which, "in the course of being thought, itself become indiscernible from its *praxis*."[71]

That the world is performative rather than *poietic* does not mean that there is no space for artistic representation in generating the space of the we or of being-in-common that the world is.[72] Art holds within its purview the "(re)presentation of one another according to which they are with one another."[73] Maurizio Lazzarato further suggests that "images, signs and statements contribute to allowing the world to happen" and "create possible worlds."[74] Contemporary performance, including the participatory art mentioned earlier, consistently engages the ethos and praxis of being-with constitutive of world. It is not only a matter of representing possible worlds but also of bringing them into being. Undoubtedly, the pieces analyzed in this chapter do represent the world in some way, taking the globe as the focus of their investigation. But this representation is also a doing, a creation of a world by representing it, performing it, and cultivating feeling toward it. The works in this chapter represent the world as a being-together on a global scale, but they also create possible worlds, both the worlds within the world and the world as world (rather than globe). Artistic practices thus have a double capacity, Lazzarato remarks, to "contribute to allowing the possible to emerge . . . and to [contribute to] its realization."[75] As governments withdraw their support from social services, which are turned over to the market, artists reassert community or the in-common as "the foundation of being"[76] that must be created continuously. Only through such infrastructure-building procedures can we repair or extend "world-sustaining relations."[77]

As praxis, being-with presences world, a shared sense that gives meaning to existence, but this sharing cannot result in communion, lest a community achieve nothing more than its own annihilation.[78] At the same time, existence is impossible without a common world, and globalization undoes this very world as common and as sense of the common. Instead of a world, we find a globe. It is not a question of reversing processes of globalization so as to return to nationalist or tribal modes of belonging and affiliation but of turning the globe into a common world. But a world, and the being-with that presences that world, must remain unfinished. The world must remain incomplete or unworked *(désœuvré)*, inoperative or in process. Unity is not the goal of the continuous enactment of being-with. Nancy's refusal of communion recalls Jacques Rancière's discussion of consensus as that which covers over the disruptive politics of dissensus. As the engine of political action, dissensus tears through the fabric of the world and its particular distribution of the sensible; consensus shifts shared sensibilities and covers over these tears to bring an end to political action. Nancy, however, does not focus so intently on such violent ruptures, because for him, the question is how to regain sense, not how to redistribute it. Indeed, the creation of a world through shared sense would create problems for Rancière's politics, since such a world would tend toward consensus. It is necessary, therefore, to emphasize the plural within Nancy's singular plural. The world is the sum of all possible worlds, but this does not mean that they are in agreement. "The unity of the world is not one: it is made of a diversity, including disparity and opposition."[79] Perhaps this is why Nancy avers, "Being is together, and it is not a togetherness."[80] Togetherness suggests unity or communion rather than being-together as singular plural. Rejecting both globalization, on one hand, and communion, on the other, Nancy situates the world, and *mondialisation,* on the boundary between them.

Teetering on the edge of both globalization and communion, how and where is *mondialisation* possible? A world is a "genuine place," says Nancy.[81] Being-together is to be in the same time and the same place, with interpersonal as well as spatial relations holding a world together as being-with or being-in-common. But what is the place of this together if it is also "the distinctness of places taken together"?[82] What does being-together-in-place look like? Where the Hell Is Matt?, *Globe Trot,* and *Mass Ornament* require technological intervention to join here with there in crafting a space of the common, or a space of being-together-in-place, on a global scale. Harding joins the globe together by traveling from site to site to perform and record his same dance, which he then edits together into individual videos. *Globe Trot* sutures people and sites together in a single choreographic sequence that unfolds around the globe as a collective endeavor. *Mass Ornament* multiplies the frames within the space of the screen to bring many dancers into view simultaneously. In each of these pieces, the dancers are linked together by the choreography. At the same time, in each of these cases, the choreography is completely uprooted; rather than being grounded in the dancers or the sites in which they dance, the choreography passes over and through their bodies without regard to who performs or where. Even when the dancers bring their specific places with them into the frame, the ability of the choreography to appear in excess of any particular body or space allows it to float as an abstraction outside of any particular instance as a commonly accessible set of gestures and movements.[83] But this choreography, passing through and across the bodies of the performers, renders the linkages among participants apparent and thus makes the in-common visible. Where the Hell Is Matt?, *Globe Trot,* and *Mass Ornament* reach toward a planetary being-in-common that can only be articulated in a representational space in which the incommensurable can co-appear. In this representational space, viewers gain a sense of the world rather than a picture of an abstract globe.

Harding's 2008 video initiates the exploration of a sense of the world, which he more fully develops in his 2012 video. In a few scenes, for example, in Papua New Guinea and South Africa, participants dance alongside Harding in their own style rather than adopting his, allowing for participation to be multiple rather than filtered through Harding's own movement vocabulary. They maintain their individuality while being in proximity to Harding. But in Gurgaon, India, embedded in a hired troupe of Bollywood dancers,[84] Harding momentarily arrests his own style of dancing to join in theirs. Deviating from his well-known aesthetic, Harding makes a radical gesture in letting go of his famous stomping step. For six beats, timed exactly to the music, he swaps out his swinging elbows for their diagonally stretched limbs, his fists for their mudras. In unison, their right legs extend and retract as their arms do the same. Soaring vocals and percussive chords amplify their movement: (right) out in out in, (left) out in. In previous videos, Harding was able to make space for others in the frame, but in 2008, he makes space for their gestures in his own body. In this way, Harding demonstrates a form of being-with that moves beyond proximity or adjacency toward an ethos, praxis, and habitus that enchain his body, through movement, to the Bollywood dancers surrounding him. Harding implicates himself in the gestures of others and, in so doing, links himself to the dancers whose gestures he incorporates, and without entirely abandoning his social location, he begins to share in their sense of the world.

SENSING A WORLD (FROM A GLOBE)

Sense is social and cultural. It is world-forming, and it encompasses but also exists beyond language. Media theorist Laura Marks glosses the senses as "a source of social knowledge,"[85] and film theorist Steven Shaviro suggests that sensuous perception of the world is meaningful without reducing sensory "data" to "self-conscious awareness or positive knowledge."[86] Anthropologist C. Nadia Seremetakis similarly describes the senses as media for the "involuntary disclosure of meaning [that is] *not* reducible to language."[87] To have a sense of the world, then, is to have an affective sense, a feeling of meaningfulness that is experienced without requiring verbal articulation but which is sensed in common. This is the task Nancy argues we are charged with: to create the world or a symbolization of the world from an "unworld."[88] This world-forming[89] "can only be a struggle—of posing the following [question] to each gesture, each conduct, each *habitus* and each *ethos*: How do you engage the world?"[90] Such is the terrain that Harding's 2012 video begins to explore, that *One Day on Earth the Music Video* takes on with particular rigor as it enacts the world by screening a sense of the world, and that *All Is Not Lost* approaches as a worldwide archive of feeling. In each piece, a community or world holds together through linkages among its inhabitants, where belonging is sharing an affective sense that is the sense of the world, a sense of community or of the in-common.

David Pogue of the *New York Times* calls Harding's 2012 video a "masterpiece," noting that, because he learns some of the dances of the countries he visits, "there's a feeling of collaboration, of immersion."[91] Shots from each location last only a few seconds, so the editing is extremely important in what vision of global modernity is crafted for viewers. "The goal was to make two years' worth of improvised flailing look like it was meticulously planned from the start."[92] Whereas he had previously performed his same stomping dance in each locale, irrespective of the location or appropriateness, treating each site as an interchangeable background, Harding gradually moves over the course of his films to a more considered form of participation. In conversation with Pogue, Harding notes that for the 2012 video, he sought advice from choreographers Aiko Kinoshita of Seattle, Washington, and Trish Sie, who made her name choreographing music videos for the band OK Go. He played the Harmonix video game *Dance Central* to "learn the nuances of some well-known moves," and then the other dancers contributed about half of the final dance movements.[93] As a result, the 2012 video has very little of Harding's familiar bouncy jig. Instead, he begins to dance with those whom he calls upon to share in the world of his films.

The first shots show Harding learning movements from other people: standing still, facing the camera in Rwanda, trying flamenco *bracero* (arm movements) in Spain, stepping through waltz foot patterns in Austria, attempting cheerleading in the United States and contemporary ballet in Syria. The next scenes show Harding teaching choreography to his hosts: disco arms in Papua New Guinea, leg crosses and finger snaps in North Korea. As the song lyrics begin, Harding and five others in Beirut advance toward the camera, snapping their fingers as they step, like the Jets in *West Side Story*. Subsequent scenes alternate between Harding trying to perform in codified movement styles from around the world and others joining him in simple choreography. Sometimes Harding even sheds his characteristic polo shirts and khaki shorts and adopts the clothing associated with a particular form or culture, for example, parts of a mask in South Africa,[94] a *thobe* in Saudi Arabia, a *pa'u* in Hawai'i, and a tuxedo in Austria.

In stark contrast to Harding's previous videos, in the 2012 Where the Hell Is Matt? video, all scenes are group scenes. He attempts to share in the gestures of others and thereby to share in their sense of the world, a world that may be in conflict with his own worldview but which difference he nevertheless attempts to broker with his body. In turn, he invites participants to share in his movements. A sequence of shots alternates between gathered crowds reaching upward diagonally toward screen left or toward screen right, and they seem not only to follow on from each other like a wave in a sports arena on a global scale but actually to reach or grasp toward each other in a gesture of support and embrace across the planet. In these moments, the choreography of the edited images suggests that populations across the planet share a sensibility and an orientation toward each other.

Figure 22. Screenshot of Matt Harding embodying a few Bollywood movements while dancing with a professional troupe in the YouTube video series Where the Hell Is Matt? (2012).

Figure 23. Screenshot of Matt Harding teaching modified disco moves to a group of men in Papua New Guinea in the YouTube video series Where the Hell Is Matt? (2012).

To allow a world to be performed in the place of a globe, Harding steps back from the role he previously occupied as proverbial king of the world. Beginning in the 2008 video and fully in the 2012 video, he takes turns following and leading, bringing his body into alignment, as far as possible, with others. Allowing these new gestures to sit uncomfortably in his body, Harding disrupts his own corporeal consensus, which was predicated on his privileged mobility. In submitting himself to the gestures and movements of others, he concedes that to exist in a world is to coexist. Without others, in Nancy's conception, there is only the abstract globe, a world without world. In learning as well as teaching new gestures and movements, Harding and the other participants link their bodies together choreographically, generating, as well as representing, a becoming-worldwide. Whatever discord might have existed in 2011 when Harding was recording, when the tensions of the Arab Spring were spilling into protest movements around the world, it disappears into the smiling faces of hundreds of people performing seemingly inconsequential dance moves. *One Day on Earth the Music Video* and *All Is Not Lost* similarly set themselves the task of generating the world as they represent it, and they also employ the contributions of the crowd to reflect a planetary reach.

On October 10, 2010 (10.10.10), November 11, 2011 (11.11.11), and December 12, 2012 (12.12.12), documentary filmmakers in every country recorded footage of whatever was happening wherever they were on that day. Participants uploaded their geotagged videos to http://www.oneday onearth.org/, where online viewers can see all submissions for each of the three years.[95] Each time, Ruddick's team pored through thousands of hours of footage to assemble a film from the contributed clips. In addition to a theatrically released film, footage for the 2012 film was edited as a music video. DJ Cut Chemist culled sounds from the *One Day on Earth* video clips and organized them into a music track, and screendance artist Cari Ann Shim Sham* edited the accompanying images as a music video. The music video (as well as parts of the feature-length film) draws more from video art aesthetics than from conventional music video[96] or documentary film. Because the music video is organized around sound, namely, music, the onscreen images reflect the circumstances in which these musical sounds were created, including dances, festivals, and parades.

A form of music visualization, *One Day on Earth the Music Video* reveals its own underlying structure. The images appear onscreen when their attached sounds are heard. For example, when a mouth harp sounds, its Mongolian player appears onscreen; when an electric guitar cuts in, its Alabaman owner appears. As instruments and sounds layer in the musical composition, the relevant images are screened, allowing viewers to identify the sounds with their sources. The images in the music video do more than just mirror the musical structure, however. The pairing is not always exact, and video clips unrelated to the soundscape are interspersed with images that manifest a clear correlation. Shim Sham* has a background in tap dance, which has likely informed her approach to editing the music video in such a way that the images engage the music in a multilayered conversation that illuminates aspects of the musical structure while also playing with and riffing on the sound track. The screen is, at times, divided horizontally or vertically in thirds. Sometimes as many as six distinct scenes appear within the frame, while sometimes a single scene will fill the entire screen. Not all of the sound clips and visual images are of music making or dancing conventionally defined, but, like Bookchin's *Mass Ornament,* the overall composition is both musical and choreographic. Scenes of a father and son pounding their woodworking tools in Afghanistan and women hammering their tall pestles into a mortar to prepare food are interspersed among other scenes of a North Korean dance festival, Maasai men jump dancing in Kenya, and a dancer voguing in New York. The images help to locate the sounds, which DJ Cut Chemist has composed into a global mélange. Without the onscreen images, the diversity of musical-cultural contributions could easily pass unnoticed as merely another example of global sampling in music production. Together, the music and images compose a sense of planetary humanity without reducing the distinctiveness of each cultural situation into a global hegemony.

What is interesting about this film is that, rather than forging global connection through the travels of a single individual like Where the Hell Is Matt?, or crafting such connectivity by subsuming others into a predetermined choreography like *Globe Trot,* the entire composition has emerged after the fact in postproduction, thus offering an image of the singular plural that maintains the singularity of the participants. Whereas *Globe*

Trot and each of the Where the Hell Is Matt? videos construct their vision of humanity or sense of the world sequentially, *One Day on Earth the Music Video* is more like *Mass Ornament* in its mutual emphasis on simultaneity and sequence. Shim Sham* has found a place for each body, movement, and location in the space of the screen, which, as an abstract space, supports the co-presence of many scenes from around the world simultaneously, and the images are also linked by the complementarity of the sounds they produce. It is not about fitting the participants to a predetermined goal but rather about fitting the end result to its contributors. *One Day on Earth the Music Video* is a clear example of being-together without togetherness, of enacting a world that does not reduce its inhabitants to the same. "Each existent belongs to more groups, masses, networks, or complexes than one first recognizes. . . . The existent does not have its own consistency and subsistence by itself: but it has it as the sharing of a community [that] is cosubstantial with the existent: to each and to all, to each as to all, to each insofar as all."[97] *One Day on Earth the Music Video* gestures toward a common space where the globe can gather itself and make-sense or make-world. This is not only a representation of the world or symbolization of the world but a world as self-composition. Performing-world produces world.

DJ Cut Chemist has sampled the globe's sounds, and Shim Sham* has edited its images, but their curatorial and organizational work amounts to an arrangement of senses of the world, leading to a world-sense, rather than a coherent and complete representation of the world as globe. Whereas the full-length film mediates viewers' experience of the world through language and narrative, namely, a story of life cycles and the interconnectedness of beings, the music video advances no narrative. It instead offers a sensory world of sound and movement, music and dance, that works through what Nancy describes as the syntactic logic of sense.[98] Sense can enchain a world in which incommensurability functions as its sole common measure,[99] through coappearance in a "space of sense [which] is a common space."[100] This common space is created as it is enacted audiovisually, and DJ Cut Chemist and Shim Sham* have orchestrated this global cacophony into a sensuous composition.

Like sense, affect has been theorized as social and as experienced to the side of language. Indeed, sense and affect cover significant shared territory.

Figure 24. Screenshot from *One Day on Earth the Music Video* (2012), directed by Kyle Ruddick, edited by Cari Ann Shim Sham*, with music arranged by DJ Cut Chemist. Content is from *One Day on Earth* (2012), directed by Kyle Ruddick.

Figure 25. Screenshot from *One Day on Earth the Music Video* (2012), directed by Kyle Ruddick, edited by Cari Ann Shim Sham*, with music arranged by DJ Cut Chemist. Content is from *One Day on Earth* (2012), directed by Kyle Ruddick.

It is through affective intensity that performance practices can cultivate—by enacting—fluencies of feeling that span emotional, sensorial, and intellectual domains, as well as feelings of being-with or being-in-common. Feminist theorist Sara Ahmed argues that feelings or emotions align "bodily space with social space" in affective economies[101] and that, as a result, we must examine how emotions function "to mediate the relationship . . . between the individual and the collective."[102] She argues that affective objects, in particular, those societally designated as happy, "might play a crucial role in shaping our near sphere, the world that takes shape around us."[103] In performing the world as happy object, *One Day on Earth the Music Video* and other pieces examined in this chapter bring the world itself into viewers' near-sphere and sensitize viewers to the world in a positive affective register rather than representing the world as a source of threat and uncertainty from which to retreat.

This is likewise the work of *All Is Not Lost,* which explicitly took form against the backdrop of era-defining crisis and catastrophe. On March 11, 2011, a 9.0 magnitude earthquake off the coast of Japan caused a severe tsunami that devastated its port cities. Coastal populations were ordered to evacuate, but many people remained—either unable or unwilling to leave their homes. Some of the residents began shooting video of the tsunami engulfing houses and roads, depositing fishing vessels in the middle of their towns, sweeping cars and even buildings out of the way. As terrible as the tsunami was, its devastation did not match what was to follow in its wake: the nuclear meltdown and release of radioactive material from the Fukushima power plant in the worst nuclear disaster since Chernobyl. As news reports updated viewers on explosions at the plant and the release of toxic radiation, there was a concrete understanding that these events were not isolated to Japan but impacted the whole world. Indeed, ocean currents would soon deposit debris and contaminated waste on far-away shores. In the weeks following the tsunami, the band OK Go began a collaboration with Google and the modern dance company Pilobolus that gestured toward a need to process this catastrophe and also for people around the world to express sympathy and support for those who had lost so much so quickly.

Directed by choreographer Trish Sie and performed by the members of OK Go and Pilobolus, *All Is Not Lost* is an interactive music video.[104] Band member Andy Ross explains, "*All Is Not Lost* is a message to the world. But at the heart of this project is a love letter to Japan. . . . We started the project in the weeks right after the Japanese earthquake, and it was hard at that time, I think, for the globe to express the sympathy and empathy we all felt for the Japanese at that time."[105] Dan Konopka adds, "Part of what I think we're hoping to achieve through this work is a kind of mediated intimacy where people are able to express their feelings and their desire to be part of a community of feeling."[106] The community of feeling that *All Is Not Lost* crafts is a distinctly global community, built of people around the world who were moved by this disaster.

For *All Is Not Lost,* the members of OK Go boldly don Pilobolus's familiar unitards—here in aqua—and join with them in shape-shifting contortions. The musicians and dancers are filmed from below through a glass surface, creating kaleidoscopic effects in the style of Busby Berkeley,[107] whose work served as an inspiration. Pilobolus is known for stacking dancers' bodies, moving into and out of positions in such a way as to create fantastical images. Here the dancers and band members spend more time standing and sitting in horizontal relation to one another than vertically on top of one another. Powered by HTML5 as an official Chrome Experiment,[108] *All Is Not Lost* begins by populating a computer user's screen with several browser windows that move through the screen space seemingly of their own accord and that occasionally form a grid to amplify the dancers' kaleidoscopic effects. In addition to forming abstract designs with their bodies, the musicians and dancers form letters with their feet, spelling out parts of the key refrain from the song: "all is lost / all is not lost"[109] Users can close the windows or move them to new locations onscreen, but this form of interaction interferes with the piece's overall visual aesthetic as well as the performers' danced messages of support.

If the media industry has a tendency to represent the contemporary world through images of death and destruction that emphasize affective registers of shock and dismay, which may or may not provoke empathic identification and action from viewers,[110] the pieces in this chapter promote images of a worldly together that bypass or short-circuit realities of violence and horror in favor of being-with. Theirs is a hopeful composition of being-in-common that covers over the conflict and struggle that is being-with, but they nevertheless optimistically extend the possibility of

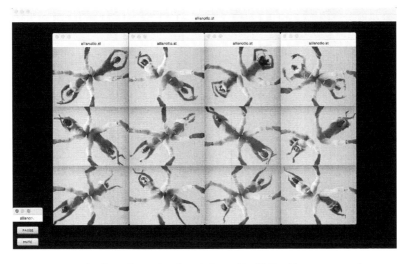

Figure 26. Screenshot from *All Is Not Lost* (2011), directed by OK Go with movement and choreography by Pilobolus and Trish Sie. Produced by Paracadute and Google.

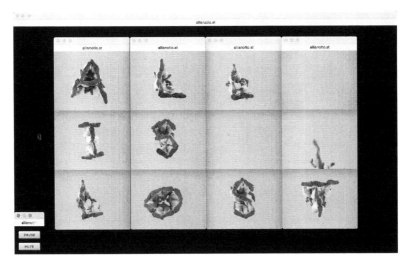

Figure 27. Screenshot from *All Is Not Lost* (2011), directed by OK Go with movement and choreography by Pilobolus and Trish Sie. Produced by Paracadute and Google.

a world in common across, and not despite, difference. *All Is Not Lost* invites users to participate in creating this world in common in a moment of catastrophe. User contributions are minor in terms of overall composition—a typed message of support, for example—but significant in terms of affective intensity. In *All Is Not Lost,* each message is performed for its author first, who then chooses whether to share the message with others. However, there is no mechanism for the intended recipients to respond, so even as contributors to the music video evidence their participation in a global community of feeling, the work's affective dimension is located primarily in the act of contributing and not in receiving an acknowledgment or response to that contribution. The intimacy of *All Is Not Lost* is therefore self-referential, an effect of reflecting back its repository of affects to contributors. This does not detract from participant experiences of this work as meaningful or cathartic for those who wish to post their messages of encouragement. But, as critics of participatory art have pointed out, it may stage a false relationality that disguises its indulgent individualism, promoting feeling in the place of action. It remains questionable, then, whether *All Is Not Lost* can generate a sense of the world from viewers' affective orientation and whether a sense of the world can be sustained in the absence of such crises as the Fukushima nuclear disaster.

Where the Hell Is Matt? from 2012, *One Day on Earth the Music Video,* and *All Is Not Lost* all offer a sense of the world as a sense of interconnectedness or a feeling of being-together, a social sense or social intelligence embedded in the ontological condition of being-with. Sensing a world is not only to sense one's way through a physical existence and surroundings—clothing, coffee cups, cars, and so on—but to feel the world as a feeling-together, to feel the links that hold a world together through the ties that bind—constantly tying and untying themselves as Nancy describes. To feel the world or sense the world as world is thus to share an affective orientation to the common, to inhabit the world as a common world. This orientation must be shared; otherwise, there is no worldly world because there is no being-with, and all that remains is the world as globe. There is no world without others, there is no sense without others, there is no meaning without others. To make-sense is to make-shared or make-common. And yet, a sense of the world must not eliminate incommensurability, which, in contrast, globalization requires.

If a sense of the world is not shared as unified affect or as the same orientation, if a sensorium is not shared, but yet shared sense is what creates a world, how, then, to create a world? How are incommensurables linked together in a common world that maintains both their singularity and their plurality? Or as Nancy asks, "how to do justice, not only to the whole of existence, but to existences, taken together but distinctly and in a discontinuous way . . . as a multiple together . . . ?"[111] The 2012 Where the Hell Is Matt? video, *One Day on Earth the Music Video,* and *All Is Not Lost* all engage in the project of performing-world and affectively sensitizing viewers to a sense of the world, but *One Day on Earth the Music Video* addresses itself to precisely the question of a "multiple together." It does not impose a single choreography that can organize the world around it[112] but allows an exposition of the world in co-motion,[113] exhibiting shared capacities for sound and movement rather than shared vocabularies of music and dance.

Like *Mass Ornament,* the world as being-with screened in *One Day on Earth the Music Video* is presented as both a simultaneous and sequential together—many performers appear onscreen at the same time, but not all possible performers. The music video includes a wide representation from many individuals and many parts of the planet, which, by extension, implies a representation of humanity writ large. Yet, its inclusive imagery does not attempt to exhaustively represent all of the Earth's inhabitants, which could only result in an image of the world as an abstract globe—as a chart or as data points that reductively eliminate "the difference of singularities"[114] mutually engaged in enacting or producing a sense of the world. Instead, the music video sustains a synecdochal relationship between *its* world and *the* world through what Virno describes as the "individualization of the universal, of the generic, of the shared experience," that constitutes the many or the multitude.[115] The planetary reach of *One Day on Earth the Music Video* supersedes that of other examples in this chapter, offering a world picture much different from theirs. Rather than a dancing subject organizing the world in advance and outside of the world, or a single choreography that organizes all the participants in a single worldly composition, in *One Day on Earth the Music Video,* a visual choreography and sound score emerge from the worldwide participation of a multitude.

Through their contributions, the planetary crowd enacts the world as a performative achievement.

The pieces explored in this chapter are global in scope, but by turning to the creativity of the crowd, they work toward the creation of a common world. They employ the crowd as a microcosm of the world, to which the labor of creating or performatively enacting a work and a world is delegated. This compositional approach, which relies on the voluntary labor of the crowd, leverages the realities of economic and cultural globalization to create a world from a globe by creating a world from a crowd. As these pieces show, the world is not given; it is enacted or performed in relation, in being-with or being-in-common. By bringing the world close, they initiate performative transformations of a global world into a worldly world. These pieces, to greater and lesser degrees, enact the world by feeling-, dancing-, sensing-, performing-world as together, thus generating a shared sense of the world. Performing-world on a global scale, these pieces not only offer representations of the globe as a world but, in that representation, contribute to the emergence of world from globe, of *mondialisation* from *globalization*.

Still, Harding's series of videos shows that, while he moves in the direction of *mondialisation* over the course of his films, that does not preclude ongoing support of operations of globalization, as becomes apparent in a more recent tour of the globe. Having made coexistence a focus, and seemingly the terminus of his videos, Harding realized that participants' desire to be part of something bigger than themselves is a desire that can be monetized. After his corporate-sponsored and self-funded trips, Harding crowdfunded a 2016 dancing tour of the globe, raising nearly $150,000 from more than four thousand fans via Kickstarter.[116] Incentives for patronage included Harding's promise to film in the city with the most funds pledged and Harding giving personalized tours of Bhutan—travel expenses not included.[117] In other words, Harding moved from soliciting volunteered labor from participants in his previous videos to soliciting funds from those who wish to participate in the 2016 experience. He successfully transformed fans' affective investment in the Where the Hell Is Matt? concept into a financial investment. In a particularly acute example of the collapse of labor and leisure, fans were willing to sponsor Harding's travels in the hope that they might also be able to donate their labor in the form of their participation, without which Harding's concept and brand could no longer function.[118] Enacting the world as worldly thus offers no total or final escape from the maneuvers of globalization, which can reassert the logic of finance in places where it had seemed to give way to *mondialisation.* The crowd, whether local or planetary in scope, must thus engage in the continuous, ongoing, and infinished work of performatively producing the world through the praxis of being-with to preserve and create alternatives to the unworld of globalization.

This same tension between world and globe manifests with different language in the following chapter, where the distinction between dance as a practice of cultural belonging and dance as a catalog of gestural belongings has distinct market implications. Dance as an expression of belonging assumes membership within a community, or world, in which dances, gestures, and movements can circulate freely as gifts—that is to say, as shared embodied objects that knit a group together as participants both share in and contribute to a corporeal common. When shared beyond the confines of a community, for example, as dance videos circulate online, they can be abstracted and extracted from their contexts, or the worlds that give them meaning. Such abstractions facilitate the misrecognition of danced gifts for a universally available given, a common inheritance available to all for mining and monetization. Issues of belonging, credit, and debt and the sociality of dance as gift thus figure prominently in the final chapter.

CHAPTER FOUR

Screen Sharing

◆ ◆ ◆ ◆

Dance as Gift of the Common

In November 2013, pop star Pharrell Williams released a twenty-four-hour online music video, *24 Hours of Happy*.[1] It features four hundred people dancing along the streets of Los Angeles alone or in small groups, moving in their own individual styles while lip-syncing to Pharrell's continuously looping song "Happy," written for the animated feature film *Despicable Me 2*. In addition to being a durational work made for the web, *24 Hours of Happy* is a clock; mousing over the screen reveals a time-telling feature. Every four minutes, the length of Pharrell's song, the spotlight shines on a new performer or group that has a single take to walk, sashay, turn, stomp, fist-pump, jump, kick, bounce, and snap their way down sidewalks and across streets. Throughout the twenty-four-hour video, there are cameo appearances by familiar faces, such as Steve Carrell, Alex Wong, Magic Johnson, and Ana Ortiz. At the top of each hour, Pharrell himself appears dance-walking through alleyways, boxing rings, and bowling alleys and singing with a gospel choir. Prompted by the lyrics to "clap along if that's what you wanna do," the performers collectively sidestep and sidewind around neighborhoods and businesses from sunrise to sunset—and then they keep going.

A few dancers perform steps that reveal expertise in a dance style, such as tap, ballet, or popping, but the majority of participants represent the dancing abilities of the general population. A Steadicam operated by Jon Beattie tracks their movement, which is sometimes mundane, occasionally on point, and frequently delightful. The continuously receding camera forces them to keep pace, and the emphasis on the dancers' forward motion shapes the movement vocabulary available, filtering all gestures—however stage, street, or silly—through the lens of pedestrian locomotion. The only edits appear at the conclusion of each iteration of the song. The camera points skyward or at the floor to set up the next take, smoothing transitions between each performance. The result is a never-ending music video without obvious cuts. Recalling the hyperdances discussed in chapter 1, video controls allow viewers to pause/play and fast-forward or rewind through different scenes, and the work includes information about the production team, participants, and view count. But *24 Hours of Happy* also exceeds the capabilities of hyperdance, being filmed in public spaces and circulated online, as we saw with dance in public in chapter 2, and incorporating contributions from the crowd, as we saw in chapter 3. Thus *24 Hours of Happy* is a fitting piece for the concluding chapter of this book.

Made for sharing, the participatory elements of *24 Hours of Happy* situate the work distinctly within a social media era. Viewers can share a moment from the video on their social media accounts, comment on any of the scenes, and, of course, purchase the music track on iTunes. In this chapter, I focus on additional ways in which *24 Hours of Happy* is shared: the independent artist Anne Marsen from the online film *Girl Walk//All Day* discussed in chapter 2 accused Pharrell of plagiarizing the concept for the twenty-four-hour music video, Pharrell's fans re-created short versions of the music video and posted videos of themselves to sites such as YouTube, and designers Julie Fersing and Loïc Fontaine have, in turn, created a website

Figure 28. Screenshot of a woman dancing in Los Angeles's Union Station from *24 Hours of Happy* (2013), featuring Pharrell Williams, directed by We Are from LA, produced by Iconocast Interactive.

Figure 29. Screenshot of a man dancing on a Los Angeles street from *24 Hours of Happy* (2013), featuring Pharrell Williams, directed by We Are from LA, produced by Iconocast Interactive.

called We Are Happy From to aggregate the distributed fan-produced content into a single dedicated site. As the proliferation of online "Happy" phenomena shows, as dance circulates through social media, the boundaries between theft, appropriation, sharing, homage, participation, and fandom blur significantly.

In *Spreadable Media*, Henry Jenkins and his coauthors suggest that commercial and cultural appropriative tendencies are embedded as fundamental flaws in Web 2.0 logic, which "transforms the social 'goods' generated through interpersonal exchanges into 'user-generated content'"[2] that can be taken up and used by anyone—including and especially those who stand to profit financially. But the traffic in images goes the other direction too, they contend, since "audiences often use the commodified and monetized content of commercial producers as raw material for their social interaction."[3] This dynamic provides a core tension that motivates my analysis throughout this chapter: the monetization of a person's or group's creative labor by industry, the reclamation of commercial products and images by individuals and communities, and the debates over cultural access and ownership that result. In the field of dance, the collision of music video and social media offers ready examples of this multisided, multisited phenomenon, where dancers upload material to the internet, which pop artists scour for inspiration for their music video routines, and which fans then reperform in their own online videos.

Imitation and replication lie at the heart of how dance travels. In considering how dance steps and dance practices circulate through digital media, fundamental questions regarding the nature of dance arise: can dances or steps be owned, and if they are not material objects, how is that ownership expressed? How does one give or receive movement? As anthropologist Michael Taussig observes in *Mimesis and Alterity: A Particular History of the Senses,* "you can't easily trade a language or steal a squint or a strange motion. But what you can do is imitate them if you want to or have to."[4] Imitating movement has very practical consequences for dancers whose movement innovations circulate beyond their spheres of influence and without attribution, for choreographers who have been unable to copyright their stage-based works, as well as for the dance enthusiasts who revel in the supposed universality and universal accessibility of dance. That dance travels via mimicry is no small thing. We saw in chapter 3 how Matt Harding progressively made room in his own body for the gestures of others as an indication of goodwill and a developing orientation toward a world rather than an abstract globe. This chapter furthers the consideration of what it means to share in the gestures of others with emphases on dance as gift, the relations of reciprocity that gifts are presumed to foster, and how movement communities negotiate the refusal of reciprocity. What is the difference between what we take as given and what we receive as gift?

Here I focus on the intensification of neoliberal economic logics in the early twenty-first century that encourages, on one hand, an ideology of free giving that obscures social and deferred costs and, on the other hand, encourages the monetization of what appears to be given or made freely available. Contemporary entrepreneurial activities mine collective archives and compel computer users to donate their personal data and the like in exchange for access to online services. We need only look at the success of Facebook or Google to understand "free" as a business model. In his parsing of sharing and pseudo-sharing behaviors on social networking sites (SNSs), business and marketing scholar Russell Belk observes that "the ubiquitous 'share' button and invitations to share from the SNS are best regarded as nicely packaged invitations to provide content to the site, encourage more participants, and in so-doing provide information that can be sold to advertisers, marketers, and research firms."[5] Gift economies directly participate in this logic of financialization, which, dance and political theorist Randy Martin has argued, "brings people together only to seem to take away what they thought they possessed."[6] Dance, as Anthea Kraut acknowledges, may simultaneously participate in gift and market economies.[7] These economies are not antithetical to each other, but each suggests proximity or distance among participants in a relationship of exchange, or the worlds in which they participate. The convergence of gift and market economies complicates perceptions of inclusivity and exclusivity, rights of access versus those of reuse or reproduction, and expanding gestural repertoires in a corporeal common as dances travel from screen to screen and body to body.

In this chapter, I offer examples from approximately 2009 to 2016 to propose that dance circulates in digital cultures as a gift but that the content of this gift belongs to a common. As dances travel beyond the communities that provide them with context, questions of cultural theft and appropriation arise, particularly where artists and entrepreneurs fail to give credit to others for their contributions. Throughout the chapter, I consider Pharrell's *24 Hours of Happy* as well as fan responses to the long-form music video and the repackaging of those fan responses by others. I also analyze questions of appropriation and what I call infelicitous acts of transfer through the examples of Karen X. Cheng's video *Girl Learns to Dance in a Year* (2013) and the online profile video *This Amazing Girl Mastered Dubstep Dancing by Just Using YouTube* (2016) featuring a young dancer, Adilyn Malcolm, both of whom claim a space for themselves as dancing autodidacts. Fan engagement with music videos like *Michael Jackson's Thriller* (1983) and dance video games like the Dance Central series provide avenues through which dance movements circulate beyond specific communities of practice and beyond any agreed-upon parameters that govern the corporeal common from which community members draw and to which they contribute. The place of these media within the global market of American popular culture facilitates the transfer of gestural information they contain.

When dances travel without authorship, attribution, or a sense of participation within a community, a decontextualization that is key to how dances circulate through digital spaces, they become positioned within a corporeal common that ostensibly can be mined by anyone. In my analysis of the 2011 controversy between American pop singer Beyoncé Knowles and Belgian choreographer Anne Theresa De Keersmaeker, as well as a 2014 rehearsal video by American choreographer Alexandra Beller that went viral, I examine how both artists and entrepreneurs obscure sources of their creative material to favor their own authorial position and how De Keersmaeker and Beller in particular responded to challenges to their authorship. A principal concern throughout the chapter is the way that the loss of local specificity is crucial to dance's broad accessibility and marketability, which creates a tension between dance as an expression of cultural belonging and as a commodity. Alternatively, positing dance as gift of the common sustained through the social ties and mutual indebtedness of practitioners may help to work against what I call infelicitous acts of transfer. My aim in this chapter is neither to advocate nor to dismiss dance as a common-pool resource but to grapple with how dance artists, practitioners, and fans leverage different corporeal commons and how the structuring concepts of credit and debt that define an era of financialization may be recuperated for understanding dance as a gift of the common.

INFELICITOUS ACTS OF TRANSFER

A few months after *24 Hours of Happy* premiered, Anne Marsen, who starred in the 2011 independent online film *Girl Walk//All Day,* accused Pharrell of pinching *Girl Walk*'s concept and posted a side-by-side video comparing scenes from the two pieces to substantiate her claim.[8] As evidence, she included a scene from *24 Hours of Happy* in which a man sports a colorful wind-breaker similar to Marsen's; scenes in which Pharrell kicks his heels and snaps his fingers; and additional scenes of participants fan-kicking their legs, dancing in pairs, or flailing about on the street. Bloggers, of course, quickly offered up their own opinions of whether Pharrell's team was engaged in creative plagiarism and if, once again, the entertainment industry had gobbled up the innovations of independent artists only to pass them off as their own.[9] Philosopher Alva Noë offered his own take on the controversy for National Public Radio, suggesting that Marsen's claims of plagiarism were specious: "Nobody stole any steps. They didn't need to. The steps were everyone's already to start with."[10] Without question, both *24 Hours of Happy* and *Girl Walk//All Day* certainly participate in the same aesthetic moment and share key traits. Just as *Girl Walk's* director, Jacob Krupnick, wanted to inspire the everyday dancer, We Are from LA, the French directing duo behind *24 Hours of Happy*, wanted to "get some freshness, some spontaneity," and, in representing diverse populations, get audiences to identify with the performers "and just say 'Why not me?'"[11] Beyond their lengthy durations, explorations of aesthetic and cultural diversity in urban U.S. contexts, and mutual embrace of amateur and everyday aesthetics, a direct relationship between the two works remains speculative. Aesthetic influence can be difficult to prove. Copying, however, is another matter entirely.

Copying is integral to the circulation of dance, embedded in training, rehearsal, performance, and reperformance as seen throughout this book. Copying is also central to debates in dance scholarship, ongoing at least since black dance studies scholar Brenda Dixon Gottschild published her 1996 book *Digging the Africanist Presence in American Performance*. In this book, Gottschild shook Eurocentric dance scholarship at its core by revealing, among other things, the influence of African American cultural

Figure 30. Screenshot of a side-by-side video showing the similarities between *Girl Walk//All Day* (2011) and *24 Hours of Happy* (2013).

practices on neoclassical choreographer George Balanchine. Ever since, dance scholars have been grappling with the politics of how dance steps and movement aesthetics travel across boundaries of race, nation, and culture. Particularly vexing is that such sharing of movement inevitably occurs amid an imbalance of power. As Priya Srinivasan notes in her analysis of the transnational circulation of classical Indian dance, "dance is embodied and passes from body to body whether we like it or not."[12] In his analysis of technique in performing arts practices, Ben Spatz similarly emphasizes that "technique does not circulate under conditions of freedom or justice."[13]

Anthea Kraut's extensive study of choreographic copyright is of signal importance for understanding the history of how dance artists have activated legal and economic language to claim authorship and ownership of movement ideas in order to protect localized worlds of meaning. She analyzes how, without recourse to copyright law, African American vernacular dancers in the Jazz Era established a system of choreographic exchange that included a code of ethics within it. Dancers imprinted certain dance moves with their signature style, and these were accompanied by unwritten agreements about the conditions under which a dancer could perform someone else's signature steps. Additionally, community policing in the form of disruptive action reprimanded violators for trespassing these norms. While mimicry fueled development, Kraut clarifies that the commercial arena constituted a different economy than that of the clubs and communities in which dancers developed their material. Thus, "when exposure and money were at stake," different rules applied; "dancers treated their 'pet steps' as a kind of intellectual property, and theft of that property constituted blatant infringement."[14] In this way, Kraut argues, African American performers found ways to embody and deploy the logic of intellectual property for their movement specialties, even as the community practice of "stealing steps" was crucial to the advancement of dance forms in the absence of official pedagogy. Playing at the boundaries between gift, theft, and sharing in a common vocabulary, stealing steps multiplied dance as a resource, while the community also placed limitations on performance to protect individual rights by visibly marking instances of trespass.

In dance studies, analyses of how gestures travel and change as they move from one cultural group to another have generally taken place within the structuring concept of cultural appropriation. Whereas appropriation as recycling or reframing holds a positive valence in the visual and literary arts as well as in postmodern-leaning circles of dance-makers, in dance scholarship, appropriation has referred negatively to instances of artists "stealing" movements, styles, or approaches—typically from socially disadvantaged groups. Within the framework of appropriation, access to material may be unauthorized, or the material may be misused in such a way as to benefit the recipient and/or harm the donor. As ethnomusicologist Kiri Miller observes in the case of learning dances from video games, "performers might mean no harm but still inflict injury."[15] In other words, acts of cultural imperialism are not limited to those pursued with obvious ill intent.

An understanding that appropriation consolidates power and prestige through acts of cultural dispossession motivates these debates, giving rise to such questions as who owns specific dance practices and who has access to them, and how artists and cultural outsiders transform publicly available gestures and movement ideas into something for private monetary gain or individual cultural capital. In her analysis of bioprospecting, or investing in the "discovery" of Indigenous knowledge that can be converted into patented pharmaceutical products, intellectual property scholar Eva Hemmungs Wirtén describes this process as "acquisition, concentration and control, and finally recirculation and regulation."[16] Her formula offers a precise account of how knowledge-as-practice, immaterial labor, and financial investment travel and is generative for considering the circulation of gestures and dances alongside and within neoliberal capitalism.[17] First, one gains access to and acquires a desired object, skill, or knowledge. Then, by accumulating influence, one restricts others' access to the same. Finally, one controls the supply and the channels of its redistribution.

This model of appropriation recalls John Locke's theory of property, in which ownership results from mixing what is unowned (or part of the common) with one's labor, enabling appropriation to function specifically as a mechanism of possession.[18] The addition of one's own labor transforms what is shared as part of a collective inheritance into what is owned as individual property. However, the transformative power of labor that Locke identified is explicitly linked to the race and gender politics of colonial expansion where appropriation is positioned as the exploitative counterpart to acculturation: colonial and settler logics created the conditions for extracting capital in the form of natural resources, Indigenous knowledges, and cultural practices. As Gottschild,[19] Kraut,[20] Srinivasan,[21] Caroline Picart,[22] Jacqueline Shea Murphy,[23] and others have shown in the field of dance, the transformative labor of some individuals, namely, white men, has been legally recognized through copyright and intellectual property protections, while the labor of others, namely, women and people of color, has not been equivalently evaluated or protected. In a legal and economic framework that favors the contributions of some over others, not all creators have been equally positioned to claim the rights of authorship or attribution, let alone derive monetary benefit from their innovations.

Eric Lott has described this imbalance as both love and theft in American race relations playing out in the field of cultural production. In mining the origin story of blackface minstrelsy, Lott focuses on the relationship between the enterprising white actor T. D. Rice and a black man named Cuff, from whom Rice has "borrowed" the apparel for his act. Onstage wearing black makeup and Cuff's clothing, Rice stirs up the audience with his antics, while Cuff waits half-naked backstage. The arrival of a steamboat, the source of Cuff's income as a porter, brings the act to an uproarious conclusion as Cuff proceeds to reappropriate his belongings to go meet the boat. Cuff's central place in the origin tale, and specifically his literal and metaphorical denuding, Lott suggests, titillates with the "threat that he may return to demand his stolen capital" and functions as an "allegory for the post-slavery economy of blackness" in which black people, as well as markers of black identity and culture, were both desired and feared by white audiences and cultural producers.[24] The narratives Lott analyzes "share an anxiety over the fact of cultural 'borrowing,'" particularly as "issues of ownership, cultural capital, and economics arise" around the stars of blackface minstrelsy.[25] Notably, Cuff can take back his material belongings, but not the nonmaterial songs, dances, or speech patterns, which, in their maligned form, made Rice a very wealthy man. Cuff cannot take them back because they were never his (alone) to begin with, and because Rice's market-oriented transformation has made them into something other than what they were—a commodity. Functioning both as a historical figure and as an archetypal character in this parable, who or what Cuff is or might have been, as manifested in corporeal practices such as song and dance, has been reconfigured as a projection of white Americans' fears and desires. As we see in Lott's retelling of Cuff's story, the stakes are nothing less than the self-possession upon which ownership of culture is founded, a self-possession that cannot be disentangled from the history of slavery.

To say that these anxieties at the nexus of race relations and market circulations are still prominent despite the prevalence of cultural hybridity and globalization is an understatement. Despite a significant shift in how dance and other movements travel from one site to another in digital global economies, the turn of the twenty-first century has not seen a shift in rhetorics of ownership and cultural imperialism. Indeed, concerns over and claims of appropriation and cultural theft have only amplified in online "call-out" culture. Accusations of appropriation attempt, in part, to correct historical wrongs, and, as media theorist Lisa Nakamura suggests of call-out culture in general, to "create better conditions for women and minorit[ies]" online.[26] Professional and amateur artists, fans, and antifans cry foul over recontextualizations of material over which they feel a sense of ownership, even when it circulates widely and beyond anyone's direct control.

Reflecting on the prevalence of white pop stars who "borrow" fad dances from their nonwhite backup singers and dancers, Gottschild has, like Lott, traced a pattern of appropriation to the minstrel era, arguing that for centuries, "whites have [had] the privilege of appropriating black cultural goods and tailoring them to their culture-specific needs."[27] From blues to jazz to hip-hop and rap, from Madonna to Eminem to Miley Cyrus, white musicians have long benefited from participating in or borrowing from black music and dance forms, prompting unresolved debates regarding the merits of their participation, compensation, and recognition by the music and dance industries. What is interesting about Marsen's claim that Pharrell's *24 Hours of Happy* plagiarized *Girl Walk//All Day* is that it inverts the racial dynamics presupposed in most discussions of appropriation, while reinforcing the gender and class dynamics found in intellectual property debates.

As African American pop artists have become prominent figures in the mainstream, they, like white artists, have been accused of appropriation. Beyoncé is a frequent target for such accusations, because she, with the choreographers in her employ, openly mines the archives of both popular and experimental dance for her music videos and choreography. Her approaches are not unique, however, since sampling, remix, and versioning have long been crucial to the project of embedding black histories within black musical practices.[28] Yet, Beyoncé seems to have received more than her fair share of criticism. Perhaps Beyoncé's sources are more discoverable than those of her predecessors and peers, because hers is an internet-savvy audience. Or perhaps the fact that Beyoncé mines both white and black archives poses a specific, uncomfortable challenge to white supremacy. Perhaps Beyoncé's status as a black female success story makes her a perfect scapegoat for a practice that is as pervasive as it is ethically ambiguous. In any case, online commentators and scholars have pointed to Beyoncé's direct quotation of choreography in the music videos *Get Me Bodied* (2009) (Bob Fosse's "Rich Man's Frug" from the 1969 film *Sweet Charity*), *Single Ladies: Put a Ring on It* (2009) (Fosse's 1969 "Mexican Breakfast" routine from *The Ed Sullivan Show* and additional choreography from *Sweet Charity*), and *Countdown* (2011) (Thierry de Mey's 1997 film adaptation of Anne Theresa De Keersmaeker's stage-based work *Rosas danst Rosas* [1983] and De Keersmaeker's 1994 film of her work *Achterland* [1990]), which I discuss in more detail at the end of the chapter. As these few examples show, like so many other aspects of cultural production, dance can function as both a *belonging,* that is to say, as an exploitable form of intellectual property, and a *mode* of belonging, or a means through which individuals demonstrate their affiliation with a group. Tensions arise, it seems, when a dance or dance practice flows from one sense of belonging to another. Importantly, it is not commodification as such that produces this tension but what commodification enables: the circulation of gestural belongings outside the communities of practice that manifest social belonging through those very gestures, and the financial profits that accrue to those who facilitate monetized circulation as compared to community participation.

Rather than take accusations of appropriation as truth claims to be proved or disproved, Srinivasan has usefully reframed such claims as "performative gestures"[29] that momentarily disrupt the too-easy translation from cultural practice to commodity that broadens access outside the boundaries of community. By calling them out, accusations of plagiarism or theft check individuals or corporate entities set up to profit from collective production, even if accusers are unable to prevent the transfer they oppose. Part of a moral economy theater scholar Elizabeth Dillon locates in the embodied public sphere, or what she calls the performative commons, such performative gestures assert "a concept of the commons and the common good, announcing a set of relations and obligations among the members of a community."[30] Accusations of appropriation call out a performative injury, a trespass of symbolic violence that results in indirect emotional suffering rather than direct physical pain. They are a reminder of the obligation to act morally and an assertion of proximity and responsibility toward others where distance, mediated by commerce, has been assumed by at least one party.

Blogger Radical Faggot offers an example of calling out cultural appropriation in their thoughtful and heartfelt post "Vogue Is Not For You": "Voguing belongs to queer people of color—specifically trans, poor, working, sex-working, homeless and young queer people of color. We created it, we need to be the ones dancing it, and we need to be the ones protecting it. . . . [It] is laughable that the privileged find such discomfort in our limiting their access to our bodies, traditions and genius."[31] In addition to criticizing the use of vogue by white, cis-gendered, or wealthy individuals, Rad Fag also critiques the desire to leverage vogue for profit from within the ballroom community, fusing decolonial performative gestures with anticapitalist ones. In Rad Fag's view, any use of vogue that is not primarily a practice of belonging that affirms the experiences of the politically disenfranchised and economically precarious is immoral.

In the performative commons of the internet, call-out commentary that serves as a reminder of mutual obligation, responsibility, and the ethics of limiting access is not generally well received. As Nakamura notes, the efforts of feminist and antiracist advocates to improve the space of the internet by drawing public attention to misogynistic, racist, homophobic, and ableist speech "are unwanted, punished, and viewed as censorship, uncivil behavior, or themselves a form of sexism [or racism, etc.]."[32] Yet these important voices of dissent highlight what is at stake as dance travels through digital spaces, disconnected from communities and packaged as commodities to circulate "freely." Such voices press against an overarching ideology that claims all knowledge, art, or culture as a universal human birthright, available for entrepreneurial transformation from collective production into private wealth. They point to something amiss in what Taussig describes as the "bewildering cross connections between gift, theft, and trade"[33] that accompanied European colonization, which globalization has only exacerbated. Where globalization has produced an abstract globe as discussed in chapter 3, call-out culture defends localized worlds of meaning and their modes of being-in-common.

In a global market economy, a model of cultural transfer based on colonial encounter is no longer sufficient to describe the commodification and circulation of cultural practices.[34] Instead of appropriation, then, I wish to speak of infelicitous acts of transfer, after performance theorist Diana Taylor. In *The Archive and the Repertoire,* Taylor argues that performances "function as vital acts of transfer"[35] of knowledge and identity. But she also notes that performances may travel among dominant and nondominant groups, influencing and changing the course of other performances. She notes, however, that this process of "mutual construction" is one that few theorists seriously consider and that such a conversation would "demand the recognition of the permanent recycling of cultural materials and processes between the Western and non-Western [and] the transformative process undergone by all societies as they come in contact with and acquire foreign cultural material, whether willingly or unwillingly."[36] Even within Taylor's own project, which analyzes the clearly exploitative scenario of transmitting Indigenous knowledges under conditions of conquest, she points beyond readings that limit acts of transfer to unidirectional appropriation.

As performance practices circulate through global economies, Taylor's "vital acts of transfer" take on a new function, not only transmitting "communal memories, histories, and values from one group / generation to the next" but also transmitting empty gestures into which new meanings and values are projected in response to changing circumstances. Older meanings continue to resonate, perhaps structurally embedded in dance forms and practices as they circulate, but, adapting to new contexts and populations with different histories and memories, new meanings may obscure the old, transforming a practice's intrinsic or social value into a market value. Although Miller correctly observes in her analysis of internet-based kinesthetic cultures that "we still have to learn from *other people's* bodies, finding a way to comprehend their kinesthetic knowledge and make it our own,"[37] to use J. L. Austin's terminology, there can be something infelicitous about such acts of transfer. Austin uses infelicity to describe the use of performative utterances (speech acts that transform the reality they describe) in contexts where their transformations cannot be realized. Examples of infelicitous performatives include performing a wedding ceremony in a theatrical play or appointing someone to a position without the authority to do so. In such instances, the performative is unhappy. Staging a marriage in a play may not change the standing of the participants in the eyes of the law, yet the legal and cultural frameworks that operate beyond the theatrical frame enable the fictional function of such a staging. Similarly, there is potentially a failure or misfire when a gesture or movement circulates as a commodity with a use-value rather than as an expression of belonging and cultural affiliation. Yet, it is precisely this failure, this abstraction and decontextualization from a world of meaning, that enables movement and physical practices to circulate across bodies regardless of community affiliation, knowledge, history, or condoned participation. Those who take up or take on these gestures ascribe new meanings to them, in accordance with, as Gottschild remarks, "their culture-specific needs."[38]

For example, learning dances through YouTube tutorials and video games rather than with and alongside amateur and practiced dancers is now commonplace. Karen X. Cheng, who now creates videos for start-ups and other companies, documented her progress learning elements of popping, tutting, roboting, and other urban dance styles in her 2013 video *Girl Learns to Dance in a Year (TIME LAPSE)*.[39] This video offers compelling evidence for the importance of a daily, deliberate physical practice: over the course of the year, Cheng's movements become more precise—the fluidity and sharpness in her gestures become more distinct, and her confidence and performance style become more apparent. Most of the video shows Cheng dancing in her home to Justice's upbeat track "D.A.N.C.E." (2007), but in a dramatic conclusion to her 365 days of dance, Cheng takes her new skills to a subway station—a preferred site of so many videos documenting urban dance phenomena. The music shifts to the smooth electronic melancholy of Dusty Brown's "This City Is Killing Me" (2010) as Cheng disembarks from a BART train. Her neon green shirt complements the neon yellow at the platform's edge; the stripe on her leggings mirrors the stripes on the train cars. Almost immediately, the beat drops, and she drops her weight, rolling a shoulder and widening her stance. Each percussive sound is met with a gesture, and a tremolo in the electronic music waves in a ripple through her extended arm and comes back into her chest as she arches backward. The camera zooms in on her upper body. As the train departs and picks up speed, she is pushed further into the foreground of the image, appearing serenely rooted even as the train's speed lends her movement more force and intensity than it actually possesses. Cheng gestures triumphantly—open chest, raised arms. It is all as if to say, "I have arrived."

On a now-defunct website featuring the video, Cheng declares, "Some of the best dancers I know have never taken a dance class. They learned by imitating what they saw on YouTube."[40] Taken on its own, the visual rhetoric of *Girl Learns to Dance in a Year (TIME LAPSE)* seems to suggest that this is the path Cheng herself pursued, relying on the presence of online tutorials and her own resources to teach herself to dance—in the

Figure 31. Screenshot of Karen X. Cheng documenting her fourth day of dedicated dance practice in *Girl Learns to Dance in a Year (TIME LAPSE)* (2013).

Figure 32. Screenshot of Karen X. Cheng gesturing triumphantly on a BART train platform in *Girl Learns to Dance in a Year (TIME LAPSE)* (2013).

space of a single year, no less. But, in fact, she credits her dance teachers on the video's YouTube page, and on her old website, she incorporated a row of class cards from San Francisco's City Dance Studios as a background design element. However, she has not provided this contextual information in the video itself, even though online videos circulate independently of additional information provided in descriptions, tags, or comment fields. The result, even if unintentional, is an erasure of influence in favor of an inspirational story of personal achievement. Furthermore, Cheng's advocacy of learning dance from YouTube plays at the tensions between approaching dance as an acontextual physical practice aligned with fitness culture versus dance as a cultural practice aligned with participation in a community.

Take, as another example, a 2016 profile video by Fusion TV on YouTube titled *This Amazing Girl Mastered Dubstep Dancing by Just Using YouTube.*[41] The young dancer Adilyn Malcolm, aka Audacious Adi, suggests that she has learned to dubstep by watching YouTube videos over a seven- or eight-month period.[42] What the video calls dubstep dancing is a freestyle dance form that combines gliding footwork with tutting, waving, popping, and strobing,[43] thus requiring physical fluency in each of these individual dance practices. The Fusion profile toggles between shots of the twelve-year-old Malcolm dancing on a gymnasium floor in jean shorts and a sports bra, revealing her small but muscled frame, and sitting in her room watching YouTube videos of dancer Marquese Scott, who is credited in the YouTube video description but not in the video itself. To learn, Malcolm says she "watch[es] the video over and over . . . until [she] figure[s] out how they do it," and further comments on how the ability to pause, rewind, and repeatedly watch these videos has enabled her to learn dubstep.[44] She further notes that she has "learned all these things on the internet,"[45] but what gets lost in attributing one's ability to learn new styles of moving to the internet or to YouTube is the labor and creativity of the individuals who distribute their content through these platforms. In other words, Malcolm did not learn to dance from the internet. What she has learned, she has learned by imitating Scott and other dancers, and perhaps also by reading the constructive criticism that more practiced dancers have left as comments on her YouTube videos.[46]

Both Cheng and Malcolm promote themselves as self-taught,[47] aligning themselves with a popular narrative of the autodidact who achieves mastery without the benefit of formal training. Of course, practice by oneself is indispensible to learning any skill, but dance remains a social

Figure 33. Screenshot of Adilyn Malcolm, aka Audacious Adi, dancing in *This Amazing Girl Mastered Dubstep Dancing by Just Using YouTube* (2016).

practice, regardless if one learns in a studio, on a street corner, or from a screen. As William Given observes in his analysis of transmissions of Lindy hop, the understanding that communally oriented improvisational dance practices "can quickly be mastered through mimesis alone" is both presumptuous and reductive.[48] Such an approach to learning takes dance practices out of the contexts that give them meaning. Furthermore, twenty-first-century narratives of quick mastery not only cheapen the accomplishments of dedicated dancers through hyperbole; they obscure the generosity of dancers who share their dances and dissect them in tutorials.[49] Regardless of whether dancers attain their movement knowledge in formal settings, to learn dances and dancing is to partake in the corporeal generosity[50] of others, to incorporate their donations of gesture and movement.

As dances circulate and multiply across bodies along the way, they lose their connection to local circumstances of production. Indeed, dance's loss of local specificity is crucial to both its marketability and its global accessibility. In his analysis of African American social dance forms in 1970s popular media, dance scholar Thomas DeFrantz has questioned the "neoliberal right of access" that renders community practices available for general consumption.[51] He laments that these dances, "at once precious and freely available,"[52] have been transformed by neoliberalism so as to "absorb participants who have no sustained contact with the corporeal fact of black people in the world."[53] Rendered fugitive from their own signification, the decontextualization of black social dance practices makes them available to repurposing for profit, which further enables broad consumption by those who neither partake in nor necessarily sustain the communities from which these practices stem. DeFrantz acknowledges that there may be little choice in the matter, but there are consequences. He cautions that "bit by bit, YouTube video by video dance game, we lose our ability to understand these dances and their larger historical-aesthetic capacities."[54] The claim to a right of access carries with it both colonial and capitalist histories. As Kraut and others have demonstrated, in categorizing black dance and performance practices as "vernacular," African American contributions to dance have been assigned to the collectively available folk idioms constituting the public domain, "effectively giv[ing] artists with greater access to the means of production license to mine and capitalize on those forms for their own creative endeavors."[55] In other words, opening access can itself be an act of dispossession.

In an era of mass distribution via television and internet technologies and neoliberal free-market principles, dance forms and steps become raw material for remixing on television shows, in dance studios, in dance video games, and for reperformance on the internet in music video cover dances and the like. Although social norms and mores come into play in determining what types of movement are considered appropriate and for whom, evaluations viewers frequently make on the basis of dancers' perceived sex and race, it is very difficult to limit physical vocabularies to the membership of a predetermined group. In legal and market terms, dance is nonexcludable: attempts at choreographic copyright notwithstanding, people cannot effectively be barred from learning and participating in dances.[56] Furthermore, dance is nonrivalrous: one person's dancing does not prevent that of another. In contrast to rivalrous goods, for which one person's usage or consumption presents a significant barrier to another's simultaneous usage or consumption, a nonrivalrous good cannot be exhausted by one person's use of it. Indeed, dance practices could be considered what Steven Weber has called anti-rival; the more people participate, the more value and affective weight they carry.[57] Dance scholar Cynthia Novack, for example, notes that practitioners of the dance form contact improvisation liken their experience to the poker player who arrives in a town where no one plays the game and who must teach others in order to play.[58] As Kraut argues, unlike other commodities in a capitalist system, dance circulates by rematerializing on other bodies.[59] If one person dances, that does not prevent another person from also dancing, and, indeed, the more people who can be persuaded to dance, the more social and financial value dancing has. It is not, therefore, acts of transfer that are at issue so much as infelicitous uses that decontextualize dance practices to facilitate their greater commodification or that recast dance movements as without history, meaning, or specific cultural relevance. As they spread, such movements become part of the public domain, or a corporeal common. In the following section, I focus on the fabrication of this corporeal common through the sharing of movement practices in dance video games as well as in acts of fandom that reproduce music video choreography for popular entertainment.

A CORPOREAL COMMON

Almost immediately after *24 Hours of Happy* appeared online, fans began recording and posting videos of themselves dancing to Pharrell's hit tune on YouTube, contributing their own videos to a growing online archive of happiness. In an interview with Oprah Winfrey, Pharrell recalls discovering that *Happy* had gone viral. He remarks, "And we were like, 'What's happening?' . . . People are putting up their own videos. It was like no longer my song."[60] *Happy* deviates somewhat from the popular trend of rigorously embodying music video choreography in cover dances, seen especially clearly with fan reperformances of Beyoncé's *Single Ladies* (2009) and Psy's *Gangnam Style* (2012), because the video avoids spectacular choreography and employs everyday movements and accessible dancing instead. In responding to the call of happiness, fans explore their own style without questioning whether their dancing is correct or "good enough." *Happy's* choreography calls upon people to perform as themselves, drawing on whatever gestural resources, footwork, and rhythmic sensibilities they can access, dancing a dance that belongs to no one because the steps, as Noë points out and DeFrantz has troubled, belong to everyone. In Paris, a notably racially diverse group strolls through plazas with iconic architecture behind them.[61] People in Warsaw clap, sway, and roller-skate.[62] Seaside views feature prominently in a video from Croatia that includes young and old participants, as well as break-dancers, ballerinas, and folk dancers.[63] And a group in Tehran dances in overcoats and jackets, incorporating a few swing dance steps and handstands.[64]

Even though the videos emphasize self-expression above conformity, key features keep the videos in direct conversation: fans record themselves in multiple locales, facing the camera, dancing or dance-walking, and usually lip-syncing. These shots are then edited together and overlaid with Pharrell's song "Happy." The effect is similar to the Where the Hell Is Matt? videos discussed in chapter 3. Some of these *Happy* videos are sponsored by local businesses or created by video production companies, and sometimes they are completely fan created. Either way, audiences leverage Pharrell's popularity to build and fortify their own sociality and marketability by taking up and sharing in the *Happy* text, perpetuating its circulation as they engage in their own social and cultural expression. The fans

Figure 34. Screenshot of dancers in the fan-produced video *Happy We Are from Tehran* (2014).

Figure 35. Screenshot of a street scene from the fan-made video *Pharrell Williams—Happy (WARSAW IS ALSO HAPPY)* (2014).

dance a happy dance without right or wrong, better or worse execution. *Happy* does not require knowledge of specialized movement vocabularies; a shimmy, a butt wiggle, a twist, a shuffle—all gestures are available to and for this dance because they are held in common.

In their book *Commonwealth,* Michael Hardt and Antonio Negri identify an "artificial" common "that resides in languages, images, knowledges, affects, codes, habits, and practices."[65] Whereas what they call the "natural" common is characteristically made up of tangible resources such as land and water in limited supply, dance practices are not scarce resources, nor can simultaneous participation by multiple parties deplete them. Indeed, like languages, habits, and affects, dance practices accrue meaning through their repetition as they spread across individuals, communities, and populations. Despite the continuing drive to privatize resources and wealth, Hardt and Negri recognize that "contemporary forms of capitalist production and accumulation, paradoxically make possible and even require expansions of the common."[66] For this reason, Randy Martin views contemporary revaluations of the common(s) with suspicion. Referencing the enclosure movement that forcibly removed eighteenth-century peasants from common lands, Martin argues that "now dispossession breeds commons without anyone needing to be moved anywhere."[67] Martin, Kraut, DeFrantz, Gottschild, and others help us see that there are conflicting logics of belonging at play in the unfettered circulation of movement. Logics of copyright and individual authorship as well as the ability of dance artists to exert control over their creative expression stand ambiguously alongside the commercial exploitation of user-generated content and the communal ownership of cultural expression, an ownership that contains within it the right to exclude nonparticipating populations. Indeed, the concept of the natural common requires adherence to practices of exclusion so as to avoid the very tragedy of the commons that Garrett Hardin famously describes in his economic fable.[68] As DeFrantz has noted, however, the neoliberal ideology of access, and more specifically a post-racial ideology of access, clamors against any right to exclude, even though regulated access has historically made the commons possible and sustainable. It is this suspension or violation of the right to exclude toward which critics of cultural appropriation point, as we saw above with Rad Fag's advocacy of limiting white, wealthy, cis-gendered access to vogue.

I do not wish to advocate for the proliferation of gestures through infelicitous acts of transfer, motivated by a neoliberal, post-racial, or still-colonial right of access. Nevertheless, regardless of whether gestures *should* circulate freely across moving bodies, they most certainly *do*. In situating dance as common, and, in the next section, as a gift of the common, I hope to emphasize that movement practices develop and circulate under conditions of mutual indebtedness, and that therefore care must be taken to distinguish what is offered as a gift from that which is "given," that is, what is broadly available because it is already held in common. In this analysis, I take seriously Taylor's call to consider performance practices as mutually constructed despite that the dancers whose labor and creativity are imbricated in the generation and circulation of danced movement may nevertheless wish to limit access to these practices. It is not my intention, then, to posit the common of dance as an antidote to cultural appropriation or capitalist expropriation. Instead, I explore the common as a model for understanding how dance circulates through early twenty-first-century digital cultures and what happens when technologically enabled decontextualization allows dancers to bypass the social norms that sustain a movement culture.

As exemplified by the fan reperformances of Pharrell's *Happy* music video, in positing dance as common, I wish to think of dancing as what theater scholar Elizabeth Dillon calls a commoning practice. Whereas Marsen accused Pharrell of stealing *Girl Walk*'s concept for *24 Hours of Happy,* fans who mimic the *Happy* music video are not accused of theft, because they do not try to pass it off as their own. Instead, the videos specifically include the song "Happy," which ensures the recognizability of their contribution to a wide-ranging, global constellation of videos referencing the *Happy* music video. In this instance, fans do not mimic the movement or structure of *Happy* to steal it but to participate in it. With their participation, fans mobilize the shared vocabularies that popular music and dance make available as a way to craft shared reference points and common ground.

Taken up and put into play, movements are shared across bodies. By allowing oneself to be permeated with others' gestures, for example, by learning a dance, one corporeally manifests belonging to a social group—even if that group is constituted in online spaces or through shared media use rather than through physical proximity.[69] As phenomenologist Rosalyn Diprose proposes, "the lived body . . . is built from the invasion of the self by the gestures of others, who [refer] to other others."[70] Reproducing the gestures of others, dancers invoke shared vocabularies in which their gestures or sequences of movement register as meaningful precisely because they are shared. Like spoken language, bodily movements are "techniques of the body"[71] that articulate a form of gestural belonging. They offer a shared sense that gives meaning to a common world supportive of social or communal interaction.

Such gestures and dances, or what I call "embodied objects," form a corporeal common through their communicability. Embodied objects are nonmaterial, corporeal objects that assume a bodily shape or sequence, and are transferable and transmissible across the bodies that are their primary medium. Gestures, steps, moves, movement phrases, dance routines, somatic practices, choreographic scores: all of these exist as movement ideas that take shape through corporeal instantiation and interpretation. They travel contagiously and accrue affective weight and meaning as they travel across the bodies that come to perform them. Embodiment activates these objects, which are similar to what philosopher Michel Serres calls "quasi-objects." He offers the example of a ball: "A ball is not an ordinary object, for it is what it is only if a subject holds it."[72] By itself, the ball is meaningless. It must be activated through game play. Similarly, gestures, steps, and dances "make sense" only when put into play or into movement. As undanced dances, abstract choreographic structures, or mental images of movement, they only function as ideas. But when put into practice, they materially transform the bodies that carry, express, and transmit them[73] and link those bodies to all the others who share a gestural or movement vocabulary.

One especially powerful example of how fans take up the contagious gestures of popular dance and, through reperformance, leverage a shared choreography to manifest a corporeal common is *Michael Jackson's Thriller*.[74] With some modifications, wedding celebrants the world over have performed this famous choreography.[75] Filipino prison inmates performed it in a video uploaded to YouTube in 2009,[76] and a 2010 Halloween flash mob in Tulsa, Oklahoma, also danced the *Thriller* choreography.[77] Students in a 2011 Zombie Walk in Flint, Michigan, danced it with lyrics performed in

American Sign Language,[78] and cowboy ghoulies danced *Thriller* in a July 2013 parade for the Stampede rodeo and festival in Calgary, Alberta.[79] Bolstered by the annual Halloween holiday in the United States and fueled by a contemporary cultural fascination with zombies, *Thriller* has proved an enduring—even viral[80]—choreography. Now more than thirty years old and still performed by fans, *Thriller* is canonical. Adapting the choreography to new sociopolitical landscapes, Jackson fans have staged more flash mobs and zombie walks in recent years than can be accounted for, including political protests and bodily expressions of cultural critique alongside acts of fandom.[81] Like internet memes, which can respond to changing circumstances, what *Thriller* means, or how it functions, is a matter of how it is employed. *Thriller* is no longer a mere fad or seasonal favorite; it is part of a global repertory of popular dance.

As with other viral choreographies, *Thriller* perpetuates itself as a shared embodied object, contagiously transmitted from one person to another. Thus *Thriller* as a cultural text is not limited to the original film by Michael Jackson and John Landis but includes all manner of fan reperformances of Michael Peters's choreography. Furthermore, online videos and public performances spread the choreography to an audience of others who additionally extend *Thriller*'s broad reach as they watch and share (in) them.

Figure 36. Screenshot of the Thrill the World flash mob event in *Thrill the World at L.A. Live ~ Official World Record Shot of 2009 Los Angeles Thriller Event* (2009).

Figure 37. Screenshot of a scene from the 2011 flash mob and student protest *Thriller por la Educación* in front of La Moneda in Santiago, Chile.

Serres elaborates on the quasi-object, "The ball isn't there for the body; the exact opposite is true: the body is the object of the ball. . . . The ball is the subject of circulation; the players are only the stations and the relays."[82] Fans render themselves physically available to *Thriller*'s choreography, serving as a medium in which it materializes and through which it circulates. Dancing fans do not simply pass the choreography along but volunteer their embodiment as a means of its circulation and transfer. Performances of *Thriller* generate and expand a corporeal common through replication, which installs the choreography in the bodies of fans who reproduce it. Each iteration refers to each of the others in a process of accrued significance through citation.

   Thriller's dancing fans demonstrate how dance not only makes use of a shared capacity for movement but organizes sharing in the gestures of others. This "syncretic sociability," as Diprose calls it, or this "intracorporeal 'transfer' of movements and gestures and body bits and pieces,"[83] establishes what she calls corporeal generosity. Bodies give themselves to and for others through movements and gestures that circulate in excess of the very bodies that produced them, to be materialized on yet other bodies. What Diprose describes in the domain of everyday gestures such as those featured throughout *24 Hours of Happy* pertains equally to codified movement vocabularies and choreographed dances. *Thriller* is just one example among many that illustrate the project of syncretic sociability within contemporary digital cultural production.

Like Diprose, dance theorist Mark Franko emphasizes generosity in his essay "Given Movement," in which he analyzes a scene from Gregory Bateson and Margaret Mead's 1936–39 film *Learning to Dance in Bali.* He focuses on a particular moment when a Balinese dance master transmits a dance to one of his students. In this scene, the master teacher guides a novice student through the motions of a dance by standing directly behind the young dancer, pressing his own body into his pupil's and moving the student's limbs. The teacher provides a physical support for the dancer as he manipulates him, moving his body through the motions of the dance. Animating the student, the teacher brings the dance to life through the student in this moment of body-to-body transmission. This example demonstrates what Franko calls an "incorporative donation."[84] The teacher "gives" the movement to the student, but as a gift, it is a "donation" that cannot be met with a response; the student incorporating the movement "gives" nothing to the teacher in return. Nor, in fact, does the teacher "give" anything to the student, but "an impulse is transmitted" from one to the other.[85] In this scenario of movement acquisition, dance is (and can only be) circulated, exemplifying cultural critic Lewis Hyde's notion of circular giving, in which "each donation is an act of social faith."[86] Circular giving presumes that all contributors and beneficiaries identify as "part of the group,"[87] which keeps everything circulating within agreed-upon parameters. *Learning to Dance in Bali* demonstrates just such a phenomenon of giving movement within the context of a predefined community. In Franko's description, a second scene of the film crucially shows an advanced student "giving" movement to a younger student while the master teacher looks on. Franko describes this scenario of gifting or giving movement as a "posteconomic" form of circulation that requires one to give (of) oneself.[88] Thus an ethical orientation accompanies this example of dance pedagogy. Dance cannot be transmitted without performers or teachers giving of themselves in the process, and to give of oneself is to offer one's labor (or one's very being) as a voluntary contribution, or a "self-donation,"[89] in Franko's terms. The student becomes the teacher, thereby keeping the dance in circulation by passing it from body to body as a gift of movement across generations.

Dance video games offer another example of the corporeal generosity that attends dance transmission, even where the framework explicitly foregrounds an economic motive. In *Playable Bodies: Dance Games and Intimate Media*, Kiri Miller aligns these games with heritage projects that support the transmission of dance through embodied performance, not unlike the project of transmission staged in *Learning to Dance in Bali*. Such games mediate the space of interaction between teacher and student, thus reworking the body-to-body relationship that is a hallmark of all sorts of dance training programs, from the highly formal to the rather informal. In the Dance Central series of video games by Harmonix, gamers stand in front of a Kinect—a peripheral motion tracking system added to the standard Xbox console—and dance to popular songs. Gamers follow onscreen animated characters that, thanks to motion capture, expertly perform the choreography, which has been devised especially for the video games and the tracking system's abilities and limitations. Flashcards notify gamers as to which moves are coming up in the sequence. Some of these steps reference specific movement histories, like "boogaloo" and "cabbage patch," while others have generic names like "step pump" and "topple." Players acquire points for creating the same shapes at the same time as the animation. The Kinect tracks players' movements and provides visual feedback when they fall out of sync with the dance onscreen. "An impulse is transmitted,"[90] but without bodily contact between teachers and students. Dance Central's choreographers move players at a distance, and the players activate the choreography within themselves, materializing it as they follow along. They incorporate the embodied objects that animate the dancers onscreen. In this way, dancing under the tutelage of a video game is not so different from learning and performing choreographies from music videos, television shows, films, or YouTube videos, as we saw with Karen X. Cheng and Adilyn Malcolm, except that dance video games evaluate players' execution of the routines. As Miller observes, Dance Central offers gamers feedback on their performances in real time, allowing them to "work through a dance curriculum and master a particular choreographic repertoire without ever submitting themselves to human evaluation."[91]

Whereas other examples in this chapter omit, defer, or occlude monetary compensation, the example of dance video games lays bare social and
economic operations that are present in many scenarios of teaching, learning, and presenting dance: participants within a movement community
generate and contribute embodied objects in a collaborative gift economy,
dance artists/teachers cull from these gestural repositories and organize
available movements into choreographed compositions or routines, and
dance artists/teachers expose these movements to broader audiences when
they sell these choreographies for corporeal consumption by novice dancers
and gamers in a market economy. While Miller calls attention to the questionable histories dance video games inherit, including the role of "racial
masquerade" in American popular music and dance,[92] she also acknowledges positively that the games encourage players to try "moves that many
players would not perform of their own accord."[93] In an interview with
Dance Central choreographer Marcos Aguirre, Miller offered Aguirre an
opportunity to comment on how he would respond to the criticism that
"these games are making some kind of cultural appropriation possible,"
to which he responded, "Nothing's being taken. . . . A lot of moves we've
learned growing up, and it's kind of like just being spread."[94] Miller notes
that both Aguirre and Chanel Thompson, another Dance Central choreographer, "referred to dance as a gift, and described feeling a calling to share
that gift."[95] Miller further observes, "Neither choreographer expressed concern about who exactly might be the recipients of these gifts, nor that they
could be misused."[96] Of particular importance for the present discussion,
Miller reflects on the choreographers' own positions, remarking, "Giving
a gift forestalls appropriation; you can't appropriate something that has
been freely given to you."[97] But Miller also notes that "the ethics of gift
economies also dictate that gifts incur obligations."[98] As theorized by Marcel Mauss and many others, gifts are paradoxically structured: they present
themselves as though outside of any obligation, but in fact, to accept a gift
is to be obliged to the giver in some way. Socialization within a cultural
group trains participants in the unstated social obligations that gifts entail.
As dance practices move outside of specific movement communities, these
social norms fall away.

By purchasing choreographic content and learning dances from a video
game platform, players partake in the gift economies that support the
development of movement material. Physical reproduction installs these

Figure 38. Split screen of MMC (MightyMeCreative) dancing the hard level as Emilia in "Pon de Replay" in *Dance Central 2*.

Figure 39. Split screen of RiffraffDC dancing the hard level as Bodie in "Moves Like Jagger" in *Dance Central 3*.

embodied objects in gamers' personal gestural repertories, enabling players to acquire ways of moving they might not otherwise have pursued. The Dance Central series thus trains players in new bodily techniques and capacities for movement. However, players pay for these embodied objects and this dance education. Whereas concert dance audiences pay for access as spectators, video game players pay to reproduce these gestures in their own bodies. With Dance Central, a corporeal common, populated with gestures through community members' "contributive participation,"[99] becomes a resource of corporeal commodities available for consumption by gamers who remain separated from the communities and individuals who have generated and continue to develop the very gestures, steps, and ways of moving that gamers pay to learn.

From these decontextualized gestures, gamers constitute other communities (and other commons), in which they post and share videos of themselves achieving high scores in accordance with the values of gaming communities. Thus a different value system recodes these danced gestures and what their performance signals to those who embody them. Dance Central demonstrates clearly how choreographers might draw from a corporeal common of collaboratively authored gestures and movements, and open access to them such that they achieve greater circulation through gamers' physical incorporation and reproduction. Furthermore, the game illustrates how opening access does not contradict but rather can support the monetization of dances that are otherwise held in common by a movement community. While all paid dance instructors rely on this same social and economic structure that enables them to receive payment for providing access to shared movement knowledge, Dance Central offers a clear example of how market and gift economies sit inside and alongside each other. As Taussig notes, "the 'gift economy' entails and perhaps depends upon mimetic facility."[100] Dance video games exemplify how a corporeal common expands beyond the parameters of a specific community as the market facilitates mimetic reproduction of these movements among those who are not otherwise affiliated with a community of practice. Severing dances from their cultural situation accelerates transmission across bodies, transforming gestures of belonging, which some may consider gestural belongings or proprietary gestures, into corporeal commodities.

The ways fans participate in *Happy, Thriller,* and Dance Central video games illustrate at varying levels how elements of a corporeal common become commodified but are then also repurposed through popular engagement, which reasserts a commonness in these movements as they become available for more generalized embodiment. *Happy*'s repertory of everyday gestures and call to fans to perform themselves make it the most easily reproducible of these three examples. While some knowledge of creating and uploading a video with a sound track is required, the only dancing expertise needed is that performers are experts at being themselves.[101] Fans thus do not replicate Pharrell's specific movements or those of the other dancers from the long- or short-form music videos; they replicate the concept or structure. This structure, however, is also shared, visible in both *Girl Walk//All Day* and the Where the Hell Is Matt? series, among many other videos made with social media content or for a social media audience. Fan performances of *Thriller* require a little more effort from those who want to embody its choreography. Rather than dancing as their own unique selves, they follow *Thriller*'s script, which indicates a particular relationship between song and choreographed movement. In performing *Thriller*'s choreography, dancers incorporate gestures that may not have previously been part of their repertory, which they work into their bodies through practice. In this process, the choreography and the movements of which it is composed change their character from corporeal commodities to shared embodied objects in a corporeal common. What fan performances of *Thriller* achieve on a global scale with a single choreography Dance Central achieves with hundreds of dances, but with a more targeted gaming audience. Instead of providing fans with a single choreography that they can master and reperform for other audiences, Dance Central opens access to all sorts of movements, styles, and routines, which are broken down so as to further facilitate their transfer. Whereas dancing fans often take pride in their virtuosic mimicry of music video choreography, Dance Central reproduces the educational scenario of coaching dancers through the acquisition of specific moves and routines. The express purpose of Dance Central is the transmission of embodied objects. What embodied objects can be gifted without forfeiture to the market and who has authority to give, retain, collect, and/or profit from a corporeal common are under constant negotiation both inside and outside of communities of practice.

But there is another approach to thinking about sharing in movement, as indicated by Idle No More's inclusion of Round Dances in their flash mob protests, discussed in chapter 2: to partake in a corporeal common is to be bound together. Moving together, synchronously or asynchronously, knowingly or unwittingly, and with whatever motivations, co-implicates each dancer in the movement of another. We might therefore modify Srinivasan's claim that dances travel from body to body "whether we like it or not"[102] and suggest that sharing in movement, gestures, and dances links bodies together—whether we like it or not. It remains true, however, that misrecognizing danced gifts for the unqualified givenness of movement perpetuates the performative injury of appropriation through infelicitous acts of transfer. The misrecognition of a gift for a given, that is to say, a common inheritance, implies a misrecognition of rights of access for rights of reproduction and monetization. This misrecognition further contributes to a genericization of movement practices as commoditized versions travel from screen to screen and body to body on a global scale. In the next section, I consider this misrecognition further through the lenses of credit and debt in gift economies.

CREDIT, DEBT, AND THE GIFT OF THE COMMON

24 Hours of Happy encouraged mimicry with its unabashedly accessible dancing performed by a largely anonymous crowd. Noting the explosion of happy dances in social media, Julie Fersing and Loïc Fontaine aggregated videos of fans performing their happiness in response to Pharrell's hit song. They created a Facebook page on which they encouraged Pharrell's fans to share their videos,[103] which they then included on their We Are Happy From website, a bright yellow page filled with a list of cities linked to more than 1,900 YouTube videos from 153 countries, which they have also located on a world map. *Happy* is made for sharing, and We Are Happy From does not let all those acts of fandom go to waste. Like the dancing fans, Fersing and Fontaine offer their aggregate of happiness as a "token of gratitude," a gift, we might say, to Pharrell and the *24 Hours of Happy* team for their "worldwide contagious happiness."[104] In answering the call to be happy, fans both produce their own happiness and simultaneously demonstrate the generative nature of collaborative consumption, in that their collective incorporation and dissemination of *Happy* makes their own movement donations available for repurposing and therefore further online consumption. Creating a collage out of thousands of contributions for online audiences, Fersing and Fontaine repackage fans' consumption of Pharrell's music video for reconsumption by online viewers. They organize the fans' largely volunteered, creative labor and transform it into a new event that will also add to their own design portfolios. As content curators, they, too, volunteer labor as an investment in themselves, demonstrating their skills for hire in their own act of fandom. Building a website collecting fan videos, they add value to *Happy* and to Pharrell as a commercial entity, and they add value to themselves in the form of desirability and hire-ability. In the example of We Are Happy From, *Happy* and its affiliated pedestrian movements travel across contexts, from the long-form music video *24 Hours of Happy,* to thousands of fan videos circulating online that both receive the song and simple dance as a gift and return that gift through reperformance, to the collation and re-presentation of these fans videos on a website. We Are Happy From is an act of fandom and volunteer labor that gives something back to Pharrell and the fans, and it simultaneously leverages fan-produced content to demonstrate the designers' own job qualifications. Even though *Happy* circulates within a commercial economy, it simultaneously activates (and is amplified by) an internet gift economy, where digital platforms cultivate and capture the circulation of intangible commodities such as the embodied objects of gesture and movement.

In this section, I consider the social functions of credit and debt as dance circulates through digital venues. I turn to the examples of Fersing and Fontaine's website We Are Happy From gathering and re-presenting fan-produced content, a rehearsal video by choreographer Alexandra Beller that went viral under the name *Baby Modern Dance,* and pop singer Beyoncé Knowles's infamous borrowing of Anne Theresa De Keersmaeker's choreography for the music video *Countdown* as well as De Keersmaeker's response. Each of these examples offers an inflection point where movement comes into or out of a common, where authorship is anonymized so as to facilitate greater transfer, and where creators reassert claims of ownership when their work is unacknowledged by those who use and

Figure 40. (*Top*) screenshots of the homepage for We Are Happy From (2013) by Julie Fersing and Loïc Fontaine showing the geographic distribution of fan-produced videos responding to Pharrell Williams's song and music video "Happy" (2013). (*Bottom*) Fersing and Fontaine have embedded fan-produced videos in their own website.

build upon it. As we have seen, however, a performative assertion of ownership is volleyed from a somewhat disadvantaged position. Backed by large companies and legal teams, popular artists such as Pharrell and Beyoncé have less need to assert ownership over their creative material, and fan responses to their work frequently solidify rather than challenge their authorial positions. When dance circulates as gift, it circulates unevenly, and with inconsistent practices of acknowledgment and credit. When creators and content aggregators refuse to credit others for their contributions, they mistake danced gifts for the givenness of movement, disavowing the mutual indebtedness that fuels the shared practices in which they participate.

In his influential and much-debated *Essay on the Gift,* Mauss sets out to discover a form of social contract that is at once voluntary and obligatory, or rather, that creates obligations through voluntary behaviors. He settles on the gift as a form of exchange, arguing that the gift contains within itself three obligations: "to give, to receive, to reciprocate."[105] With this triune expectation, the gift ensures its continuation beyond any one instance of transfer or transmission and further ensures that, while gift giving may be asymmetrical in terms of the participants' status or wealth, it is not unidirectional. The gift assumes an obligation on the part of the recipient, generally in proportion to the perceived value of the gift. For this reason, would-be recipients refuse gifts for being "too much" when their value implies a proportional obligation beyond that to which they are willing to commit. Gifts can be dangerous—fairy tales are full of duplicitous and deadly gifts, Trojan horses that arrive with false humility and expose the gift recipient to risk in the very act of acceptance. When offered, seemingly, without ill intent, gifts remain suspect in the ways they create social bonds between a donor and a recipient. Professional codes of ethics therefore routinely prohibit service providers from accepting gifts from clients and constituents, and other rules abound that regulate giving and accepting gifts.

Following Mauss, many commentators have remarked upon the gift as paradox. Mary Douglas contends that there are no free gifts,[106] Pierre Bourdieu describes gift giving as a social game in which everyone is aware of the rules yet must "refuse to know" them,[107] and Jacques Derrida calls the gift "the very figure of the impossible."[108] Two competing claims are embedded in the gift: that, as Derrida suggests, the gift is given freely, or free of social ties and reciprocal obligations, and that, as Mauss contends, the gift is given with obligations already attached. In his analysis of the gift, Olli Pyyhtinen describes the paradox thus:

> While the gift, almost without exception, occurs within exchange, when it is explained entirely based on exchange, the gift is annulled, for in exchange nothing is really given, irrevocably and without return. And the other way around, when one looks at the gift solely in terms of free giving, dissociated from relations of reciprocity, one fails to see the circles of exchanges in which the gift takes place and to which it gives rise. Thus, the gift cannot be what it "in reality" is (reciprocity / exchange), and it is what it cannot be (free giving).[109]

So the gift is neither free nor not-free; reciprocation is both demanded and disavowed. Upon acceptance of the gift, the recipient incurs an obligation that cannot be discharged in the form of mere compensation. According to Mauss, the recipient thereby enters into an irrevocable bond with the giver. Yet social propriety dictates that both giver and receiver must feign ignorance of this obligation.

While pretending to ignore mutual obligations may facilitate and strengthen social ties, *actually* ignoring the social bond and reciprocal imperative damages those ties. Refusing to acknowledge generosity and to respond in kind violates, as Diprose says, the very "condition of personal, interpersonal, and communal existence."[110] She therefore finds that injustice stems, in part, from an asymmetrical recognition of generosity: outsized celebration of the generosity of some coupled with selective amnesia regarding the generosity of others. "Some bodies accrue value, identity, and recognition through accumulating the gifts of others and at their expense."[111] As seen in the reperformances of *Happy* and *Thriller,* fan videos contain within them an acknowledgment, a thank-you to the artists whose work they duplicate and embody. Sometimes fans indicate thanks by dedicating their videos to the artist who inspired their reproduction. Sometimes, to deter take-down notices from music copyright holders, they add a note that no infringement is intended and that theirs is an expression of admiration and appreciation. Serres reminds us of the importance of expressing gratitude: "No exchange could take place, no gift could be given . . . if the final receiver did not say 'thank you' at the end of the line." This phrase is indispensible, he says. "Without it, there have been wars."[112] When a recipient accepts a gift with no acknowledgment and no thought of return, it may be considered a form of theft. This is because, as Mauss contends, "the gift necessarily entails the notion of credit."[113] "What is credit?" Maurizio Lazzarato asks: "A promise to pay a debt."[114]

The term *credit* describes both the situation of acknowledging an individual's contributions to a group enterprise and a measurement of the capacity for indebtedness. In "giving credit where it's due," as the saying goes, one expresses gratitude as well as obligation to the individual or group from whom one has borrowed. Giving credit is an acknowledgment of social debts, or the "reciprocal bonds of productivity between people" for which cultural theorist Richard Dienst advocates reserving the term *indebtedness*.[115] But when credit is employed in finance, it is tied to repayment. Credit cards and credit lines establish an estimated loan amount that a borrower "is good for," and purchases made on credit carry with them a built-in penalty in the form of interest. The inability to pay off a debt within a predetermined time frame can lead to further penalties, including hindering one's ability to borrow in the future. The same term describes an obligation born of gratitude within a group endeavor and a monetary debt.[116]

These two notions of credit align with the two notions of belonging as affiliation and as property discussed earlier. In manifesting affiliation or belonging to a group, one gives credit in the manner a community has accepted as an appropriate mode of attribution or acknowledgment. In scholarly communities, for example, individuals belong to a community of ideas. Citation and attribution ensure that contributors receive recognition for their work within intellectual communities as members collectively borrow and build on circulating ideas, while also reflecting, as Thomas Jefferson famously opined, "the moment [an idea] is divulged, it forces itself into the possession of every one."[117] Similarly, kinesthetic and gestural communities form around movement practices, but no dancer owns the gestures or movements of which their choreographies or improvisations are composed. Like ideas, languages, and bodily techniques, embodied objects are held in common; they are not static belongings but dynamic expressions of belonging. Thus attribution stands in the place of owner-ship. Social norms of attribution may not carry beyond the boundaries of a community, however, and belonging as property may come into play as a way to distinguish between the rights and responsibilities of community participants who engage in circular giving with regard to communal prac-tices or products (what Russell Belk calls sharing in) versus access to these practices or products offered to community outsiders for a fee (sharing out).[118] In this way, belonging also aligns with a financial understanding of credit. If movements "belong" to an individual or community as property, then in using them, one owes something to their creators for the right to use and reproduce them. If movements cannot be owned or licensed, how-ever, then no one owes anybody anything for the right to use them. Cul-tural brokers and entrepreneurs thus benefit the most financially by acting as intermediaries between gift and market economies, reconfiguring what is commonly produced into a saleable format.

Digital platforms facilitate the slippage between gift and commodity, since posting and sharing content online have the effect of orphaning that content, stripping away affiliations and contextual information. Such con-tent is attributed to the internet or anonymous creatives rather than indi-vidual contributors. "As a result," notes media and communications scholar James Meese, "creators have little opportunity to benefit either economi-cally or reputationally from this system."[119] For example, in her post "A Cau-tionary Tale: What Can Happen When Your Personal Video Goes Viral," choreographer Alexandra Beller recounts how she uploaded a video from rehearsal one evening, only to watch it go viral over the next several days without reference to her or her dance company.

Beller is a contemporary dance maker based in New York, and she was rehearsing her work *milkdreams* (2015), an investigation of children's move-ment inspired by her young sons.[120] One day, she brought her fourteen-month-old son, Ivo, into the studio and asked her dancers to follow his movements. This is a variation on a common technique called *flocking,* which is regularly incorporated into modern dance classes and rehearsals as a way of sharing in movement. Typically, in a flocking exercise, a group follows the lead of whichever dancer is at the front of the group. As the group changes its spatial orientation, the leadership also changes. Beller altered this movement score by asking her dancers to keep following her son. In a re-posted video clip of Beller's rehearsal,[121] the (unidentified) dancers Lea Fulton, Christina Robson,[122] and Simon Thomas-Train follow Ivo as he squats, stands on his tiptoes and falls, turns circles, and collapses onto the floor. The video takes contemporary explorations of "de-skilling" as an aesthetic beyond the amateur into the realm of child development. According to Beller, she documented a playful moment in rehearsal and shared it with her online followers without a thought for how it might circulate beyond that intended audience. Like Pharrell, who was surprised to see that his song and video were no longer his, Beller was surprised to see how popular her video became. Unlike Pharrell, however, whose "Happy" song traveled with fan performances of the video's concept, social media users posted and shared Beller's video, titled *Baby Modern Dance*, without any connection to Beller or her company, depriving her of the monetary compensation that could have come through YouTube advertising, for example, and also depriving her of the opportunity to build her theater audience through exposure. Beller recalls, "I didn't have any experience with this, nor any idea what, if anything, it required of me. I watched, fascinated, as it got picked up and spread by *Huffington Post*, BuzzFeed, Perez Hilton: 50 million views, 200 million, 300 million views

Figure 41. Screenshot of the rehearsal video for *milkdreams* (2015), choreographed by Alexandra Beller. Pictured are dancers Lea Fulton, Christina Robson, Simon Thomas-Train, and Beller's son, Ivo.

on each site. Then it started getting posted by less famous sources, and I noticed my name was no longer on it, but advertisements were."[123]

Beller missed an opportunity literally to capitalize on what she thought was a moment worth sharing with her followers and friends because she did not anticipate the potential for monetization. As a result of this miscalculation, it was thus not Beller but content aggregators and re-posters who benefited financially, as well as those who used the same idea for product advertisements. Beller remarks in language reminiscent of Anne Marsen, "I've seen the concept—my concept—borrowed and reused to monetize products in television commercials and online marketing campaigns."[124] As with Marsen's claim that Pharrell stole *Girl Walk*'s concept, Beller feels that hers was likewise pilfered. Still, as with Marsen, it is difficult to ascertain what has been misappropriated. Beller is not the first contemporary choreographer to ask dancers to imitate the movements of a baby, nor are the techniques of flocking or mirroring unique to Beller's choreographic process. Ivo, who was at the time in the process of acquiring movement as a toddler, was gathering the embodied objects of gestures and movement from the dancers he observed due to having a choreographer as a parent. Ivo copies the dancers, the dancers copy Ivo, Beller captures this copying on video, and content aggregators capture its monetary value. As Meese contends, internet platforms and procedures for sharing are frequently structured to sever content from creators. Whereas Beller posted the video as a small gift, a triviality, to share with her friends and fan community, others' sharing of that gift assisted in its anonymization and transformation into monetizable content. As is commonly the case with viral videos, its value could only be recognized in retrospect as an effect of its having been shared. Prior to its viral spread, it had little value. Indeed, if Beller had known how profitable it could have been, she likely would not have given it away freely. "If I had ONE PENNY for every time the video has been viewed, I'd have $10 million," Beller laments in her Kickstarter video for the production of *milkdreams*, indicting "the disconnect between how we ingest, share, take and discard each other's material, versus supporting, nurturing, and collaborating on it."[125] Traveling outside the context for which it was intended, Beller's video became disarticulated from the relations of reciprocity she needs to financially support her work as an artist.

In his analysis of Mauss, anthropologist David Graeber differentiates between open and closed reciprocity. Open reciprocity "implies a relation of permanent mutual commitment"[126] and is a form of generosity reserved for the closest of relationships—between friends or family members, for example. Open reciprocity allows for expenditure without exchange, in the way that family members will help each other out or dancers will collectively build from what each has to offer when they improvise together. Closed reciprocity, in contrast, is governed by a quid pro quo that preserves the ability to conclude relationships with the balancing of accounts. There is no sense that the relationship endures beyond the point of transaction. Graeber further allows that closed relationships can become more open, and vice versa, as the nature of a relationship changes, but in Graeber's view, closed reciprocity resembles a market economy, where relationships conclude at the point of sale, more than the ideals of a gift economy. Gift economies retain the connection between giver and gift (or contributor and contribution), mediated by the recipient. Market economies, as Marx observed, alienate producers from (the products of) their labor, and compensation, in theory, terminates the relationship with payment for services rendered—whether in the context of a factory, a dance studio, or a video game.

In the example of dance video games seen earlier, gamers offer monetary payment toward a debt of access, seemingly bringing the relation to a conclusion by purchasing the game. Gamers thus do not accrue any debts vis-à-vis movement communities, because theirs is a closed relationship mediated by the video game platform and the choreographers who open access through commodification. In Beller's case, she volunteered content only to be made aware of its value in retrospect as it became commodified. Viewers did not pay to view her video, but neither was there a sense of reciprocity in the form of attribution. In the place of Beller's gift is an unacknowledged debt insofar as she has neither been compensated, nor been given credit.[127] However, if one contends that gifts cannot be paid off, even if they circulate as commodities, then one must further consider the social debts that structure the gifting of dance, which insists upon an open system of reciprocity regardless of whether money ever changes hands.

Whereas theorists of the gift emphasize the obligatory gift and the paradoxical gift "with strings attached" as lying at the heart of community,

Maurizio Lazzarato follows Nietzsche in arguing that it is debt that lies at the foundation of social relations. The principle of exchange, Lazzarato argues, presupposes parties that are on equal footing, but acknowledging the force of debt in structuring social relations also acknowledges that there is an imbalance of power in every relation, and this influences the flow of capital. Imbalance "does not mean that exchange does not exist, but rather that it functions according to a logic not of equality but of disequilibrium and difference."[128] Debt not only operates economically, according to Lazzarato; it produces subjectivity in conjunction with a morality and, following Foucault, forms of life. Credit and debt have become powerful metaphors for contemporary life, bringing social and even biological life itself into the logic of finance. Financial solvency has become a measurement of moral character. Only those who are "morally bankrupt" would disregard the social debts that accompany a gift, "ignor[ing] the fact," as Graeber remarks, "that we rely on other people for just about everything."[129] However, because credit relations always exist with an imbalance of power, the valuation of character reflects that imbalance with curious effect.[130]

Although presumably currency holds a consistent value in relation to itself regardless of where it came from—my dollar is the same as your dollar—the debt economy and financialization have eviscerated this basic principle of exchange. The value of currency has become a matter of speculation, an evaluation of the value of one's promise to repay reflected in credit limits and interest rates. The inequalities built into the credit relations that fuel a debt economy thus net different results for different parties, in which some parties are indemnified against their debts and others are not: the more capital one has, whether financial or social, the more capacity one has for debt, which is measured and described financially as credit. This additional capacity for debt does not result in increased indebtedness, however, as excess capital indemnifies against the burden of debt. In Richard Dienst's phrasing, capitalism produces "credit without debt for the few (who can wield the power of investment without accountability) and debt without credit for the many (who bear the hazards without exercising a choice)."[131] In other words, the more capacity one has for debt, the less one is expected to repay, and the less capacity one has for debt, the more one is expected to make good on the promise of repayment. By extension, there is potentially an inverse correlation between the credit one has (or takes) and the credit one gives. In the creative realm, one gives credit to others because one is not indemnified against one's social debts and has a need for the ties they create. But when one is of such stature that social ties are unimportant to continued success, one is perhaps less likely to credit the contributions of others and more likely to take credit undeservingly. "Within relations of presumed inequality, no presumption of reciprocity exists," Graeber remarks,[132] fostering a scenario in which, as Dienst contends, "capital always tries to take credit for everything people can do in common."[133]

The conflict between Belgian choreographer Anne Theresa De Keersmaeker and American pop singer Beyoncé Knowles, briefly mentioned earlier in this chapter, offers another example of how credit and debt play out vis-à-vis social capital and choreographic authorship in the field of dance. Beyoncé famously borrows from music, fashion, dance, and visual artists for her music videos, garnering accusations of plagiarism from both the aggrieved and fans. Her music video Countdown,[134] which is a collage of popular media references, reproduces sections of De Keersmaeker's choreography from her dance works Rosas danst Rosas[135] and Achterland,[136] both of which were adapted for film. De Keersmaeker was not a featured participant or collaborator on Countdown. She was not consulted on the inclusion of her work, nor was she compensated. No presumption of reciprocity exists between De Keersmaeker and Beyoncé, not only because Beyoncé no longer needs the social ties that attribution and return gifts maintain but also because her cultural capital indemnifies her against any such social debts. Although De Keersmaeker did issue a statement challenging the use of her choreography in Beyoncé's music video,[137] she did not ultimately pursue a lawsuit. Instead, discovering that YouTube had transformed her choreographic gift into a given, that is, a universally available common inheritance, De Keersmaeker paradoxically reasserted her authorship by giving a simplified section of the work to the public for remixing, thereby explicitly submitting her choreography to the common herself.[138]

A signature work developed early in De Keersmaeker's career and filmed by Thierry de Mey, Rosas danst Rosas explores feminine and feminist themes through a series of gestures that repeat in ever-changing combinations,

resulting in a spare and highly structured exposition of everyday movements. In the scene used in *Countdown*, four seated women run their fingers through their hair, prop their elbows on their knees and chins on their
fists, reach and fling their arms out of boredom and despair, and collapse
forward. Each action recurs relentlessly. Although the women do not
heighten the drama with performances of emotional states that accompany the otherwise angst-ridden gestures, the driving music and repetitive
choreography convey a sense of frustration and confinement.

In the course of their dance education, college students frequently learn
the "chair scene" as repertory—the embodied history of concert dance—
so this choreography is already widely shared within a global community
of modern dance practitioners. De Keersmaeker's response to Beyoncé's
use of her material was to further open access to the choreography, for-
malizing the long-standing practice of learning repertory informally by
copying it from film and video. For the *Re: Rosas!* project (ongoing from
2013), De Keersmaeker and the fABULEUS team posted a tutorial for
the choreography online along with the original music. They extended an
invitation to perform and adapt De Keersmaeker's choreography by
changing the sequence of movements, the music, the setting, the number
of dancers, and so forth. As a point of comparison, when Beyoncé's fans
began posting online videos of themselves performing the *Single Ladies*
choreography,[139] she responded by sponsoring a contest for which fans
were required to "adhere precisely" to the music video's choreography.[140]
Illustrating the pervasiveness of both delegated artistic processes, discussed in chapter 3, and choreographic unworking, discussed in chapter 1,
De Keersmaeker's *Re: Rosas!* places the famous chair scene from *Rosas
danst Rosas* in the hands of anyone who wishes to perform it and upload
an interpretation to the project website. In unworking the choreography,
turning it over to the crowd for reinvention and rediscovery, De Keersmaeker offers it as a site through which participants can express their
being-in-common, their participation in a community of movement built
on gestural indebtedness.

Affirming her authorship through the very process of engaging the
crowd to unwork the choreography, De Keersmaeker provided a mechanism for danced interpretations to come back to her, inviting contributors

Figure 42. Homepage for the *Re: Rosas!* project (2013), which provides an overview of the project, videos teaching the choreography, a downloadable music file (bottom of the screen), an invitation to participate (top right), and the three most recent contributions (right banner).

to upload videos directly to the *Re: Rosas!* website. Like We Are Happy From, for which Fersing and Fontaine gathered fan-produced videos, *Re: Rosas!* similarly gathers these contributions in a single location. In 2013, the fABULEUS project team also compiled and edited videos of the *Rosas danst Rosas* chair scene from around the globe, "from Australia to Burkina Faso and from Mexico City to Shanghai," into a single video, which they posted on YouTube.[141] Since then, the project has continued to grow. More than 360 rerenderings of the chair scene had been posted to the project website by the end of 2016. In groups or solo, participants reinvent the dance. They perform in subways, on rock faces, in rivers, in bathrooms and living rooms, on escalators, and elsewhere. Performances by young women read differently from those of solo men or groups of small children, all flinging themselves through its movements. Abstracted from the performers who originated the roles (*Rosas danst Rosas* gestured to the idea that the members of the company, called Rosas, were dancing themselves) and their experiences of femininity and feminism in the 1980s, the gestures take on alternate possibilities.

Notably, the extracts of De Keersmaeker's choreography utilized in
Beyoncé's *Countdown* sample everyday gestures, club dancing, and even
tap dance, which reside in an uncredited movement common from which
postmodern dance routinely pulls, as Brenda Dixon Gottschild has demonstrated.[142] Disrupting the presumed hierarchy between concert and social
dance, the horizontal logic of a postmodern aesthetic, Randy Martin observes, "suddenly brings to notice troves of movement riches once consigned to the periphery."[143] In the case of Beller, this movement periphery
extended all the way to the bodily logics of toddlers in the process of learning how to control their own motion. Both De Keersmaeker and Beller
illustrate this practice of developing choreography within a postmodern
aesthetic by turning to a movement common for their compositions. You-
Tube, where De Keersmaeker's choreography circulated beyond her control
and where Beyoncé's creative team discovered it, ensures that the process of
concertizing vernacular dance[144] is reversed as well, flattening hierarchies
of movement practices and vernacularizing concert dance choreography.
Just as film and television disseminated the dance routines and movement
innovations of individuals and communities of dancers in decades prior,
YouTube and other video-sharing sites now enable the broad circulation
of steps, gestures, and choreographies within and through the internet's
gift economies with little regard for authorial claims. Although they differ
in their approaches to what can be considered a common from which to
glean dance movement, both De Keersmaeker's use of vernacular dance
forms and pedestrian movements and Beyoncé's use of choreographic material from experimental dance artists recognize that these cultural practices
and products circulate as gifts. Both approaches exemplify a Derridean
interpretation of the gift, which contends that gifts are given freely and
without obligation, while also illuminating the financial and authorial investments in identifying (or occluding) the source of the gift.

In his short volume *Given Time,* Jacques Derrida dismantles Mauss's
three obligations to give, receive, and reciprocate through which the gift
creates mutual ties of indebtedness. Derrida counters, "For there to be a
gift, there must be no reciprocity, return, exchange, countergift, or debt.
If the other gives me back or owes me or has to give me back what I give
him or her, there will not have been a gift."[145] Derrida's gift refuses recognition and reciprocation. It must be completely forgotten.[146] "So we are

speaking here of an absolute forgetting—a forgetting that also absolves, that unbinds absolutely and infinitely more, therefore, than excuse, forgiveness, or acquittal."[147] With his emphasis on the forgetfulness embedded in giving and accepting gifts, however, I contend that Derrida more accurately describes the social operations of privilege than those of giving or receiving gifts.

Privilege, as unacknowledged inheritance, produces advantage even as it masks itself. Nothing has been given, nothing is owed, and yet these nothings add up to an immaterial something that both possesses and produces value. This privilege, born of disavowal and antisocial amnesia regarding the contributions of others, belongs to the parasite, which Michel Serres understands to be the direct product of the gift on Derrida's model.[148] Privilege allows for the purposeful or accidental mistaking of the gifted for the given—taking without thought of return, without thanks, and without recognition of the donations of others. As the corporeal common expands—populated by unacknowledged gifts that become part of the given via physical reproduction and circulation through digital media—it becomes fertile ground for entrepreneurial intervention and investment. But the expansion of the common can also open up a space of gratitude and a sense of indebtedness for movement that is shared.

Dance practices and choreographies are constructed from embodied objects that populate a corporeal common, but unlike giving material gifts, movement donors cannot be rid of the dances they give. As Thomas Jefferson observed of transmitting an idea, "no one possesses [it] the less, because every other possesses the whole of it."[149] As gifts, dances change bodies without changing hands. Dances are fugitive in one way, but in another, they never leave their location. Dancing is an invitation or an offering, not a giving-away but a gesture of giving that retains dancing for oneself in the act of distribution. Dance cannot be possessed, only circulated and propagated in relation to a common that establishes what is given to be shared.

Yet, what is given for some is not given for all, as neoliberal ideals of universal access would suggest, because there is no single common, only many commons. As Hardt and Negri argue, "contemporary forms of capitalist production and accumulation . . . require expansions of the common."[150] The expansion of the common is not only an expansion of what

knowledges, practices, and products can be made available for monetization, but an expansion of the common as singular rather than multiple,
governed by universal access rather than communal norms that govern
practices of sharing in and sharing out. This expansion underwrites the
repeated misrecognition of gifts of a particular common for the given of
a universal common. Embodied objects thus travel, through infelicitous
acts of transfer, from situated fields of knowledge and practice to a common inheritance posited as universal. However, it is not only capital that
demands the expansion of the common by mining particular commons.
As Martin observes, postmodern choreographers turning to peripheral
movement practices as sources for choreographic innovation likewise
expand the movement common. Indeed, the craft of dance is the recapitu-
lation and exposure of gestures held in common, which artists organize,
situate, recycle, and re-present as gifts through scenarios of transmission
such as choreography and dance pedagogy.

In this chapter, I have argued that danced offerings circulate, accrue meaning and value as they travel from body to body, lose their cultural specificity as they increase in accessibility, and become fodder for entrepreneurial
as well as communal innovation. As with all embodied objects, dancing
is never given once and for all; dance movements and practices find
both their source and their destination in a corporeal common, from
which they are gifted again and again. How far this corporeal common
reaches is a matter of debate, however, and tensions arise between movement communities that assert dance as a mode of belonging and digital
cultural practices that circulate movement beyond the boundaries of community. In positing dance as gift of the common, I wish to undo the privileged Derridean account in which gifts circulate without thought of
return and suggest instead that a Maussian interpretation of the structure
of the gift better grasps how dance's circulation through digital media is
underwritten by dancers' corporeal generosity and gestural indebtedness.
As common, dances circulate freely through digital media, but as gifts,
they circulate with social obligations attached. Attending to these social
obligations offers an opportunity to maintain an ethical orientation toward
sharing in the movement and gestures of others.

Perpetual Motion: Dance, Digital Cultures, and the Common explores the uses and meanings of dance in digital and online environments from 1996 to 2016. Throughout, I attend to shifts in dance performance, reception, dissemination, and circulation brought about by popular digital media technologies. Whereas early examples of dance on the web and CD-ROM, such as those I explore in chapter 1, are mostly limited to artistic investigations of hypertextual and combinatory aesthetics, social media platforms give amateurs and enthusiasts a means of joining with professional dance artists to spread popular dances by digitizing, sharing, and embodying them. Participating in digital cultures, dancers across the amateur and professional spectrum physically articulate a space and sense of the common through their shared movements. In chapter 2, these performances of the common act to recuperate and loosen public spaces as common spaces in the wake of violence and pressures to curtail freedom of movement. In chapter 3, dances participate in performing a common world, which is enacted through gestures that link communities together. Employed in the broad participation of the crowd, dance additionally transforms and performs-world onscreen. Finally, in chapter 4, dances circulate among and between communities, raising questions about the ethics of dance's corporeal transmission through digital media. Circulating beyond communities of practice, commonly accessible gestures are mistaken for a given field of movement that is universally available. Throughout *Perpetual Motion*, I have considered how digital cultures engage dance and movement in the production and performance of a common and the purposes and effects of these performances.

Notes

INTRODUCTION

1. *Passe-Partout,* iPad app, concept and design by Abbott Miller, choreography by Justin Peck, performance by Justin Peck and Daniel Ulbricht, video direction by Ben Louis Nicholas, music by Aaron Severini, produced by 2wice Arts Foundation.

2. Gia Kourlas, "You're the Choreographer, an iPad's Your Stage," *New York Times,* June 25, 2014.

3. Kourlas.

4. Kourlas.

5. See esp. Elinor Ostrom, *Governing the Commons: The Evolution of Institutions for Collective Life* (Cambridge: Cambridge University Press, 1990).

6. Ramsay Burt, *Ungoverning Dance: Contemporary European Theatre Dance and the Commons* (New York: Oxford University Press, 2017), 19.

7. See, e.g., Judith Hamera, *Dancing Communities: Performance, Difference and Connection in the Global City* (Houndsmills, U.K.: Palgrave Macmillan, 2007).

8. Michael Hardt and Antonio Negri, *Commonwealth* (Cambridge, Mass.: Belknap Press, 2011), 250.

9. Hardt and Negri, xviii.

10. Hardt and Negri, ix.

11. Hardt and Negri note, "One primary effect of globalization, however, is the creation of a common world, a world that, for better or worse, we all share, a world that has no 'outside'" (vii).

12. Kimberly Christen, "Gone Digital: Aboriginal Remix and the Cultural Commons," *International Journal of Cultural Property* 12 (2005): 315.

13. Christen, 336.

14. Randy Martin, *Financialization of Daily Life* (Philadelphia: Temple University Press, 2002), 20.

15. Martin, 141.

16. Kimberly Christen, "Does Information Really Want to Be Free? Indigenous Knowledge Systems and the Question of Openness," *International Journal of Communication* 6 (2012): 2874. Her emphasis.

17. Brenda Dixon Gottschild, *Digging the Africanist Presence in American Performance: Dance and Other Contexts* (Westport, Conn.: Praeger, 1998). Jacqueline Shea Murphy, *The People Have Never Stopped Dancing: Native American Modern Dance Histories* (Minneapolis: University of Minnesota Press, 2007).

18. Jane Desmond, "Dancing Out the Difference: Cultural Imperialism and Ruth St. Denis's 'Radha' of 1906," *Signs* 17, no. 1 (1991): 28–49. Priya Srinivasan, "The Bodies beneath the Smoke or What's Behind the Cigarette Poster: Unearthing Kinesthetic Connections in American Dance History," *Discourses in Dance* 4, no. 1 (2007): 7–48.

19. Susan Manning, *Modern Dance, Negro Dance: Race in Motion* (Minneapolis: University of Minnesota Press, 2006).

20. For a critical account of this phenomenon in the realm of popular dance, see Thomas F. DeFrantz, "Unchecked Popularity: Neoliberal Circulations of Black Dance," in *Neoliberalism and Global Theatres: Performance Permutations,* ed. Lara Nielson and Patricia Ybarra, 128–40 (New York: Palgrave, 2012), which I take up in chapter 4.

21. Diana Taylor, *The Archive and the Repertoire: Performing Cultural Memory in the Americas* (Durham, N.C.: Duke University Press, 2003), 2.

22. Elizabeth Maddock Dillon, *New World Drama: The Performative Commons in the Atlantic World, 1649–1849* (Durham, N.C.: Duke University Press, 2014), 4.

23. Dillon, 7.

24. These include *Biped* (1999) choreographed by Merce Cunningham, *Ghostcatching* (1999) choreographed by Bill T. Jones, and *How Long Does the Subject Linger on the Edge of the Volume* (2005) choreographed by Trisha Brown. Marc Downie joined Kaiser and Eshkar for *How Long.*

25. Deirdre LaCarte's Hampster Dance was a popular 1990s website featuring rows of hamsters dancing to "Whistle Stop" from Disney's 1973 animated film *Robin Hood.* For more information, see the "Hampster Dance" entry on Know Your Meme, accessed August 1, 2017, https://knowyourmeme.com/memes/hampster-dance.

26. See esp. Peggy Phelan, "The Ontology of Performance: Representation without Reproduction," in *Unmarked: The Politics of Performance* (London: Routledge, 1993), 146–166, and Rebecca Schneider, *Performing Remains: Art and War in Times of Theatrical Reenactment* (New York: Routledge, 2011).

27. Mark Franko and Annette Richards, "Actualizing Absence: The Pastness of Performance," in *Acting on the Past: Historical Performance across the Disciplines* (Hanover, Penn.: Wesleyan University Press, 2000), 2.

28. See, e.g., Paul Grainge, ed., *Ephemeral Media: Transitory Screen Culture from Television to YouTube* (London: Palgrave Macmillan, 2011).

29. Chesapeake Digital Preservation Group, "'Link Rot' and Legal Resources on the Web: A 2014 Analysis by the Chesapeake Digital Preservation Group," accessed August 1, 2017, http://cdm16064.contentdm.oclc.org/cdm/linkrot2014.

30. Wendy Hui Kyong Chun, "The Enduring Ephemeral, or the Future Is a Memory," *Critical Inquiry* 35 (2008): 153, 160.

31. For a further consideration of ephemerality in the contexts of dance and digital media, see my chapter "'Complex Temporalities': Digitality and the Ephemeral Tense in Adam H. Weinert's 'The Reaccession of Ted Shawn'" in *The Routledge Dance Studies Reader,* 3rd ed., ed. Jens Richard Giersdorf and Yutian Wong, 364–73 (London: Routledge, 2019).

32. See Gay Morris and Jens Richard Giersdorf's excellent overview of choreography as a methodological approach in the introduction to their coedited book *Choreographies of 21st Century Wars* (New York: Oxford University Press, 2016), 1–24.

1. INTERACTIVITY AND AGENCY

1. The twelve scenes are (1) "Ouverture," (2) "Ghost," (3) "Pluie," (4) "Machination," (5) "Slow Down," (6) "Frontal," (7) "Docks," (8) "Fragile," (9) "Melting," (10) "High," (11) "Nuages," and (12) "Coda."

2. *Somnambules,* web, art conception, libretto, camera, and programming by Nicolas Clauss; music, libretto, camera, and executive production by Jean-Jacques-Birgé; dance by Didier Silhol (2003), accessed July 13, 2016, http://www.somnambules.net/.

3. *Somnambules.*

4. Works of comparable scale were created for CD-ROM, but few were created specifically for the web.

5. See Espen Aarseth, *Cybertext: Perspectives on Ergodic Literature* (Baltimore: Johns Hopkins University Press, 1997).

6. See Harmony Bench, "Screendance 2.0: Dance and Social Media," *Participations: Journal of Audience and Reception Studies* 7, no. 2 (2010), http://www.participations.org/Volume%207/Issue%202/special/bench.htm.

7. *Trilogy,* choreography and performance by Carolien Hermans (2003), accessed June 29, 2006, http://www.du.ahk.nl/mijnsite/trilogy/trilogy.htm. Site now defunct.

8. *Invisible,* choreography and artistic direction by Magali and Didier Mulleras; stage/light design and multimedia/video by Nicolas Grimal; music/sound design

by Magali and Didier Mulleras; dance by Magali and Didier Mulleras, Elisabeth Nicol, and Severine Prunera (2003), accessed March 25, 2018, https://vimeo .com/5436189.

9. *5th Wall,* iPad app, concept and design by Abbott Miller, choreography and performance by Jonah Bokaer, video direction by Ben Louis Nicholas, music by So Percussion (2013).

10. *Windowsninetyeight: lo-fi kitchen sink dancing,* CD-ROM, dance and visual art by Ruth Gibson, art by Bruno Martelli (Igloo, 1996–98).

11. *Move-Me,* web, created by Simon Fildes and Katrina McPherson (Ricochet Dance and Goat Media, 2004), accessed July 13, 2016, http://move-me.com/.

12. Gilles Deleuze, *Cinema 1: The Movement Image,* trans. Hugh Tomlinson and Barbara Habberjam (1983; Minneapolis: University of Minnesota Press, 1986), 13.

13. Wendy Hui Kyong Chun, "The Enduring Ephemeral, or the Future Is a Memory," *Critical Inquiry* 35 (2008): 148.

14. Lev Manovich, *The Language of New Media* (Cambridge, Mass.: MIT Press, 2001), 55.

15. Jens F. Jensen, "'Interactivity': Tracking a New Concept in Media and Communication Studies," *Nordicom Review: Nordic Research on Media and Communication* 19, no. 1 (1998): 185.

16. Jon Katz, "Birth of a Digital Nation," *Wired,* April 1, 1997, accessed March 25, 2018, https://www.wired.com/1997/04/netizen-3/.

17. George P. Landow, *Hypertext: The Convergence of Contemporary Critical Theory and Technology* (Baltimore: Johns Hopkins University Press, 1992).

18. Landow quoting Barthes, *S/Z,* trans. Richard Miller (1970; New York: Farrar, Straus, and Giroux/Hill and Wang, 1974), 5.

19. Margaret Morse, "The Poetics of Interactivity," in *Women, Art, and Technology,* ed. Judy Malloy (Cambridge, Mass.: MIT Press, 2003), 18. Original emphasis.

20. Morse, 19.

21. Mark B. N. Hansen, *New Philosophy for New Media* (Cambridge, Mass.: MIT Press, 2004), 24.

22. David Z. Saltz, "The Art of Interaction: Interactivity, Performativity, and Computers," *Journal of Aesthetics and Art Criticism* 55, no. 2 (1997): 118.

23. As a vector-based animation program, Flash was especially popular for creating noninteractive web-based cartoons circa 1999. For a time, Flash was the software of choice for online game developers.

24. Though Web 1.0 and Web 2.0 seem to indicate a linear progression, the emergence of social media has introduced an additional layer of web experience but has not replaced previous modes of information distribution.

25. *Progressive 2,* web, Richard Lord, director and choreographer (1996), accessed October 15, 2004, http://www.bigroom.co.uk/consumers/webdances.php. Site now defunct.

26. *Waterfall,* CD-ROM, directed and choreographed by Richard Lord, performance by Emma Diamond, music by Kate Heath (Big Room Ventures, 2002).

27. *Big,* web, camera by Katrina McPherson, editing by Simon Fildes, choreography by Crystal Pite (2002), accessed July 13, 2016, http://hyperchoreography.org/big.html.

28. *The Truth: The Truth,* web, directed by Katrina McPherson, choreography by Fin Walker and Paolo Ribeiro (2004), accessed July 13, 2016, http://hyperchore ography.org/thetruth.html.

29. *Triad HyperDance* is a web-based, interactive documentation of the 1998 telematic performance *Triad NetDance* directed by Marikki Hakola. Modern dancer Molissa Fenley in New York and butoh performer Akeno in Tokyo were joined by video transmitted over the internet and projected into the Kiasma museum in Helsinki, the primary performance venue, where the video feeds were mixed with digital media and music. *Triad HyperDance,* web, concept and direction by Marikki Hakola, choreography and performance by Akeno and Molissa Fenley, music by Otna Eahket (1999), accessed July 13, 2016, http://www.kroma.fi/triad/info/triadhyper.html.

30. *Drift,* web, directed by Koert van Mensvoort, dance by Nancy Mauro-Flude (Music Artefact, 2003), accessed July 13, 2016, http://www.mensvoort.com/work/drift-dancer-without-a-body.

31. Following Deleuze's typology of cinematic signs or images, Galloway delineates a number of "acts" unique to gameplay. He describes the ambience act as a state of equilibrium wherein environmental "micromovements" let the player know the game is in play mode but in which points are neither gained nor lost. Alexander R. Galloway, *Gaming: Essays on Algorithmic Culture* (Minneapolis: University of Minnesota Press, 2006), 10–11.

32. In addition to Morse, "The Poetics of Interactivity," see Sokë Dinkla, "From Participation to Interaction: Toward the Origins of Interactive Art," in *Clicking In: Hot Links to a Digital Culture,* ed. Lynn Hershman Leeson, 279–90 (Seattle, Wash.: Bay Press, 1996), as well as Steve Dixon, *Digital Performance: A History of New Media in Theatre, Dance, Performance Art, and Installation* (Cambridge, Mass.: MIT Press, 2007).

33. For a more thorough treatment of the performativity of code in hyperdance, see my essay "Computational Choreographies: Performance in Dance Online" in *International Journal of Performance Arts and Digital Media* 5 (2014): 155–69.

34. Rita Raley, "Reveal Codes: Hypertext and Performance," *Postmodern Culture* 12 (2000), para. 9, accessed March 25, 2018, http://pmc.iath.virginia.edu/text-only/issue.901/12.1raley.txt.

35. Raley, para. 10.

36. Hans Dieter Huber, "Only!4!!!!!!!!!!!!!!!!!!!!!!!4-for your private eyes. A structural analysis of http://www.jodi.org" (2002), accessed April 1, 2009, http://www.hgbleipzig.de/artnine/huber/writings/jodie/indexe.html.

37. Carolien Hermans, "Trilogy," accessed July 13, 2016, http://www.du.ahk.nl/people/carolien/papers/TrilogyPaper.htm.

38. Hermans.

39. See Umberto Eco, *The Poetics of the Open Work*, trans. Anna Cancogni (Cambridge, Mass.: Harvard University Press, 1989).

40. Hermans, "Trilogy," n.p.

41. Susan Kozel, *Closer: Performance, Technologies, Phenomenology* (Cambridge, Mass.: MIT Press, 2007), 182.

42. Kozel, 189.

43. Morse, "Poetics of Interactivity," 21.

44. Hal Foster, "Chat Rooms," in *Participation*, ed. Claire Bishop (Cambridge, Mass.: MIT Press, 2006), 193.

45. Alexander Galloway and Eugene Thacker, *The Exploit: A Theory of Networks* (Minneapolis: University of Minnesota Press, 2007), 124.

46. Hansen, *New Philosophy for New Media*, 24.

47. *Latitudes*, web, choreography by Molissa Fenley (November 1996), accessed May 3, 2009, http://www.diacenter.org/fenley/title.html. Site now defunct.

48. *Yearbody*, web, choreography by Dawn Stoppiello, web design by Mark Coniglio (November 1996–October 1997), accessed October 15, 2005, http://www.troikaranch.org/yearbody.html. Site now defunct.

49. *Be to Want I*, web, choreography by Marianne Goldberg, performed by Christianne Brown (1996), accessed July 13, 2016, http://kairos.technorhetoric.net/3.2/response/Kendall/goldberg/Be_to_want_I.html. Site semifunctional.

50. *Tree*, web, part 2 of *Before and After Geography*, choreography by Ralph Lemon (2000). This was part of his *Geography Trilogy* (1995–2005), with digital artists Vivian Selbo and Carl Skelton (May 3, 2009), accessed July 13, 2016, http://www.cavil.com/tree/. Site semifunctional.

51. For commentary on some of these and other early hyperdances, particularly works prior to 1998, see Sita Popat, *Invisible Connections: Dance, Choreography, and Internet Communities* (London: Routledge, 2006).

52. Rita Raley, "The Digital Loop: Feedback and Recurrence," *Leonardo Electronic Almanac* 10, no. 7 (2002).

53. André Lepecki, *Exhausting Dance: Performance and the Politics of Movement* (New York: Routledge, 2006), 16.

54. Lepecki, 13.

55. Following anthropologist Nadia Seremetakis, Lepecki calls these "still-acts." See Seremetakis, "The Memory of the Senses (parts I–III)," in *The Senses Still:*

Perception and Memory as Material Culture in Modernity, ed. N. Seremetakis, 1–43 (Chicago: University of Chicago Press, 1996).

56. See, e.g., Simon Ellis and David Corbet's work for iPod, *Microflicks* (2006–7), accessed July 17, 2016, http://slightly.net/microflicks/.

57. Raley, "Digital Loop."

58. Gilles Deleuze, *Cinema 2: The Time Image*, trans. Hugh Tomlinson and Robert Galeta (1985; Minneapolis: University of Minnesota Press, 1989), 2.

59. Deleuze, 62.

60. Deleuze, 67.

61. Deleuze, 128.

62. *Trilogy*. Hermans takes this passage from Henri Bergson's *Matter and Memory*.

63. *Trilogy*.

64. Deleuze, *Cinema 2*, 4.

65. Videos of these other instantiations are available online. For links, see http://www.mulleras.com/invisible/accueilinv.html, accessed July 5, 2016.

66. Deleuze, *Cinema 2*, 59.

67. Manovich, *Language of New Media*, xxxiii.

68. Gilles Deleuze, *Difference and Repetition*, trans. Paul Patton (1968; New York: Columbia University Press, 1994), xvi.

69. Deleuze, 29.

70. Deleuze, 222.

71. Deleuze, 65–66.

72. Deleuze, 15.

73. Hansen, *New Philosophy for New Media*, 24.

74. See Elizabeth Grosz's reading of Nietzsche's philosophy of time in *The Nick of Time: Politics, Evolution and the Untimely* (Durham, N.C.: Duke University Press, 2004).

75. Deleuze, *Cinema 2*, 55.

76. Deleuze, *Difference and Repetition*, 14.

77. Ruth Gibson and Bruno Martelli, "Read-Me File," *windowsninetyeight*, n.p.

78. *Windowsninetyeight*.

79. Jeffrey Sconce, *Haunted Media: Electronic Presence from Telegraphy to Television* (Durham, N.C.: Duke University Press, 2000), 200–203.

80. Deleuze, *Cinema 1*, 132.

81. Deleuze, *Difference and Repetition*, 41. My emphasis.

82. Qtd. in Maurice Blanchot, *The Infinite Conversation*, trans. Susan Hanson (1969; Minneapolis: University of Minnesota Press, 1993), 280. Original emphasis.

83. Deleuze, *Cinema 1*, 133.

84. Deleuze, 132.

85. Deleuze, 131.

86. Deleuze, 132.

87. Gilles Deleuze, *Nietzsche and Philosophy*, trans. Hugh Tomlinson (1962; New York: Columbia University Press, 1983), 45.

88. See esp. Rebecca Schneider, *Performing Remains: Art and War in Times of Theatrical Reenactment* (New York: Routledge, 2011).

89. See Mark Franko, ed., *The Oxford Handbook of Dance and Reenactment* (New York: Oxford University Press, 2018).

90. André Lepecki, "The Body as Archive: Will to Re-enact and the Afterlives of Dances," *Dance Research Journal* 42, no. 2 (2010): 31. Lepecki is using the term virtual here in the Bergsonian/Deleuzian sense as that which can be actualized and not in reference to a digital representation or simulation.

91. Mark Franko, "Introduction: The Power of Recall in a Post-ephemeral Era," in Franko, *Oxford Handbook of Dance and Reenactment*, 1. Original emphasis. Here Franko is reflecting on choreographer Susanne Linke's 1988 engagement with Dore Hoyer's 1962 dance work *Affectos Humanos*.

92. Manuel DeLanda, *A New Philosophy of Society: Assemblage Theory and Social Complexity* (London: Continuum, 2006), 12.

93. DeLanda, 50.

94. Jean-Luc Nancy, *The Inoperative Community*, trans. Peter Connor, Lisa Garbus, Michael Holland, and Simona Sawhney (Minneapolis: University of Minnesota Press, 1991).

95. Jean-Luc Nancy, *The Muses*, trans. Peggy Kamuf (Stanford, Calif.: Stanford University Press, 1996), 98.

96. Eco, *Poetics of the Open Work*, 6.

97. Kenny Mathieson, "Simon Fildes and Katrina McPherson, Part 1," *Northings*, March 1, 2006, accessed July 13, 2016, http://northings.com/2006/03/01/simon-fildes-and-katrina-mcpherson-part-1/.

2. DANCE IN PUBLIC

1. Peter Gabriel, "In Your Eyes" (Geffen Records, 1986), CD single.

2. *Girl Walk//All Day*, web, directed by Jacob Krupnick; performance by Anne Marsen, Daisuke Omiya, and John Doyle; music by Girl Talk (2011–12), accessed December 31, 2013, http://www.girlwalkallday.com/.

3. For an excellent visualization of all music samples used as well as the timing and duration, see "Girl Talk: 'All Day' Visualized," accessed December 31, 2013, http://www.fastcompany.com/1707948/infographic-girl-talks-latest-mashup-masterpiece-deconstructed#self.

4. See esp. Beth Genné, "'Dancin' in the Street': Street Dancing on Film and Video from Fred Astaire to Michael Jackson," in *Rethinking Dance History: A Reader*, ed. Alexandra Carter, 132–42 (London: Routledge, 2004).

5. Melanie Kloetzel and Carolyn Pavlik, eds., *Site Dance: Choreographers and the Lure of Alternative Spaces* (Gainesville: University Press of Florida, 2009), 1.

6. Stephen Koplowitz, lecture, February 15, 2013, Wexner Center for the Arts, Columbus, Ohio.

7. Judith Butler, "Bodies in Alliance and the Politics of the Street," European Institute for Progressive Cultural Policies, September 2011, http://eipcp.net/transversal/1011/butler/en.

8. Butler.

9. Oberwetter v. Hilliard, 639 F.3d 545 (D.C. Cir. 2011). The charges were not pursued after the district court found the requisite paperwork incomplete.

10. The ruling continues: "As the Supreme Court has observed, an area 'is not transformed into "public forum" property merely because the public is permitted to freely enter and leave the grounds at practically all times.' *United States v. Grace,* 461 U.S. 171, 178 (1983)," Oberwetter v. Hilliard (11).

11. See esp. *TURF FEINZ RIP RichD Dancing in the Rain Oakland Street* | *YAK FILMS* (October 27, 2009), accessed July 16, 2016, https://www.youtube.com/watch?v=JQRRnAhmB58&list=PLC98CB20C4167995C&index=4, and *TURF FEINZ 'RIP Oscar Grant' Fruitvale BART Oakland* | *YAK FILMS* (December 31, 2010), accessed July 16, 2016, https://www.youtube.com/watch?v=atyTZ8prhCg&list=PLC98CB20C4167995C&index=8.

12. Elizabeth A. Povinelli, *Economies of Abandonment: Social Belonging and Endurance in Late Liberalism* (Durham, N.C.: Duke University Press, 2011), 3.

13. Naomi Bragin, "From Oakland Turfs to Harlem's Shake: Hood Dance on YouTube and Viral Antiblackness," in *The Oxford Handbook of Screendance Studies,* ed. Douglas Rosenberg (New York: Oxford, 2016), 542.

14. Randy Martin, *Critical Moves: Dance Studies in Theory and Politics* (Durham, N.C.: Duke University Press, 2007), 217–18.

15. Denice Szafran has made the important argument that not all flash mobs are perceived as playful by longtime inhabitants of specific sites in which a flash mob might occur. See Denice Szafran, "Scenes of Chaos and Joy: Playing and Performing Selves in Digitally Virtu/Real Places" (PhD diss., State University of New York at Buffalo, 2011). Her examples do not include dancing flash mobs, however, and I find that the presence of dance, whether informal or professionally choreographed, offers viewers a different frame of reference that diffuses threat.

16. *Girl Walk//All Day.*

17. Take, for example, the group choreographies developed by Rudolf Laban and his students, their ideological parity with German National Socialism, and the eventual use of their principles for the spectacularization of Hitler's power. As another example, see Rachmi Diyah Larasati's work on the state's appropriation and reinvention of regional court dance practices to promote a unified anticommunist Indonesia under the Surharto regime. Larasati, *The Dance That Makes You*

Vanish: Cultural Reconstruction in Post-genocide Indonesia (Minneapolis: University of Minnesota Press, 2013).

18. Marc Augé, *Non-places: Introduction to an Anthropology of Supermodernity,* trans. John Howe (1992; London: Verso, 1995).

19. See Hannah Arendt, *The Human Condition* (Chicago: University of Chicago Press, 1958).

20. See esp. Jacques Rancière, *The Politics of Aesthetics,* trans. Gabriel Rockhill (2000; London: Continuum, 2004).

21. See, e.g., Richard Grusin, *Premediation: Affect and Mediality after 9/11* (Houndsmills, U.K.: Palgrave Macmillan, 2010).

22. Michael Hardt and Antonio Negri, *Multitude: War and Democracy in the Age of Empire* (New York: Penguin, 2004), 14.

23. Indeed, the original name for the military operation in response to the attacks of 9/11, Operation Infinite Justice, pointed to the very interminability of the War on Terror.

24. Hardt and Negri, *Multitude,* 20.

25. Hardt and Negri, *Commonwealth,* 255.

26. Jacques Rancière, *Hatred of Democracy,* trans. Steve Corcoran (2005; London: Verso, 2006), 74.

27. Butler, "Bodies in Alliance." For an excellent reading of the physical rhetoric of Black Lives Matter protests, see Anusha Kedhar, "'Hands Up! Don't Shoot!': Gesture, Choreography, and Protest in Ferguson," *Feminist Wire,* October 6, 2014, accessed July 16, 2016, http://www.thefeministwire.com/2014/10/protest-in -ferguson/.

28. See esp. Kazys Varnelis, ed., *Networked Publics* (Cambridge, Mass.: MIT Press, 2008).

29. Presciently, Raymond Williams described the latter phenomenon as "mobile privatization" in his 1974 analysis of television. Williams, *Television: Technology and Cultural Form* (London: Fortuna, 1974).

30. Kathrin Peters and Andrea Seier give the name "home dances" to videos of privately performed dances publicly posted to YouTube or other video-sharing sites. See "Home Dance: Mediacy and Aesthetics of the Self on YouTube," in *The YouTube Reader,* ed. Pelle Snickars and Patrick Vonderau, 187–203 (Lithuania: Logotipas, 2009).

31. Planking is the phenomenon of standing or lying flat (like a plank) in various comical, unexpected, or dangerous circumstances. A photograph documenting the event is generally then posted to the internet. In horsemanning, two or more people combine efforts to stage a trick photograph in which it appears that the subject of the photograph is missing his or her head, which appears somewhere else in the frame. The reference is to the tale of the Headless Horseman. Tebowing is the practice of prayerfully kneeling on one knee like the quarterback

Tim Tebow. Hadoukening is a staged photograph named for a *Street Fighter* video game attack, which features a central figure that appears to be releasing a massive surge of energy that causes the people and/or objects surrounding him or her to be blown back. The photograph is timed to catch participants midair.

32. See Angela Trimbur, *Dance Like Nobody's Watching: Laundromat* (December 11, 2011), accessed July 16, 2016, http://www.youtube.com/watch?v=eVVX tknZVfo; *Dance Like Nobody's Watching: Airport* (December 31, 2012), accessed July 16, 2016, http://www.youtube.com/watch?v=S32bgx36G-o&list=SPBF2BA5 E35CD0B8B8; and *Dance Like Nobody's Watching: Mall* (April 13, 2012), accessed April 20, 2013, http://www.wimp.com/dancewatching/.

33. See, e.g., wheresmymarbles, *Official Hello Video Dance Like Nobody's Watching "Walmart"* (December 8, 2011), http://www.youtube.com/watch?v=yVD6jqt GHOM; Betan, *Dance Like Nobody's Watching: Icelandic Mall* (April 22, 2012), accessed July 17, 2016, https://www.youtube.com/watch?v=D6rr9Ze3Zqk; Kristín Rut Eysteinsdóttir, *Dance Like Nobody's Watching-stina stud* (May 12, 2012), accessed July 17, 2016, https://www.youtube.com/watch?v=-6B-fvdrm7A; Joseph Deiana, *Dance Like Nobody's Watching—Rue de Béthune, Lille (JdenVrai)* (May 6, 2012), accessed July 17, 2016, https://www.youtube.com/watch?v=bUosTSTdbcs; Kanal von PrinzessinTeodora, *Dance Like Nobody's Watching—Munich* (September 12, 2012), accessed July 17, 2016, https://www.youtube.com/watch?v=SFc5BKOqeLo; toxismokie ferreira, *Dance Like Nobody's Watching: Coffee Shop* (September 13, 2012), accessed July 17, 2016, https://www.youtube.com/watch?v=wc1IpRnqz9Y.

34. See Roland Barthes, *Camera Lucida: Reflections on Photography,* trans. Richard Howard (1980; New York: Hill and Wang, 1981).

35. See Philip Auslander, "The Performativity of Performance Documentation," *PAJ* 84 (2006): 1–10.

36. Julie Bloom, "'Girl Walk//All Day': A Conversation with the Director," *New York Times,* December 6, 2011, accessed December 31, 2013, http://artsbeat .blogs.nytimes.com/2011/12/06/girl-walkall-day-a-q-and-a-with-the-director/.

37. Bloom.

38. That dance in public is often working in the service of capital is not something I can explore deeply in this chapter.

39. Mark Franko, "Dance and the Political: States of Exception," in *Dance Discourses: Key Words in Dance Research,* ed. Marina Nordera and Suzanna Franco (London: Routledge, 2007), 15.

40. Jan Cohen-Cruz, ed., *Radical Street Performance: An International Anthology* (New York: Routledge, 1998), 6.

41. Performance theorist Shannon Jackson critiques the outsourcing of precisely this type of social labor to the artist class as the neoliberal state withdraws from the public and the collective well-being of the persons therein. See Jackson, *Social Works: Performing Art, Supporting Publics* (New York: Routledge, 2011).

42. Butler, "Bodies in Alliance."

43. *Adbusters* is a magazine whose mission is described thus: "We are a global network of culture jammers and creatives working to change the way information flows, the way corporations wield power, and the way meaning is produced in our society." Accessed April 19, 2013, http://www.adbusters.org/.

44. Martin, *Critical Moves,* 182.

45. Jeffrey Hou, *Insurgent Public Space: Guerilla Urbanism and the Remaking of Contemporary Cities* (London: Routledge, 2010), 3.

46. Judith Nicholson, "Flash! Mobs in the Age of Mobile Connectivity," *Fibreculture Journal* 6 (2005), http://six.fibreculturejournal.org/fcj-030-flash-mobs-in-the-age-of-mobile-connectivity/.

47. Jeffery Schnapp and Matthew Tiews, "Introduction: A Book of Crowds," in *Crowds,* ed. Jeffrey Schnapp and Matthew Tiews (Stanford, Calif.: Stanford University Press, 2006), xvi.

48. Life's for Sharing, *The T-Mobile Dance* (January 16, 2009), accessed July 17, 2016, http://www.youtube.com/watch?v=VQ3d3KigPQM.

49. Elsewhere, I have used the term *flash choreography* to mark the increased professionalization of dancing flash mobs, which are expertly choreographed and managed by production companies like Flash Mob America rather than being grassroots efforts. Though I would argue that *flash choreography* is a more accurate term than *dance mob,* which implies little to no difference from flash mobs except for the inclusion of styled bodily motion, I defer to popular parlance in my use of the terms *dance mob* and *dancing flash mob* in this book. See Harmony Bench, "Screendance 2.0: Social Dance-Media," *Participations* 7, no. 2 (2010): 183–214.

50. The YouTube video *The T-Mobile Dance* has far outlived the original television commercial, reaching new and repeat viewers—more than 38 million on the official video alone by October 2013. It is common for YouTube users to repost popular content, which is sometimes removed after copyright complaints. The number of views reported here, then, is limited to the count given on the T-Mobile Life's for Sharing YouTube channel.

51. Georgiana Gore, "Flash Mob Dance and the Territorialisation of Urban Movement," *Anthropological Notebooks* 16, no. 3 (2010): 126.

52. Gore, 130.

53. Flash Mob America, a flash mob production company started in 2009 and still going strong in 2016, states that its mission is to "create joy through surprise." Flash Mob America, accessed July 7, 2014, http://www.flashmobamerica.com/.

54. "'Harlem Shake' on a Plane Has FAA Investigating; See the Video," National Public Radio, March 1, 2013, accessed July 17, 2016, http://www.npr.org/blogs/thetwo-way/2013/03/01/173226781/harlem-shake-on-a-plane-has-faa-investigating-see-the-video.

55. Susan Leigh Foster, "Why Not 'Improv Everywhere'?," in *The Oxford Handbook to Dance and Theater*, ed. Nadine George-Graves (Oxford: Oxford University Press, 2015), 199.

56. *The T-Mobile Dance.*

57. FOX TV, *Glee—Il FlashMob* (December 23, 2009), accessed July 17, 2016, http://www.youtube.com/watch?v=NhbK2bMTRbI; *yes glee flash mob Tel Aviv* (January 12, 2010), http://www.youtube.com/watch?v=ZB22aIYHLII; SonyMusic IrelandLtd, *Glee Flash Mob—Grafton Street—Dublin, Ireland* (February 1, 2010), accessed July 17, 2016, http://www.youtube.com/watch?v=x1zVigP_T9k&p=C77 24D0671B57B0B&playnext=1&index=31.

58. PercyGreen17, *Beyonce 100 Single Ladies Flash-Dance Piccadilly Circus, London for Trident Unwrapped* (April 20, 2009), accessed July 17, 2016, http://www.youtube.com/watch?feature=player_embedded&v=OLj5zphusLw.

59. DellAust, *Dell Streak Flash Mob Sydney—Full Version* (September 23, 2010), accessed July 17, 2016, http://www.youtube.com/watch?v=zkvW2he2loc&feature=player_embedded.

60. Flash Mob America, *Official Suave Professional Hairography Flash Mob w/ Sofia Vergara—Times Square* (May 13, 2010), accessed July 17, 2016, http://www.youtube.com/watch?v=jVhPbBfxCvk.

61. U.S. President George W. Bush urged Americans to travel—"get on the airlines, get about the business of America"—while New York mayor Rudy Giuliani said his city was in need of "the best shoppers in the world." British prime minister Tony Blair encouraged U.K. residents to "go about their daily lives: to work, to live, to travel and to shop," and Canadian president Jean Chrétien said that late 2001 was an excellent time to "go out and get a mortgage, to buy a home, to buy a car." See Elisabeth Bumiller, "A Nation Challenged: The President," *New York Times*, September 28, 2001; "America's New War: Giuliani on Local Radio Show," CNN, September 21, 2001, http://transcripts.cnn.com/TRANSCRIPTS/0109/21/se.20.html; George Jones and Michael Smith, "Britain Needs You to Shop, Says Blair," September 28, 2001; Peter O'Neil, "'Get a Mortgage, Buy a Car,' PM Urges," *Vancouver Sun*, September 28, 2001.

62. "Amazon Posts a Profit," CNN Money, January 22, 2002, accessed July 17, 2016, http://money.cnn.com/2002/01/22/technology/amazon/.

63. Rachel Signer, "Girl Walk: Jacob Krupnick Talks the Talk," Bomb—Artists in Conversation, June 4, 2012, original emphasis, accessed December 31, 2013, http://bombsite.com/issues/1000/articles/6602.

64. Signer.

65. Arendt, *Human Condition*, 206.

66. Hannah Arendt, *On Revolution* (1963; repr., New York: Penguin, 1990), 30–31.

67. Augé, *Non-places*, 77–78.

68. Augé, 78.

69. Augé, 79.

70. Augé, 95.

71. Augé notes that non-places can become places if they foster social ties for those who spend time there: "For me, place has never been an empirical notion. Anything can become a place, every space can become one, if in one manner or another encounters take place there that create social ties." "Places and Non-places—a Conversation with Marc Augé," *On the Move,* January 26, 2009, http://onthemove.autogrill.com/gen/lieux-non-lieux/news/2009-01-26/places-and-non-places-a-conversation-with-marc-auge. Site now defunct.

72. Augé, *Non-places,* 103.

73. Augé, 103.

74. Augé, 103.

75. Bars are a notable exception in a U.S. context, where zoning restrictions may require businesses that sell alcohol but that are not categorized as dance clubs to prohibit dancing on their premises.

76. Michel Foucault, *Discipline and Punish: The Birth of the Prison,* trans. Alan Sheridan (1975; New York: Random House, 1995), 201.

77. Foucault, 202–3.

78. Foucault, 200.

79. Arendt, *Human Condition,* 200.

80. "Equality is not a goal to be attained but a point of departure, a supposition to be maintained in all circumstances." Jacques Rancière, *The Ignorant Schoolmaster: Five Lessons in Intellectual Emancipation,* trans. Kristin Ross (1987; Stanford, Calif.: Stanford University Press, 1991), 138.

81. Mark Colonomos, *Dance Walking Fitness Ben Aaron. Time to Dance Walk Baby* (April 21, 2012), accessed July 17, 2016, http://www.youtube.com/watch?v=Ib3Duz_6a9M.

82. Choreographer Merce Cunningham famously offered, "You have to love dancing to stick to it. It gives you nothing back, no manuscripts to store away, no paintings to show on walls and maybe hang in museums, no poems to be printed and sold, nothing but that single fleeting moment when you feel alive." Cunningham, "You Have to Love Dancing to Stick to It," in *Changes: Notes on Choreography,* n.p. (New York: Something Else, 1968).

83. Arendt, *Human Condition,* 207.

84. Arendt, 220.

85. Arendt, 177.

86. See Sianne Ngai, *Our Aesthetic Categories: Zany, Cute, and Interesting* (Cambridge, Mass.: Harvard University Press, 2012).

87. John Lennon, "Imagine" (Apple Records, 1971), LP vinyl.

88. Tom McCormack, "Dance Dance Revolution: The Political Dimensions of *Girl Walk*'s Modern City Symphony," Museum of the Moving Image (June 14, 2012), accessed July 17, 2016, http://www.movingimagesource.us/articles/dance-dance-revolution-20120614.

89. See "'Terrorist Plots Targeting New York City" for a listing of known terrorist plots since September 11, 2001, accessed May 15, 2014, http://www.nyc.gov/html/nypd/html/pr/plots_targeting_nyc.shtml.

90. McCormack, "Dance Dance Revolution."

91. Bloom, "Girl Walk//All Day."

92. Jacques Rancière, *The Emancipated Spectator*, trans. Gregory Elliott (2008; London: Verso, 2009), 54.

93. Rancière, 56.

94. Rancière, 72.

95. Rancière, 75.

96. José Esteban Muñoz, "'Gimme Gimme This . . . Gimme Gimme That': Annihilation and Innovation in the Punk Rock Commons," *Social Text* 31, no. 3 (2013): 96.

97. See Jacques Rancière, *Dis-agreement: Politics and Philosophy*, trans. Julie Rose (1995; Minneapolis: University of Minnesota Press, 1999).

98. Jacques Rancière, "The Paradoxes of Political Art," in *Dissensus: On Politics and Aesthetics*, ed. and trans. Steven Corcoran (London: Continuum, 2010), 139.

99. Rancière, 140.

100. Rancière distinguishes among ethical, representative, and aesthetic regimes of art. For a fuller explanation, see especially *The Politics of Aesthetics*. For an extended meditation on the aesthetic regime, see Jacques Rancière, *Aisthesis: Scenes from the Aesthetic Regime of Art*, trans. Zakir Paul (2011; London: Verso, 2013).

101. Rancière, *Emancipated Spectator*, 72.

102. Jill Bennett, *Practical Aesthetics: Events, Affects and Art after 9/11* (London: I. B. Tauris, 2012), 6.

103. Rancière, "Paradoxes of Political Art," 139.

104. Tim Groves has compiled an extensive list of rallies, Round Dances, and other events from 2012 on a Google Map, January 19, 2013, accessed July 17, 2016, https://maps.google.ca/maps/ms?msid=204534403836525039663.0004d13bdc1d5b9ad39cf&msa=0&ll=42.032974,-62.929687&spn=126.64569,246.445313&dg=feature.

105. Paul Kuttner, "Case Study: Idle No More and the Round Dance Flash Mob," Beautiful Trouble, accessed July 25, 2014, http://beautifultrouble.org/case/idle-dance-flash-mob/.

106. Kuttner.

107. Reyna Crow, "Mall of America Threatens Arrest of Idle No More," *Popular Resistance: Daily Movement News and Resources,* December 25, 2013, accessed July 17, 2016, http://www.popularresistance.org/mall-of-america-threatens-arrest-of -idle-no-more/.

108. Sheila Regan and Bill Sorem, "Two Arrested in Idle No More Round Dance Attempt at Mall of Americas," *Popular Resistance: Daily Movement News and Resources,* January 2, 2014, accessed July 17, 2016, http://www.popularresistance .org/two-arrested-in-idle-no-more-round-dance-attempt-at-mall-of-americas/.

109. José Muñoz, "The Brown Commons: The Sense of Wildness," *Journal of Native Theory Dialogue,* March 20, 2013, accessed July 17, 2016, https://www .youtube.com/watch?v=F-YInUlXgO4.

110. Rancière, *Politics of Aesthetics,* 39.

111. For an analysis of how Native American performance troupes have historically negotiated a similar false dichotomy between dance as entertainment and as spiritual practice, see Shea Murphy, *The People Have Never Stopped Dancing.*

112. Rancière, *Emancipated Spectator,* 58–59.

113. Rancière, 53.

114. Jacques Rancière, "Contemporary Art and the Politics of Aesthetics," in *Communities of Sense: Rethinking Aesthetics and Politics* (Durham, N.C.: Duke University Press, 2009), 40.

115. Rancière, 48.

116. Rancière, 47–48.

117. Rancière, 41.

118. "Flo6x8," accessed July 29, 2014, http://flo6x8.com/flo6x8.

119. "Somos un grupo de gente de a pie que tenemos una serie de inquietudes comunes y que compartimos nuestra afición por el arte flamenco y nuestra crítica al sistema financiero. Entre las inquietudes que nos mueven destaca el hartazgo no sólo del expolio de la vida en el planeta a cargo de los bancos, sino también del silencio generalizado con que se responde a este expolio, su naturalización y la impunidad con que se perpetra." "Flo6x8." Thanks to Jeannine Murray-Román for the translation.

120. The video from which these translated lyrics were taken is no longer available online. For the original Spanish language video, see *flo6x8: Bankia, pulmones y branquias (bulerías)* (uploaded May 24, 2012), https://www.youtube.com/watch?v =iop2b3oq1Oo.

121. "No nos creemos muy importantes para plantarles cara a los bancos. Entre nuestros delirios no destaca la megalomanía. Más bien nos vemos como liliputienses escarbando en sus gélidas fisuras con piolets de cartón piedra. Pero por algún sitio hay que empezar." "Flo6x8." Thanks to Jeannine Murray-Román for the translation.

122. "Flo6x8."

123. Qtd. in Jason Webster, "How Flash Mob Flamenco Took on the Banks," *BBC News Magazine*, April 17, 2013, accessed July 17, 2016, http://www.bbc.com/news/magazine-22110887.

124. Qtd. in Andy Robinson, "The Deeping Spanish Debt Crisis," *The Nation*, July 3, 2012, accessed July 17, 2016, http://www.thenation.com/article/168716/deepening-spanish-debt-crisis#.

125. See Danielle Goldman's *I Want to Be Ready: Improvised Dance as a Practice of Freedom* (Ann Arbor: University of Michigan Press, 2010) for an excellent Foucauldian analysis of improvisatory social and theatrical dance forms of the mid- to late twentieth-century United States as practices of freedom.

126. Rancière, "Paradoxes of Political Art," 141.

127. "A New Law Limits NYC Street Musicians," *Buzzkers: Sounds of the Street*, April 23, 2013, accessed July 17, 2016, http://www.buzzkers.com/a-new-law-limits-nyc-street-musicians/.

128. Matt Flegenheimer and J. David Goodman, "On Subway, Flying Feet Can Lead to Handcuffs," *New York Times*, July 28, 2014, accessed July 17, 2016, http://www.nytimes.com/2014/07/29/nyregion/29acrobats.html?_r=1.

129. Veronica Carchedi, "'Park Performers' to Lose Stage in Washington Square," *Washington Square News*, May 1, 2013, accessed July 17, 2016, http://www.nyunews.com/2013/05/01/performer/.

130. "Musician or Performer Permit," *NYC*, accessed July 30, 2014, http://www1.nyc.gov/nyc-resources/service/3003/musician-or-performer-permit.

3. A WORLD FROM A CROWD

1. See Latika Linn Young, "Dorky Dance.Com: Dorky Dancing, Vlogging and the Rise of Self Produced Dance on the Internet" (master's thesis, Florida State University, 2007).

2. "About Matt," accessed May 3, 2009, http://www.wherethehellismatt.com:80/about.shtml. Site now defunct.

3. "Meet Matt," accessed January 13, 2007, http://www.stridegum.com/whereismatt_textOnly.asp. Site now defunct.

4. The title with which each video opens is "Dancing," but I use the title as it is listed on YouTube. Matt Harding, *Where the Hell Is Matt? 2005* (June 24, 2006), accessed July 13, 2016, https://www.youtube.com/watch?v=7WmMcqp670s. Harding, *Where the Hell Is Matt? 2006* (June 20, 2006), accessed July 13, 2016, https://www.youtube.com/watch?v=bNF_P281Uu4. Harding, *Where the Hell Is Matt? 2008* (June 20, 2008), accessed July 13, 2016, https://www.youtube.com/watch?v=zlfKdbWwruY. Harding, *Where the Hell Is Matt? 2012* (June 20, 2012), accessed July 13, 2016, https://www.youtube.com/watch?v=Pwe-pA6TaZk.

5. For additional perspectives on dance and world/world-making, see esp. Gabriele Klein and Sandra Noeth, eds., *Emerging Bodies: The Performance of World-making in Dance and Choreography* (Bielefeld, Germany: transcript, 2011), and Susan Leigh Foster, ed., *Worlding Dance* (Basingstoke, U.K.: Palgrave, 2009).

6. Antonio Negri, *Art and Multitude,* trans. Ed Emery (2009; Cambridge: Polity Press, 2011), xii.

7. Negri.

8. *Globe Trot,* directed and edited by Mitchell Rose and choreographed by Bebe Miller (2014), accessed July 7, 2016, http://www.mitchellrose.com/globetrot/.

9. *Mass Ornament,* by Natalie Bookchin (2009), accessed June 30, 2016, https://bookchin.net/projects/mass-ornament/.

10. *One Day on Earth the Music Video,* directed by Kyle Ruddick, edited by Cari Ann Shim Sham*, music by Cut Chemist (2012), accessed July 27, 2016, https://vimeo.com/39875998.

11. *All Is Not Lost,* directed by OK Go, Pilobolus, and Trish Sie, produced by Paracadute and Google (2011), accessed July 27, 2016, http://www.allisnotlo.st/index_en.html.

12. Paolo Virno, *A Grammar of the Multitude,* trans. Isabella Bertoletti, James Cascaito, and Andrea Casson (Los Angeles, Calif.: semiotext(e)), 38.

13. Jean-Luc Nancy, *The Creation of the World or Globalization,* trans. and introduction by François Raffoul and David Pettigrew (Albany: State University of New York Press), 47.

14. Nancy, 109.

15. James Surowiecki, *The Wisdom of Crowds: Why the Many Are Smarter than the Few and How Collective Wisdom Shapes Business, Economies, Societies, and Nations* (New York: Anchor Books, 2004).

16. Nicolas Bourriaud, *Relational Aesthetics* (Dijon, France: Les Presses Du Reel, 1998), 13.

17. Bourriaud, 13.

18. Shannon Jackson, *Social Works: Performing Art, Supporting Publics* (New York: Routledge, 2011), 14.

19. See Claire Bishop, "Antagonism and Relational Aesthetics," *October* 110 (Fall 2004): 51–79.

20. Jen Harvie, *Fair Play—Art, Performance, and Neoliberalism* (Basingstoke, U.K.: Palgrave Macmillan), 36.

21. Harvie, 37.

22. Harvie, 42.

23. See Hal Foster, "Chat Rooms," in *Participation: Documents of Contemporary Art,* ed. Claire Bishop, 190–95 (Cambridge, Mass.: MIT Press, 2006).

24. See Virno, *A Grammar of the Multitude.*

25. Sarah Elgart, "Globe Trotting with Mitchell Rose," *Cultural Weekly*, June 11, 2014, accessed July 13, 2016, http://www.culturalweekly.com/globe-trotting -mitchell-rose/.

26. Jean-Luc Nancy, *Being Singular Plural*, trans. Robert Richardson and Anne O'Byrne (1996; Stanford, Calif.: Stanford University Press, 2000), 83.

27. Matt Harding, "Athens, Greece, No Dancing at the Parthenon," May 10, 2006, accessed July13, 2016, http://www.wherethehellismatt.com/journal/2006/ 05/athens_greece_n.html.

28. See Matt Harding, *Where the Hell Are Matt's 2006 Outtakes* (March 12, 2007), accessed July 13, 2016, https://www.youtube.com/watch?v=tT8jA_pps30, and Harding, *Where the Hell Are Matt's 2012 Outtakes* (July 11, 2012), accessed July 13, 2016, https://www.youtube.com/watch?annotation_id=annotation_40189&feat ure=iv&src_vid=Pwe-pA6TaZk&v=l4quCAG4eCc.

29. Harding, "Athens, Greece." Original emphasis.

30. Nancy, *Creation of the World*, 40.

31. Gabriella Giannachi, *Virtual Theater: An Introduction* (London: Routledge, 2004), 17.

32. See Samuel Weber, "Television: Set and Screen," in *Mass Mediauras: Form, Technics, Media* (Stanford, Calif.: Stanford University Press, 1998), 108.

33. Giannachi, *Virtual Theater*, 17. Original emphasis.

34. Giannachi.

35. Harding's parodists draw attention to this point by dancing in the comparatively mundane spaces available to them: bedrooms, kitchens, bus stops, parks, and so on. A search for "Where the Hell Is Matt parody" on YouTube results in hundreds of such videos.

36. It should come as no surprise that Harding and his team were hired to produce (but not dance in) the video celebrating the fiftieth anniversary of the song "It's a Small World after All." See *"it's a small world" 50th Anniversary Global Chorus | Disney Parks* (March 21, 2014), accessed July 16, 2016, https://www .youtube.com/watch?v=weZrqrN9Jpo&list=LL__TABIHzr7fUz5pQL2GU4w.

37. Nancy, *Creation of the World*, 40.

38. Martin Heidegger, "The Age of the World Picture," in *Off the Beaten Track*, ed. and trans. Julian Young and Kenneth Haynes (1938; Cambridge: Cambridge University Press, 2002), 67–68. Original emphasis.

39. Charles McGrath, "A Private Dance? Four Million Web Fans Say No," *New York Times*, July 8, 2008, accessed July 13, 2016, http://www.nytimes.com/ 2008/07/08/arts/television/08dancer.html?pagewanted=all.

40. "The Guy Who Danced around the Globe," *Washington Post*, October 22, 2006, accessed July 13, 2016, http://www.washingtonpost.com/wp-dyn/content/ article/2006/10/20/AR2006102000373.html.

41. As of August 11, 2014, the 2006 video had 18.8 million views and the 2008 video had 47.6 million.

42. McGrath, "A Private Dance?"

43. McGrath.

44. Celene, "Seattle, Washington: Dancer Comments," June 20, 2008, accessed July 13, 2009, http://wherethehellismatt.typepad.com/blog/2008/06/seattle -washi-5.html#comment-119562366.

45. Roemarie, "Seattle, Washington: Dancer Comments," June 20, 2008, accessed July 13, 2009, http://wherethehellismatt.typepad.com/blog/2008/06/seattle-washi -5.html#comment-119577564.

46. Devin Weiss, "Seattle, Washington: Dancer Comments," June 20, 2008, accessed July 13, 2009, http://wherethehellismatt.typepad.com/blog/2008/06/ seattle-washi-5.html#comment-119581358.

47. Rose provides a list of all the filmmakers and film sites on his website. See the "Globe Trot Shot Locations and Filmmakers" list, accessed July 27, 2016, http://www.mitchellrose.com/globetrot/shot-list/.

48. See Rose's website, accessed July 18, 2016, http://www.mitchellrose.com/ globetrot/.

49. Mitchell Rose, "Crowd-Sourced Filmmaking: Despair Is Your Friend," *International Journal of Screendance* 5 (2015): 64.

50. Rose calls this style of editing "hyper-matchcutting."

51. Rose, 64.

52. Siegfried Kracauer, "The Mass Ornament," in *The Mass Ornament: Weimar Essays,* ed. and trans. Thomas Y. Levin (1927; repr., 1963; Cambridge, Mass.: Harvard University Press, 1995), 79.

53. Participating in a history of "appropriation art," Bookchin's crowdsourced content has different ethical implications as well. Like other visual artists of recent years who turn to social media content for both inspiration and material, Bookchin collected videos from YouTube as "found objects" for *Mass Ornament.* Although these videos were made publicly available and accessible on the internet, works like *Mass Ornament* raise the question of ownership and privacy rights that individuals forfeit when they participate in social media. For an analysis of *Mass Ornament* in terms of privacy and publicity, see Wendy Hui Kyong Chun, *Updating to Remain the Same: Habitual New Media* (Cambridge, Mass.: MIT Press, 2016), 172–74.

54. Burt, *Ungoverning Dance,* 87.

55. Burt, 87.

56. Jean-Luc Nancy, "Of Being-in-Common," in *Community at Loose Ends,* ed. Miami Theory Collective, trans. James Creech (Minneapolis: University of Minnesota Press, 1991), 4.

57. Nancy, *Being Singular Plural,* 29.

58. Nancy, 43.

59. Jean-Luc Nancy, *The Sense of the World*, trans. Jeffrey S. Librett (1993; Minneapolis: University of Minnesota Press, 2008), 14.

60. Nancy, *Being Singular Plural*, 65.

61. Nancy, *Creation of the World*, 41–42.

62. Nancy, *Being Singular Plural*, 9.

63. J. L. Austin, *How to Do Things with Words* (Cambridge, Mass.: Harvard University Press, 1962), 16.

64. Austin remarks, for example, that a wedding ceremony performed within the context of a theatrical play is "infelicitous," as the circumstances of the utterance invalidate its performative power. Scholars have argued that theatrical representation may yet be performative in another way, not by bringing about the specific change indicated by the words spoken, for example, legally binding two people in a marriage, but by bringing about social change. This position does not recognize the law or "authority" as such as the arbiter of language's transformative capacities.

65. Judith Butler, *Bodies That Matter: On the Discursive Limits of Sex* (New York: Routledge, 2011), 232.

66. Judith Butler, *Gender Trouble: Feminism and the Subversion of Identity* (New York: Routledge, 2006), 173.

67. Carrie Noland, *Agency and Embodiment: Performing Gestures/Producing Culture* (Cambridge, Mass.: Harvard University Press, 2009), 189.

68. This formulation recalls Hannah Arendt's understanding of politics and the political sphere, with its emphasis on action *(praxis)* and rejection of fabrication *(poiesis)*. See esp. Arendt, *Human Condition*.

69. Virno, *A Grammar of the Multitude*, 52.

70. Nancy, *Being Singular Plural*, 41.

71. Nancy, *Creation of the World*, 9

72. As we see in immersive or participatory artwork, however, contemporary artistic practice is not limited to representation, and therefore neither is it limited to *poiesis*. As Rancière has observed in his analysis of politics and aesthetics, artistic practices share with politics an ability to disrupt a perceptual field and alter the distribution of the sensible, incorporating and making intelligible the part that has no part. In this way, artistic practices not only represent the world but enact new possibilities of the world by activating new senses of the world. It is the dissensual aspect of artistic practice that Rancière links to politics. See Rancière, *Politics of Aesthetics*.

73. Nancy, *Being Singular Plural*, 58.

74. Maurizio Lazzarato, "Struggle, Media, Event," May 2003, accessed July 18, 2016, http://www.republicart.net/disc/representations/lazzarato01_en.htm.

75. Lazzarato.

76. Nancy, *Being Singular Plural*, 23.

77. Lauren Berlant, "The Commons: Infrastructures for Troubling Times," *Environment and Planning D: Society and Space* 34, no. 3 (2016): 393. Berlant further cautions that "resilience and repair don't necessarily neutralize the problem that generated the need for them, but might reproduce them" (393–94).

78. See Nancy, *Inoperative Community*.

79. Nancy, *Creation of the World*, 109.

80. Nancy, *Being Singular Plural*, 60.

81. Nancy, *Creation of the World*, 42.

82. Nancy, *Being Singular Plural*, 61.

83. This uprootedness is a result of the choreography being situated in what I have elsewhere called "no-place," a fundamental site that accompanies dance within the Western concert tradition, enabling, for example, dance to appear in the blank space of an emptied proscenium theater. No-place is a site that performs its own emptiness prior to the arrival of dance within its architectural frame. See Harmony Bench, "Media and the *No-place* of Dance," *Forum Modernes Theater* 23, no. 1 (2008): 37–47.

84. See *How the Hell Did Matt Get People to Dance with Him?* (September 12, 2008), accessed July 13, 2016, https://www.youtube.com/watch?v=ue1GZ4IUFiU.

85. Laura U. Marks, *The Skin of the Film: Intercultural Cinema, Embodiment, and the Senses* (Durham, N.C.: Duke University Press, 2000), 195.

86. Steven Shaviro, *The Cinematic Body* (Minneapolis: University of Minnesota Press, 1993), 27.

87. C. Nadia Seremetakis, *The Senses Still* (Chicago: University of Chicago Press, 1996), 6. Original emphasis.

88. Nancy, *Creation of the World*, 34.

89. World-forming, for Nancy, succeeds world-becoming, though not in a chronological way. World-becoming accompanies the retreat of God as subject or master of the world, which requires that the world be thought in itself and not as an object of God's contemplation or love.

90. Nancy, *Creation of the World*, 53.

91. David Pogue, "Behind the Dancing Matt Videos," *New York Times*, July 12, 2012, accessed July 13, 2016, http://pogue.blogs.nytimes.com/2012/07/12/behind-the-dancing-matt-videos/?_php=true&_type=blogs&_r=0.

92. Pogue.

93. Pogue.

94. African masks encompass not only the carved face covering but also the ceremonial attire as well as the music and dance that work collectively with the dancer to enliven a mask. Harding wore only some of the garments in this scene.

95. The experiment in collaborative filmmaking was supported by international organizations such as Oxfam, UNESCO, and the United Nations and was awarded the 2012 Vimeo Social Change Award.

96. See Carol Vernallis, *Experiencing Music Video: Aesthetics and Cultural Context* (New York: Columbia University Press, 2004).

97. Nancy, *Creation of the World*, 110.

98. Nancy, *Sense of the World*, 15.

99. Nancy, *Creation of the World*, 62.

100. Nancy, *Sense of the World*, 88.

101. For an explication of schools of thought regarding the relationship of affect and emotion, see Gregory Seigworth and Melissa Gregg, *The Affect Theory Reader* (Durham, N.C.: Duke University Press, 2010), 6–8.

102. Sara Ahmed, "Affective Economies," *Social Text* 22, no. 2 (2004): 119.

103. Sara Ahmed, *The Promise of Happiness* (Durham, N.C.: Duke University Press), 24.

104. OK Go frequently incorporates dance into their music videos and repeatedly engages with old and emerging technologies in crafting quirky, one-of-a-kind music videos. Two examples include the video for Here It Goes Again, performed on treadmills—arguably the video that made OK Go famous beyond its musical fan base—and I Won't Let You Down, performed on Honda UNI-CUB "personal mobility devices" (http://world.honda.com/UNI-CUB/), shot with drone-mounted video cameras, and accompanied online by an interactive tool that allows viewers to create their own animated choreographies. Emimusic, *OK Go—Here It Goes Again* (February 26, 2009), accessed July 18, 2016, https://www.youtube.com/watch?v=dTAAsCNK7RA. *I Won't Let You Down* (October 7, 2014), accessed July 18, 2016, http://iwontletyoudown.com/#.

105. OK Go, *OK Go—a Message for Japan (with Subtitles)* (July 27, 2011), accessed July 18, 2016, https://www.youtube.com/watch?v=akyxuKZgy7Q#t=45.

106. OK Go.

107. The Hollywood films featuring Esther Williams's synchronized swimming are perhaps a better point of comparison than Berkeley, particularly since the aqua unitards seem to be a tongue-in-cheek reference to the aquatic musical form that Williams pioneered.

108. Despite the piece being a Google Chrome Experiment, in 2016, I was only able to play it properly in the Safari web browser.

109. OK Go, *All Is Not Lost* (July 25, 2011), accessed July 27, 2016, https://www.youtube.com/watch?v=ur-y7oOto14.

110. See Mary Ann Doane, "Information, Crisis, Catastrophe," in *Logics of Television: Essays on Cultural Criticism*, ed. Patricia Mellencamp, 222–39 (Bloomington: Indiana University Press, 1990). See also Saidiya V. Hartman, *Scenes of Subjection: Terror, Slavery, and Self-Making in Nineteenth Century America* (New York: Oxford University Press, 1997), on the problems of empathic identification.

111. Nancy, *Creation of the World*, 61.

112. See chapter 4 for further consideration of choreography as quasi-object able to organize bodies in relation to itself.

113. Susan Leigh Foster, *Dances That Describe Themselves: The Improvised Choreography of Richard Bull* (Middletown, Conn.: Wesleyan University Press, 2002), 108.

114. Nancy, *Creation of the World*, 53.

115. Virno, *A Grammar of the Multitude*, 25.

116. Matt Harding, "Where the Heck Is Matt," https://www.kickstarter.com/projects/wheretheheckismatt/where-the-heck-is-matt.

117. Kickstarter campaigns are structured like other fund drives, offering rewards in return for monetary support. Products and services on offer vary widely from campaign to campaign.

118. Harding stands outside of typical arts communities, but as an internet celebrity engaged in practices of production similar to those of contemporary artists, many of whom are also making work for internet audiences, Harding's turn toward a pay-to-play structure is both a model for and a cautionary tale of artrepreneurialism in the new economy.

4. SCREEN SHARING

1. *24 Hours of Happy*, web, directed by We Are from LA, produced by Iconoclast Interactive, performed by Pharrell Williams (November 2013), accessed July 8, 2016, http://www.24hoursofhappy.com/.

2. Henry Jenkins, Joshua Green, and Sam Ford, *Spreadable Media: Creating Value and Meaning in a Networked Culture* (New York: NYU Press, 2013), 83.

3. Jenkins et al., 83.

4. Michael Taussig, *Mimesis and Alterity: A Particular History of the Senses* (New York: Routledge, 1993), 93.

5. Russell Belk, "Sharing versus Pseudo-Sharing in Web 2.0," *Anthropologist* 18, no. 1 (2014): 13.

6. Martin, *Financialization of Daily Life*, 16.

7. Anthea Kraut, *Choreographing Copyright: Race, Gender, and Intellectual Property Rights in American Dance* (Oxford: Oxford University Press, 2016), 7.

8. See "How Pharrell's 'Happy' Video Owes a Lot to an Uncredited Indie Film," *Spin*, April 17, 2014, accessed July 8, 2016, http://www.spin.com/2014/04/pharrell-happy-looks-like-girl-walk-all-day-video-interview/. See also Anne Marsen, "Pharrell Loves My Work," Vimeo, April 17, 2014, accessed July 8, 2016, https://vimeo.com/92226001.

9. Interestingly, I have not uncovered any accusations that *24 Hours of Happy* drew its concept from *Uniqlock*, an advertising campaign by the Japanese clothing company Uniqlo, where Pharrell has his "I am other" clothing line. *Uniqlock*, which ran from 2007 to 2010, is a twenty-four-hour time-telling, music-playing, dancing advertisement for the company's season. *Uniqlock* was created by the production company Projector under the direction of Koichiro Tanaka, with music

by Fantastic Plastic Machine and featuring the Japanese dance crew U-Min. Like *24 Hours of Happy, Uniqlock* marks the top of each hour with special video clips. Accessed May 3, 2009, http://www.uniqlo.jp/uniqlock/. Site now defunct.

10. Alva Noë, "Imitation or Celebration? The Joy of Dancing in the Streets," *NPR 13.7 Cosmos and Culture*, April 25, 2014, accessed July 17, 2016, http://www.npr.org/sections/13.7/2014/04/25/306747324/imitation-or-celebration-the-joy-of-dancing-in-the-streets.

11. Lyndy Stout, "Searchlight: We Are from LA," Young Director Award, December 6, 2013, accessed July 8, 2016, http://youngdirectoraward.com/search light-we-are-from-la/.

12. Priya Srinivasan, *Sweating Saris: Indian Dance as Transnational Labor* (Philadelphia: Temple University Press, 2012), 167.

13. Ben Spatz, *What a Body Can Do: Technique as Knowledge, Practice as Research* (London: Routledge, 2015), 31.

14. Kraut, *Choreographing Copyright*, 140.

15. Kiri Miller, *Playable Bodies: Dance Games and Intimate Media* (New York: Oxford University Press, 2017), 133.

16. Eva Hemmungs Wirtén, *Terms of Use: Negotiating the Jungle of the Intellectual Commons* (Toronto: University of Toronto Press, 2008), 53.

17. This series of operations is easily seen in the fitness industry, for example, with Pure Barre, Bikram Yoga, and Zumba, all of which are registered trademarks that rely on the availability of commonly available gestures and inherited movement sequences that can then be arranged, branded, and sold.

18. John Locke, *Two Treatises of Government* (1690; repr., London: Whitmore and Fenn, 1821), accessed July 15, 2016, https://books.google.com/books?id=K5 UIAAAAQAAJ.

19. Brenda Dixon Gottschild, *Digging the Africanist Presence in American Performance: Dance and Other Contexts* (Westport, Conn.: Praeger, 1998).

20. Kraut, *Choreographing Copyright*.

21. Srinivasan, *Sweating Saris*.

22. Caroline Picart, *Critical Race Theory and Copyright in American Dance: Whiteness as Status Property* (New York: Palgrave Macmillan, 2013).

23. Murphy, *People Have Never Stopped Dancing*.

24. Eric Lott, "Love and Theft: The Racial Unconscious of Blackface Minstrelsy," *Representations* 39 (1992): 25.

25. Lott, 39.

26. Lisa Nakamura, "The Unwanted Labour of Social Media: Women of Color Call Out Culture as Venture Community Management," *New Formations: A Journal of Culture, Theory, Politics* 86 (2015): 109.

27. Brenda Dixon Gottschild, *The Black Dancing Body: A Geography from Coon to Cool* (New York: Palgrave, 2003), 104.

28. For a consideration of how African American musicians rework inherited archives of sound, see esp. Trisha Rose, *Black Noise: Rap Music and Black Culture in Contemporary America* (Middletown, Conn.: Wesleyan University Press, 1994); Joseph Schloss, *Making Beats: The Art of Sample-Based Hip-Hop* (Middletown, Conn.: Wesleyan University Press, 2014); and Mark Anthony Neal, "Now I Ain't Saying He's a Crate Digger: Kanye West, 'Community Theaters' and the Soul Archive," in *The Cultural Impact of Kanye West,* ed. Julius Bailey, 3–12 (New York: Palgrave, 2014).

29. Srinivasan, *Sweating Saris,* 84.

30. Dillon, *New World Drama,* 7.

31. Radical Faggot, "Vogue Is Not for You: Deciding Whom We Give Our Art To," May 31, 2015, accessed July 8, 2016, http://radfag.com/2015/05/31/vogue-is-not-for-you-deciding-whom-we-give-our-art-to/.

32. Nakamura, "Unwanted Labour," 111.

33. Taussig, *Mimesis and Alterity,* 95–96.

34. This is not to deny the pernicious effects and residual affects of the colonial era, which for many has not ended.

35. Diana Taylor, *The Archive and the Repertoire: Performing Cultural Memory in the Americas* (Durham, N.C.: Duke University Press, 2003), 2.

36. Taylor, 10.

37. Kiri Miller, *Playing Along: Digital Games, YouTube, and Virtual Performance* (Oxford: Oxford University Press, 2012), 183. Original emphasis.

38. Gottschild, *Black Dancing Body,* 104.

39. See karenxcheng, *Girl Learns to Dance in a Year (TIME LAPSE)* (July 9, 2013), accessed July 17, 2016, https://www.youtube.com/watch?v=daC2EPUh22w.

40. Karen X. Cheng, "Hi, I'm Karen. I Learned to Dance in a Year," accessed July 15, 2015, http://www.danceinayear.com/. Site now defunct; snapshot available at https://web.archive.org/web/20130709205654/http://www.danceinayear.com/.

41. Fusion, *This Amazing Girl Mastered Dubstep Dancing by Just Using YouTube* (January 25, 2016), accessed July 17, 2016, https://www.youtube.com/watch?v=OgzdDp5qfdI&nohtml5=False.

42. Fusion.

43. Dubstep more accurately refers to a type of electronic dance music to which these dance movements are performed. Thanks to Alexandra Harlig for breaking this down for me.

44. Fusion, *This Amazing Girl.*

45. Fusion.

46. Alexandra Harlig, "DO Read the Comments, and Watch the Videos: The Discursive Negotiation of Genre, Ethics, and Sociality for Popular Dance Audiences on YouTube," paper presented at Popular Dance: Curating, Collecting,

Reflecting, PoP Moves Annual Conference, University of Roehampton, U.K., October 24, 2015.

47. Adilyn Malcolm, *Audacious Adi—Don't Let Me Down (HD)* (March 27, 2016), accessed July 17, 2016, https://www.youtube.com/watch?v=hnE60ZmKJwM.

48. William Given, "Lindy Hop, Community, and the Isolation of Appropriation," in George-Graves, *Oxford Handbook to Dance and Theater*, 740.

49. The current practice of learning dances from YouTube and video games was preceded historically by dancers picking up steps from movies, television shows, and variety acts.

50. See Rosalyn Diprose, *Corporeal Generosity: On Giving with Nietzsche, Merleau-Ponty, and Levinas* (Albany: State University of New York Press, 2002).

51. DeFrantz, "Unchecked Popularity," 128.

52. DeFrantz, 128.

53. DeFrantz, 130.

54. DeFrantz, 139.

55. Kraut, *Choreographing Copyright*, 175.

56. Some communities take measures to protect sacred or ritual dances, for example, by expressly prohibiting circulation beyond their membership.

57. Steven Weber, *The Success of Open Source* (Cambridge, Mass.: Harvard University Press, 2004), 153–54.

58. Cynthia Novack, *Sharing the Dance: Contact Improvisation and American Culture* (Madison: University of Wisconsin Press, 1990), 69.

59. Kraut, *Choreographing Copyright*, 180.

60. Oprah Prime, "Pharrell Williams," episode 81, Oprah Winfrey Network, first aired April 13, 2014.

61. Rohân Houssein, *Happy We Are from Paris* (December 3, 2013), accessed July 15, 2016, https://www.youtube.com/watch?v=hZ5rR0WlEkQ. The racial and ethnic diversity represented in the video has prompted some comments from viewers regarding the demographic makeup of Paris and who should be able to represent the city.

62. KetothPL, *Pharrell Williams—Happy (WARSAW IS ALSO HAPPY)* (January 5, 2014), accessed July 15, 2016, https://www.youtube.com/watch?v=B8Jaqp HdBuI.

63. Baraba Bilonic, *Pharrell Williams—Happy (Split , Croatia)* (March 14, 2014), accessed July 15, 2016, https://www.youtube.com/watch?time_continue=144&v =GcccM2BAshE.

64. Ah T, *Happy We Are from Tehran* (May 19, 2014), accessed July 15, 2016, https://www.youtube.com/watch?time_continue=58&v=RYnLRf-SNxY. According to an article in the *Guardian*, the performers in the video were sentenced with deferred punishments of lashings and prison time for their involvement. "Iranian

Pharrell Williams Fans behind Happy Video Sentenced," *Guardian*, September 19, 2014, accessed October 10, 2014, https://www.theguardian.com/world/2014/sep/19/iranian-pharrell-williams-fans-happy-video-sentenced.

65. Hardt and Negri, *Commonwealth*, 250.

66. Hardt and Negri, ix.

67. Martin, *Financialization of Daily Life*, 141.

68. See Garrett Hardin, "The Tragedy of the Commons," *Science*, New Series 162, no. 3859 (1968): 1243. See also Elinor Ostrom's work for further analysis of how communities manage shared physical or natural resources, including *Governing the Commons*.

69. See, e.g., Miller, *Playing Along*.

70. Rosalyn Diprose, "Performing Body-Identity," *Writings on Dance* 11–12 (1994): 15. The social relation may, however, be maintained through exclusion. Gestures reflect training and skill regarding their execution that may not be immediately available to everybody, and some may not be available even after spending a good deal of time and energy toward their mastery.

71. Marcel Mauss, "Techniques of the Body," in *Techniques, Technology, Civilization* (1935; repr., New York: Durkheim Press, 2006), 77.

72. Michel Serres, *The Parasite*, trans. Lawrence R. Schehr (1980; Minneapolis: University of Minnesota Press, 2007), 225.

73. See Carrie Noland, *Agency and Embodiment: Performing Gestures/Producing Culture* (Cambridge, Mass.: Harvard University Press, 2009).

74. *Michael Jackson's Thriller*, directed by John Landis, choreography by Michael Peters, performance by Michael Jackson and Ola Ray, narrated by Vincent Price (Epic, 1983), uploaded October 2, 2009, accessed July 13, 2016, https://www.youtube.com/watch?v=sOnqjkJTMaA.

75. rockwoodcomic, *The Wedding Dance* (August 30, 2006), accessed July 13, 2016, https://www.youtube.com/watch?v=OPmYbPoF4Zw; Drew, *Wedding Thriller* (August 7, 2007), accessed July 13, 2016, https://www.youtube.com/watch?v=YT6InvLJUzA; Z0z07024, *Persian Wedding in Tehran via Michael Jackson's Thriller* (January 9, 2011), accessed July13, 2016, https://www.youtube.com/watch?v=Q37y17NAwhg; *Wedding Thriller Dance Japan* (January 18, 2010), accessed July 13, 2016, https://www.youtube.com/watch?v=KRLvcPsWaRE; Karen Geisler, *Michael Jackson Thriller Indian Wedding Dance* (September 8, 2015), accessed July 13, 2016, https://www.youtube.com/watch?v=_VF2mvm2C38.

76. byronfgarcia, Thriller (July 17, 2007), accessed July 13, 2016, https://www.youtube.com/watch?v=hMnk7lh9M30. See J. Lorenzo Perillo, "'If I Was Not in Prison, I Would Not Be Famous': Discipline, Choreography, and Mimicry in the Philippines," *Theatre Journal* 63, no. 4 (2011): 607–21, for an analysis of this video's penal and neocolonial politics.

77. Ida Red, *"Thriller" Flash Mob in Tulsa* (November 5, 2010), accessed July 13, 2016, https://www.youtube.com/watch?v=tai8wuLcNLg.

78. Jeff Smith, *Flint Zombie Walk Presents Michael Jackson's Thriller* (August 11, 2011), accessed July 13, 2016, https://www.youtube.com/watch?v=h9ioYPOY1Ac.

79. Thrill Calgary, *Dancing Zombie Cowboys: Stampede Parade 2013 Highlights* (July 19, 2013), accessed July 13, 2016, https://www.youtube.com/watch?v=mw2rXooGTyI.

80. See Harmony Bench, "Screendance 2.0: Social Dance-Media," *Participations: Journal of Audience and Reception Studies* 7, no. 2 (2010), accessed July 16, 2016, http://www.participations.org/Volume%207/Issue%202/special/bench.htm.

81. For a consideration of "Thriller" in the context of Occupy Wall Street's political protest, see Tavia Nyong'o, "The Scene of Occupation," *The Drama Review* 56, no. 4 (2012): 136–49. For an analysis of the use of "Thriller" in Chilean student protests, see Camila González Ortiz, "Choreographic Meanings: Performance and Student Movement in Chile," Hemispheric Institute Encuentro, 2014.

82. Serres, *Parasite*, 226.

83. Diprose, *Corporeal Generosity*, 54.

84. Mark Franko, "Given Movement: Dance and the Event," in *Of the Presence of the Body: Essays on Dance and Performance Theory*, ed. André Lepecki (Middletown, Conn.: Wesleyan University Press, 2004), 113.

85. Franko, 132.

86. Lewis Hyde, *The Gift: Imagination and the Erotic Life of Property* (New York: Vintage, 1983), 20.

87. Hyde, 20.

88. Franko, "Given Movement," 120.

89. Franko, 121.

90. Franko, 132.

91. Miller, *Playable Bodies*, 32. I question the extent to which dance games promote "mastery" of a choreography or movement repertoire as compared to mastery of a point system for scoring dance performance, but I do not question the extent to which gestural transmission *does* occur through dance video games.

92. Miller, 65.

93. Kiri Miller, "Multisensory Musicality in Dance Central," in *The Oxford Handbook of Interactive Audio*, ed. Karen Collins, Bill Kapralos, and Holly Tessler (Oxford: Oxford University Press, 2014), 294.

94. Miller, *Playable Bodies*, 172–73.

95. Miller, 173.

96. Miller, 173.

97. Miller, 174.

98. Miller, 174.

99. Robert Stebbins, *Amateurs, Professionals, and Serious Leisure* (Montreal: McGill-Queen's University Press, 1992).

100. Taussig, *Mimesis and Alterity*, 99.

101. Alexandra Harlig, "Social Texts, Social Audiences, Social Worlds: The Circulation of Popular Dance on YouTube 2010–2015" (PhD diss., Ohio State University, 2019).

102. Srinivasan, *Sweating Saris*, 167.

103. Julie Fersing and Loïc Fontaine, We Are Happy From, Facebook, January 20, 2014, accessed June 4, 2016, https://www.facebook.com/wearehappyfrom/.

104. Julie Fersing and Loïc Fontaine, We Are Happy From, accessed June 4, 2016, http://www.wearehappyfrom.com/.

105. Marcel Mauss, *The Gift: The Form and Reason for Exchange in Archaic Societies*, trans. W. D. Halls (1950; 1990 repr., London: Routledge, 2002), 50.

106. Mary Douglas, "Foreword: No Free Gifts," in Mauss, *Gift*, ix–xxiii.

107. Pierre Bourdieu, *Outline of a Theory of Practice*, trans. Richard Nice (1972; Cambridge: Cambridge University Press, 1977), 6.

108. Jacques Derrida, *Given Time: 1. Counterfeit Money*, trans. Peggy Kamuf (1991; Chicago: University of Chicago Press, 1992), 7.

109. Olli Pyyhtinen, *The Gift and Its Paradoxes: Beyond Mauss* (Farnham, U.K.: Ashgate, 2014), 36–37.

110. Diprose, *Corporeal Generosity*, 15.

111. Diprose.

112. Serres, *Parasite*, 45.

113. Mauss, *Gift*, 46.

114. Maurizio Lazzarato, *The Making of the Indebted Man: An Essay on the Neoliberal Condition* (2011; Los Angeles, Calif.: Semiotext(e), 2012), 45.

115. Richard Dienst, *The Bonds of Debt: Borrowing against the Common Good* (London: Verso Press, 2011), 30.

116. David Graeber's *Debt: The First 5,000 Years* (Brooklyn, N.Y.: Melville House, 2011), 13, turns on this equation: "what does it mean when we reduce moral obligations to debts?"

117. Thomas Jefferson to Isaac McPherson, August 13, 1813, accessed July 6, 2016, http://press-pubs.uchicago.edu/founders/documents/a1_8_8s12.html.

118. Russell Belk, "Sharing," *Journal of Consumer Research* 37 (2010): 715–34.

119. Jame Meese, "'It Belongs to the Internet': Animal Images, Attribution Norms, and the Politics of Amateur Media," *M/C Journal* 17, no. 2 (2014), http://journal.media-culture.org.au/index.php/mcjournal/article/view/782Not/0.

120. Erin Bomboy, "A Day with Alexandra Beller Discussing Her Latest Work 'milkdreams,'" *The Dance Enthusiast*, June 8, 2015, accessed June 4, 2016, https://www.dance-enthusiast.com/features/view/milk-dreams.

121. Alexandra Beller, "Milkdreams (Baby Modern Dance)," performed by Ivo, Lea Fulton, Christina Robson, and Simon Thomas-Train (May 26, 2015), accessed June 17, 2016, https://www.youtube.com/watch?v=jYA3TBwarwE. Note that in this upload, Beller incorporates the title of the viral version, *Baby Modern Dance,* into her own title.

122. Many thanks to Benny Simon for his help in identifying Robson.

123. Alexandra Beller, "A Cautionary Tale: What Can Happen When Your Personal Video Goes Viral," *From the Green Room: Dance/USA's eJournal,* May 14, 2016, accessed July 17, 2016, https://www.danceusa.org/ejournal/2016/05/02/cautionary-tale-when-your-personal-video-goes-viral.

124. Beller.

125. Beller.

126. David Graeber, *Toward an Anthropological Theory of Value: The False Coin of Our Own Dreams* (Basingstoke, U.K.: Palgrave, 2001), 220.

127. Indeed, as Beller details, her attempts to monetize her own content by contracting with a licensing company backfired. The video has since been removed from many websites, and there is no longer a record of the millions of views Beller's video received as it traveled across platforms. See "A Cautionary Tale."

128. Lazzarato, *Making of the Indebted Man,* 75.

129. Graeber, *Theory of Value,* 219.

130. Lazzarato does not explore the differential consequences for the production of subjectivity, which are profound.

131. Dienst, *Bonds of Debt,* 151.

132. Graeber, *Theory of Value,* 225.

133. Dienst, *Bonds of Debt,* 30.

134. Beyoncé Knowles, Terius Nash, Shea Taylor, Ester Dean, Cainon Lamb, Julie Frost, Michael Bivins, Nathan Morris, and Wanya Morris, *Countdown,* performed by Beyoncé Knowles, produced by Beyoncé Knowles, Shea Taylor, and Cainon Lamb (Columbia, 2011), accessed July 27, 2016, https://www.youtube.com/watch?v=2XY3AvVgDns.

135. *Rosas danst Rosas,* choreographed by Anne Teresa De Keersmaeker, music by Thierry De Mey, premiered at the Kaaitheater Festival in Brussels, Belgium (1983). De Mey created a film of *Rosas danst Rosas* in 1997.

136. *Achterland,* choreographed by Anne Teresa De Keersmaeker, music by György Ligeti and Eugène Ysaÿe, premiered in Brussels, Belgium, 1990. De Keersmaeker created a film of *Achterland* in 1994.

137. "Anne Teresa De Keersmaeker Responds to Beyoncé Video," *The Performance Club,* October 10, 2011, accessed July 17, 2016, http://theperformanceclub.org/2011/10/anne-teresa-de-keersmaeker-responds-to-beyonce-video/.

138. Dance scholar Ramsay Burt interprets De Keersmaeker's gesture differently. He contends that her release of the choreography demonstrated "an

acknowledgement that contemporary dance knowledge is a shared resource—a commons—rather than a commodity from which to generate financial profit." Burt, *Ungoverning Dance*, 71. While I agree with Burt that dance knowledge is a shared resource, I disagree with his assertion that choreographies built from this shared resource are not commodities. By and large, professional choreographers have financial interests in their work, even if profits may be meager or they receive government support, and thus have vested interest in controlling how their work circulates.

139. This choreography repurposed Broadway choreographer Bob Fosse's work, which, in turn, sampled African American social and jazz dance vocabularies.

140. "Beyoncé Announces Official 'Single Ladies' Dance Video Contest," accessed July 17, 2016, Beyonceonline, http://www.beyonceonline.com/us/news/beyonc%C3%A9-announces-official-single-ladies-dance-video-contest.

141. Rosas VZW, *Re: Rosas, the Trailer (Extended Version)* (October 8, 2013), accessed July 27, 2016, https://www.youtube.com/watch?v=winhUJUgSMg.

142. Gottschild, *Digging the Africanist Presence*.

143. Randy Martin, "A Precarious Dance, a Derivative Sociality," *The Drama Review* 56, no. 4 (2012): 70.

144. Janet Schroeder, "Ethnic and Racial Formation on the Concert Stage: A Comparative Analysis of Tap Dance and Appalachian Step Dance" (PhD diss., Ohio State University, 2018).

145. Derrida, *Given Time*, 12.

146. Derrida, 16.

147. Derrida, 16.

148. Serres, *Parasite*.

149. Jefferson to McPherson.

150. Hardt and Negri, *Commonwealth*, ix.

Index

HARMONY BENCH is associate professor of dance at The Ohio State University.